The
ART
Of
AIDS

ROB BAKER

The ART of AIDS

CONTINUUM · New York

Cover & page 1 of insert: Frank Moore's paintings, *Arena* (cover) and *The Great American Traveling Medicine Show* (p. 1), courtesy of the artist and Sperone Westwater Gallery.

Page 2 of insert: Jeffrey photo by William Gibson/Martha Swope Assoc. Courtesy of Boneau/Bryan-Brown, press representatives.

Page 3 of insert: Angels in America photos by Joan Marcus. Courtesy of Boneau/Bryan-Brown, press representatives.

Page 4 of insert (top): Album cover of John Corigliano's Symphony No. 1, courtesy of John Corigliano and Erato Records. Photos of NAMES Project AIDS Memorial Quilt (on album cover) © 1987 by Matt Heron.

Page 4 of insert (bottom): Photo of William Parker by Kevin Lynn, courtesy of John Gingrich Associates.

Page 5 of insert (top): Photo by Rob Baker.

Page 5 of insert (bottom): Zero Patience photo courtesy of Cinevista.

Pages 6 & 7: Dance performance photos © Janet P. Levitt.

Pages 8: Poster art by Gran Fury, Little Elvis, and the Silence = Death Collective.

1994
The Continuum Publishing Company
370 Lexington Avenue, New York, NY 10017

Printed in the United States of America

Library of Congress Cataloging-in-Publication Data

Baker, Rob
        The art of AIDS / Rob Baker.
                p. cm.
        ISBN 0-8264-0653-X (alk. paper)
        1. AIDS (Disease) and the arts—United States. 2. AIDS (Disease) and the arts. I. Title.
NX180.A36B35 1994   94-15703
700'.1'03—dc20   CIP

In Memory of

PETER LA BELLA (1 9 5 3 – 1 9 8 7)
& GARY WALKER (1 9 4 6 – 1 9 9 3)

&

To Gerardo & Life

ACKNOWLEDGMENTS

For helping me shape the massive amount of material that went into this book, I wish to give special thanks to my editor, Cynthia Eller, who has an uncanny ability to balance enthusiasm with a sharp objective eye; and William Harris, a friend since our days together at the *Soho Weekly News*, whose suggestions during and after my research and writing have proven invaluable. In addition to Cynthia and Billy, I also want to thank the other readers of the manuscript, Peter Born, Anne Glusker, and W. Gay Reading, all of whom made splendid suggestions about structure or detail.

I also want to express gratitude to the following people for taking time to discuss the project with me: Gerald Arpino, Philip Caggiano, John Carlin, Karen Cooper, John Greyson, Brian Hanna, William K. Hoffman, Jeff Lunger, Joseph L. Mazo, Greg Mehrten, Frank Moore, Jim O'Quinn, Paul Rudnick, Nicky Silver, Thomas Sokolowski, and Sandy Zeig. The reference librarians at the New York Public Library, both at the main branch and at the Library for the Performing Arts, were all helpful and polite, especially Katherine Nickeson of the Dance Collection.

I'll always owe a special debt of gratitude to Daniella Dooling, both for her piece about Peter La Bella and me for the 1990 Day Without Art at Yale and for first telling me about the paintings of Frank Moore, which became such a key inspiration for this project. At the same time, this book would probably not have been possible without her grandmother, Dorothea Dooling, who introduced me to the healing mountains of Montana (and so much more) after Peter's death.

The book needed peace and quiet for its first draft. Carol Kramer's Kinderhook hideaway was the perfect solution: it wasn't quite Montana, but it was a bit more accessible to New York City (though in January and February of 1994, Kinderhook was almost as snowbound and frigid as its western counterpart).

James Sarfati is wonderfully responsible for the look of this book, inside and out, and Peter Frandsen, the only person who's ever been able to take a decent picture of me besides Daniella, took the jacket photo.

Clem E. and Billy L. provided strong support, by phone and in person, during the difficult genesis of this work. I thank them, along with Gerardo Mendoza (my very own Antonio Banderas), who helped keep house and home (and two cats in heat) together through this ordeal and our ensuing move to Lexington, Kentucky, to start a new life in a bluegrass state.

—Rob Baker, April 17, 1994

Contents

Art

Theater

PRELUDE

Circles of Dance

he dancer stands in the center of the stage, his hands and arms stained dark red, up to the elbows: blood, the most dangerous of body fluids and one of the two most notorious signifiers or conduits of AIDS. It's a clinical, asexual symbol, but containing all the mystery and terror of the condition itself. This silent, ambiguity-packed statement remains frozen in time and space for a long, eerie moment, then the image thaws quickly as the dancer's body pulses into life, resonating in resistance to the bloody, arbitrary diagnosis.

Blond hair flying, Lance Gries is a dynamo of barely contained energy, moving about the stage wearing loose-fitting off-white trousers. His upper torso is thin but muscular: hard, wiry, offering a statement of tough resilience. He turns in silence, cradles and shelters an invisible partner, stretches out the red arms to the audience (in accusation? supplication? anger? despair?). Three other dancers, in what look like hospital robes or tunics of an unspecified Eastern religion, move just outside the circle of light in which Gries remains: caught, confined, trying to bring them inside. He beckons to them, tries to clasp hands with them, to take care of them, comfort them, share their experience. Mostly he is alone, struggling inside the circle, rising and falling back to the floor: running, dropping, rising again, arms arcing into space, reaching out, questioning. After several minutes of silence, the sound of composer John Adams' "Shaker Loops" winds its way in, counterpointing the pent-up anger, fear, and violence with its promise of simple truths, gentle forbearance.

It's Monday, October 18, 1993, and *A Demand Performance* is a benefit organized by DIFFA (Design Industries Foundation for AIDS, a group of powerhouse go-getters from the fashion industry who have frequently taken the lead in mounting such AIDS benefits) in collaboration with

Broadway Cares/Equity Fights AIDS at the New York State Theater at Lincoln Center. Eighteen choreographers are presenting mostly new works as a dance gala in memory of persons who have died of AIDS. No similar celebration in the dance world has occurred since 1987, which has been the cause of no little concern among many in that community, one that's been hit particularly hard by the epidemic—though little acknowledgment has been made of that, outside the obituary pages, which sometimes lie.

This performance has a particular poignancy about it, being dedicated to the memory of Christopher Gillis, a dancer and choreographer who had been planning a piece for this evening's performance when he died of AIDS just two months ago. Working from his notes and instructions, his sister Margie, also a dancer, and several friends have brought the work to fruition; it will be premiered tonight.

When I arrived an hour ago, after a nervous crosstown bus ride, the second-floor promenade was already crammed with tuxedoed men and women dressed to the nines, spooned into a cramped space with five or six hors d'oeuvres tables, a plethora of competing decors, and far too many bars for someone relatively new to sobriety. Loud cocktail party conversation was at a fever pitch, and everyone seemed to be sporting a red ribbon, prominently displayed in almost strident political correctness.

This was certainly not what I had imagined, planned on, wished for. The ambiance seemed all wrong. This was not an atmosphere in which I function well—or even minimally. I saw two people I knew, uttered quick hellos, then fled as quickly as possible to my seat.

The first few dances had gone by in a fog. They were all serviceable, nicely danced, interestingly costumed by various designers of the moment. But nothing seemed to really have any relevance to AIDS, until now: Gries's "Carry On, Carry On," which beautifully captures the dilemma of the contemporary artist in the age of AIDS: how to deal with this intruder, this disease, in our bodies, in our midst.

Then, after two brief interludes, comes Gillis's "Vers Champs Élysées," its title nicely cloaked in mystery—perhaps a reference to the main thoroughfare of Paris, perhaps to that place name's own translation, the Elysian Fields, where the ancient Greek heroes went home to rest. The dance, to the "Pié Jesu" section of Gabriel Fauré's *Requiem,* features a man (danced by Ken Tosti) facing death in a circle of light, his energy running out, his strength failing as he struggles and falls, then tries to rise again, always with a faraway look in his eyes; he points, attempting to understand the gesture and follow it. His hands clutch his head at one point, perhaps wishing to still the dream or the pain inside. Joao Mauricio portrays the lover (there is no namby-pamby ambiguity here, as in most male dance duets: no closeted interpretation of "shadow self" or platonic friend is possible), following his every move, caregiving, trying to ease his pain, his passage, cradling his head, gently helping him into his sick-bed. At one point, Mauricio wakes up just in time to catch Tosti as he falls, then seems afraid to look away, to sleep or leave, for fear of missing the final moment. But sleep comes at last, and a trio of women dancers arrive and take over the caregiving. When the end comes, the living partner cradles the other in his arms, in a frozen moment with obvious reference to Michaelangelo's Piéta, then arranges the motionless body on the floor.

Two more special moments come in the second half. A solo by Margie Gillis to "Torn Roots, Broken Branches," a sad song by Sinead O'Connor, is a sweeping power-packed homage to her brother Christopher, part mourning, part celebration: the plant of the title resolutely refuses to go gentle into that good night. Ms. Gillis—costumed by Norma Kamali in a long dress and a big droopy hat over her braided hair—swirls and swoops, carrying the costume and her long braided hair with her through the arcs and sweeps. She also takes the audience's hearts and breath along with her, helping bring the evening's grief (and her own very personal loss) to resolution.

The feeling of catharsis continues in the last dance, a powerful excerpt from Twyla Tharp's *In the Upper Room*, a fitting closing eulogy to dancers and dancing now lost to time: expansive, ecstatic, ethereal, with ribbons flying from the dancers' costumes (Kamali again), spinning forth its own epiphany.

Then it's over: we're back onto crosstown buses, out into a world for the most part without tuxedos, red ribbons, or the benefits of remembering.

What is this all about, this response? Red ribbons, tuxedos, hors d'oeuvres, and flower arrangements? But is AIDS *not* about these things, these expressions? Or at least about them as well? Are they not equally as valid as a dance made by a dying man or the sweeping onstage grief of his sister? And where am I in all this, gratuitously taking notes on 3 x 5 cards, in seat First Ring Right AA 34, judging the events onstage and off, trying to make a book out of them?

These four dances in particular were highlights of the program and also stood out as very different responses to the threat that AIDS poses to the arts. Lance Gries, especially, zeroed in on the numbing anger and grief felt by survivors who have lost too many friends and lovers, colleagues and mentors, to the epidemic—and remain trapped in a circle of their own sadness, unable to affect the tragedy taking place all around them. Christopher Gillis reveresed that imagery: here the person with AIDS, the person dying, is the one inside the circle, but the care and concern of those attending him can (and do) help ease his passage. But whether the circle excludes or includes, both dances are unabashedly about AIDS, without abstraction, without ambiguity, without apology.

The Margie Gillis and Tharp pieces, on the other hand, represent a different but equally valid response. Their dances also circle and spiral, but here the subject is allusive, abstract, contained. The vocabulary is still full of feeling, but less direct somehow: the two women sublimate those emotions into their art, inside their imagery. The Tharp piece, in fact, wasn't made about AIDS at all and dates form 1986. But the choreographer picked it as her statement for the evening, and it has a particular poignant power in this context.

Maybe all the evening's works were really about AIDS: about a multicultural artistic community devastated and frightened by an enemy bent on destoying the very beauty, form, and life that is that community's stock in trade.

Still, at times, the evening resembled nothing so much as an upscale anti-war campaign, and indeed it was that, too—the kind of cocktail-party-to-relieve-social-angst that Tom Wolfe once lambasted back in the sixties. Stop the War, Stop the Injustice, Stop the Disease. But is this really just about STOPPING AIDS or FINDING A CURE, even? Even if one accepts the single-virus theory (and an increasing number of us don't), the likelihood of a cure—a single, definitive cure—remains slim. It's astonishing how people—activists and bystanders alike—insist on that, though most people today rather readily acknowledge that no cure is ever likely to be found for cancer or heart disease. The single answer, the magic bullet, the panacea—devoutly to be wished for, so little likely to be achieved.

And where does that leave us, other than wondering what this epidemic really means, to us, to life, to art? What is art, other than an exploration of meaning, personal and universal? It encompasses all the questioning that that entails, all the posed but incomplete answers, all the rage and denial, all the pain and struggle.

When I began this book I assumed that my writing about AIDS was about my own grieving, my own coming to terms with memories of those I have lost and fears for those (including myself, of course) who are at risk, at war. Yes, Peter, my lover of nine years, died of AIDS the Sunday after Thanksgiving in 1987. And so did my cousin Gary, all the way out in Oregon, last June. But I also lost another cousin this summer to alcoholism and suicide, and my mentor and spiritual guide two years ago, to leukemia at the ripe old age of 80. Life goes on. Death goes on. AIDS goes on. They're not neatly compartmentalized, separate entities of experience or emotion.

And AIDS itself is not just about dying, not just about finding a cure, not just about its own demise. Ultimately, AIDS is not even just about itself, but about how we are, what part of us is sick and what part is well, what part of us can be better, what part can care for ourselves, for others. It is no coincidence that AIDS, internationally, is a disease of the disenfranchised, of the outsider. But its lesson is for everybody; it is a part of everyone, part of each whole. By including it in our view of our self, our community, and our world, we can begin to see the complete picture. The art of AIDS is about exactly that—a voice full of contradictions: sometimes soft, sometimes shrill, full of hope and full of despair, struggling to make meaning out of its own meaninglessness. There's no single right or wrong to all this, no exclusive vision, no point of view that should be ignored or dismissed—except those grounded in, and promoting, hate and despair...and maybe we learn something even from them.

If this crisis has brought us to anything, to any common good, it has brought us to awareness, to community, to conscience. And that experience goes beyond AIDS, goes beyond death and dying, goes beyond causes and blames, beyond cures and treatments; it goes beyond any answer or question that any of us, alone or even together, can bring. It changes everything, transforming us—and our art—from here on out.

1

The Art of AIDS: An Overview

*I*n the dozen or so years since the advent of AIDS, the various artistic communities which have been so deeply affected by the epidemic—the worlds of painting and sculpture, classical and popular music, dance, theater, photography, film and video—have responded to the crisis in various ways, from very public big-name benefits to very private works of anger and eloquence, despair and hope. It is these artistic statements—the dances, the songs, the paintings, the plays—by people with AIDS or about their struggle, that this study intends to examine. Some of these statements have received wide media attention, but for every NAMES Project AIDS Memorial Quilt or *Angels in America* or *Philadelphia*, there are literally dozens of less familiar works which address the same burning issues but which the general public seldom hears about. This book is a compendium of many of those statements, geared to give the reader a chance to reflect on the scope of this art of AIDS: how these diverse responses are related, how they challenge or reinforce each other, how they open up deep questions about the very soul of our society—sick and well, male and female, rich and poor, gay and straight.

Like AIDS itself, this art of AIDS at first seems chaotic, unmanageable. We'd be a lot more comfortable if it would just go away, but it won't. AIDS has altered not only the way we live, but also the way we look at life and the way we see and make art. We need to understand these changes in art and in ourselves, to reexamine the deep and often disturbing responses that are being elicited. What is needed is not a quick and easy way to judge or categorize these responses, but an approach that will allow them speak and sing their own stories. Eulogies and elegies can coexist with calls-to-arms and manifestos, figurative paintings with abstractions. No response to this epidemic is invalid.

This study will try to present the scope and depth of these responses by examining each of the art forms in turn, as well as some interdisciplinary correspondences. Obviously not every single song or dance or play about AIDS has been included: a book could easily be written on each specific area, delving into the forms in greater detail (as indeed has been done elsewhere with literature about AIDS). The wish here is more for a kind of generalist overview, a glimpse at the big picture.

I have selected a few major examples in each area of the visual or performing arts, not because they are necessarily better or more important than the others (though at times this may be true), but because they are especially representative of certain responses to AIDS. And I have tried in general to balance less familiar works in each area with works which have achieved broad critical acclaim. ("Don't forget the set designers and stage managers," a friend urged as I started this study. I've tried to keep that in mind throughout.)

Though AIDS is by no means a gay disease—and there are grave dangers in misrepresenting it as such, both for the gay population and for the general public—this study will focus primarily on gay representations of AIDS in the arts, mainly because of the simple truth that most artistic responses to AIDS thus far have been made by gay artists. This will and should change in the future. But thus far, with very rare exceptions, most of the AIDS art which has focused on the heterosexual community has done so not out of any conscientious attempt to balance the demographics of representation but out of sheer homophobia and fear of sexuality, period.

Much discussion has arisen about the language which has been used to describe this epidemic, especially in the mainstream press. AIDS, or acquired immune deficiency syndrome, is not technically a disease, but a condition which causes the human immune system to collapse, allowing opportunistic infections to take over. It is these "AIDS-related" complications that kill, not AIDS per se, or the virus called HIV that is now generally accepted (perhaps too readily) to be the sole cause of the condition. Yet though it is technically incorrect to say that a person "died of AIDS" or that AIDS is a disease, in a practical sense, it's almost impossible to avoid such references. And it seems no more incorrect to say that a person died of AIDS than to say someone died of old age or (even more mysteriously) "natural causes."

What seems much more crucial is to avoid three widespread misconceptions which occur constantly in the media and in private conversations about AIDS: (1) equating AIDS with homosexuality; (2) equating testing positive for the HIV virus with "having AIDS" (and thus jumping to the debatable conclusion that the results of a highly untrustworthy medical test means a death sentence); and (3) equating AIDS with sex in general, be it gay or straight, rather than with irresponsible, unprotected, or compulsive sex (or the transfer of infected blood).

I'm also solidly in favor of referring to people who have the condition of "full-blown" AIDS as exactly what they are: people with AIDS (PWAs) or people living with AIDS (PLWAs): they are not, nor do they wish to be referred to as, "AIDS victims," a term which immediately puts them into a category of "other" and robs them of dignity and respect. If we use a language of stigma and death, we end up stigmatized and dying. If, on the other hand, we choose a language of conscience and survival, we at least have a fighting chance.

One final disclaimer: I have tried to keep my own opinions and judgments at bay, but a life-and-death subject like AIDS renders objectivity virtually impossible at times, so that personal responses almost demand to have their say. I have therefore included an appendix, comprised of some poems that I wrote over a six-year period as I tried to come to grips with my own lover's illness and death; and some occasional "interludes" in the main text, detailing my own journey as a caretaker, a commentator, and a critic of the art of AIDS. These personal notes, like my discussions of the various works being made, are offered as simply another way to approach the deep enigma of AIDS, a continuing mystery that affects both the way we live and the way we perceive the world.

2

Being in Philadelphia

here is a scene halfway through Jonathan Demme's *Philadelphia*, the first major Hollywood film about AIDS, in which the Tom Hanks character, a gay lawyer with the syndrome, tries to describe his condition to the straight black lawyer (played by Denzel Washington) who is handling his lawsuit against the law firm that fired him for being ill—and gay. To get his message across to the sympathetic but distinctly homophobic Joe Miller, Andrew Beckett resorts, literally, to grand opera—specifically, the aria by Maddalena in Giordano's *Andrea Chenier*, as interpreted by the diva to end all divas (certainly to gay opera queens): Maria Callas.

Demme thus takes a considerable risk, right in the middle of an already chancy film project which is dealing straightforwardly with both AIDS and homosexuality. Having broached that double taboo head on, the director pushes his mainstream and probably relatively conservative audience one step further, asking these moviegoers to confront grand opera, the most elitist of art forms, not just as quiet background music but as character development, blasting forth at full volume, delivered edgily by a singer not exactly famous for the soothing quality of her vocal timbre.

What's the point? To add a touch of melodrama? To reinforce the stereotype that all gay men relish grand opera, as some critics have suggested? Or to try, however haltingly, to actually *contain* some of the rage, pain, and despair that people with AIDS confront, day in and day out, in facing their own mortality? To try to describe an indescribable horror—to make some sort of sense out of the sheer senselessness of the epidemic itself—is at the heart of all art about AIDS. And the scene works stunningly, if uneasily (perhaps because of its uneasiness), epitomizing those disturbed and disturbing feelings.

Interestingly, Demme and screenwriter Ron Nyswaner have not picked one of Callas's more famous arias. Andrew therefore can make it his own personal property, avoiding the baggage of associations others may have with the singer's "Casta Diva" from *Norma* or "Sempre Libera" from *La Traviata*. Andrew's identification with "La mamma morta"[1] can thus serve as his own statement, and the declamatory pathos he finds in it certainly fits the moment: In the aria, the character Maddalena recalls how her mother had been killed trying to save her child from a burning house during the French Revolution. The house had been torched by an angry mob: the sort of action often experienced by outsiders, foreigners, and other gypsy minorities (including people with AIDS as well in recent years).

Andrew translates the libretto for Joe, as the music swells to a dramatic climax. The image on the screen shifts back and forth between Andrew declaiming and Joe listening: something begins to melt, to change in Joe's face. An understanding is born, the kind that can't be put into words. The recorded aria ends with an upsurge of passion, and Andrew is left emotionally drained, standing beside his IV stand. The reality of his own situation returns. Joe, who had come to Andrew's house to prepare him for taking the stand in his own defense the following day, announces that no further rehearsal for the trial is necessary. "You're ready," he declares, foreshadowing Andrew's own positive declaration to his lover Miguel at the end of the film ("I think I'm ready"), signaling that that trial, too, is almost over.

But it is the scene that follows the operatic exposition that captures most tellingly what Demme and his screenwriter seem to be trying to get at in this episode: Miller leaves Beckett's apartment, turns around and starts to go back and knock on the door; he hears Andrew listening again to the aria inside the apartment and changes his mind, walking away and getting into his car. The aria on the soundtrack—softer now, less strident—follows him all the way home as he confronts his own commonplace humanity (his house, his baby, his wife asleep in bed). The music thus underscores the same universal promises of love overcoming sorrow, of not having to face life (or death) alone. It's a turning point, of sorts, for Miller and the audience: something is understood, a shared decency, a sense of conscience. The uneasy bond between Miller and Beckett (between black and white, between straight and gay, between the well and the sick) is firmly cemented at last: the course of their allied challenge against injustice is set.

Demme's gamble seems to have paid off: *Philadelphia* has been a considerable box office and critical success, bringing in over $72 million dollars in the first eighteen weeks of its release, almost tripling the $25 million it cost to produce. More importantly, of course, it has brought the theme of AIDS to the attention of a wider general public than any previous film—an audience that, thanks to its casting (and the well-calculated intentions of Demme and his producers) is straight as well as gay, black as well as white, poor as well as middle class. No preaching to the converted here; in fact, the most vitriolic attacks on the film have come not from right-wing homophobes but from gay activists like the ever-vocal Larry Kramer (see Chapter 17), who, almost predictably, declared it "worse than no movie about AIDS at all."

Philadelphia wears its laurels well: it is a good barometer of most of the issues about AIDS which will be considered in this book. The film manages to examine a whole subset of complex questions about AIDS: the similarities (and differences) between AIDS discrimination and racism, and between racism and homophobia; the dilemma of public acknowledgment of both AIDS and homosexuality; the importance to the AIDS community of support groups and political organizations; the myriad ways in which misinformation about the epidemic (and homosexuality) is spread; the actual clinical details of the effects of AIDS-related illnesses on the body, mind, and feelings of those who are ill.

The most problematic of these issues is how to conscientiously delineate the relationship of AIDS to homosexuality. Unlike most TV producers and other Hollywood directors who have tried to sublimate or downplay the fact that the gay subculture was originally the population most devastated by AIDS, Demme deals directly with the issue of homosexuality from the very start. Andrew is openly gay in his non-professional life. He has a good-looking, well-adjusted Latino lover named Miguel (Antonio Banderas), a solid group of politically aware out-of-the-closet gay and lesbian friends, and a family who welcome him and Miguel to family gatherings as if to do so were the most natural thing in the world.

Andrew is not, however, out at the office: a big law firm in Philadelphia

where he is being groomed as the golden boy. Early in the film, he is given
a very important computer copyright infringement case: it's clear that the
good old boys at the firm trust him to run with the ball for a major endplay
around the opposition. But at the end of the session in which he's given the
assignment, one of the senior partners notices a purplish spot on Andrew's
forehead. What's that, boy? the senior partner asks. Andrew assures him
he just got hit playing racquetball.

But Andrew is already sick, with several of the symptoms that signal his
condition could be progressing to full-blown AIDS. The spot is, in fact, a
Kaposi's sarcoma lesion, the mark of a once-rare cancer that is now a defining characteristic of AIDS. As he works feverishly to draw up the complaint for the complex copyright case, he drives himself to exhaustion,
working mostly at home, in part so that his co-workers won't notice the
progress of his disease. On the day the complaint is due, he leaves the finished draft for the company's suit on his secretary's desk. Then while visiting some friends at the local gay community center, he has an intestinal
attack (again AIDS related) and is taken to the hospital. But when he's
beeped by his law office in the emergency room, Andrew realizes someone
has sabotaged him: the complaint has disappeared, both from his secretary's desk and his computer. He rushes to the office—still in very bad
shape physically—and the complaint is found, misfiled, at the last possible
moment. The next day he is fired by the firm, supposedly for incompetence
because of the "bungled" complaint.

Andrew knows better: now that they have seen him looking sick, he
realizes, they've put two and two together. Someone who suspected his
condition had apparently trumped up the incident of the lost complaint,
and he's been fired because the partners presume he has AIDS. He decides
to sue. Finding a lawyer is no easy task. He has already been to nine other
lawyers (who all turned down his case) when he approaches Joe Miller, an
ambulance-chasing personal injury lawyer whom he had opposed in a pol-
lution case in the film's opening scene. Beckett tells Miller what he wants
and Miller balks: he wants nothing to do with this case, obviously, being
equally uncomfortable with Beckett's being gay and his having AIDS.

There's something terribly believable—and for the filmgoing public
identifiable—about both Miller's homophobia and his fear of AIDS (he goes
for an HIV test merely because Andrew visited his office and shook his
hand, somewhat to the amusement of his old-timer family physician). It is
this attitude of a straight black lawyer—no hotshot, no political radical,

but a decent, flawed human being (played, not insignificantly, by black matinee idol Washington)—that makes *Philadelphia* work. Miller's education into tolerance comes slowly. Interestingly, it begins at home, where his wife declares he's always had a problem with prejudice against gays. When she asks him if he knows anyone who's gay, Joe draws a blank. So she gives him a list that properly stuns him: everyone from the guy who's putting in their new kitchen cabinets to her Aunt Teresa. "Your Aunt Teresa is gay?" Miller says, obviously in shock. "That beautiful, sensuous, voluptuous woman is a *lesbian?*"[2]

In one of the film's most effective scenes, a gay librarian in a law library snottily asks Andrew (after bringing him the documents he had requested on a case about HIV-related discrimination) if he would "not be more comfortable in a private research room?" Miller, who has previously declined to take Andrew's case, happens to be at the library at the same time and observes the prejudicial slur. He comes over to Andrew to offer his support, and the librarian withdraws.

Joe and Andrew then read the "relevant precedent" aloud together, a Supreme Court decision that concludes: "Subsequent decisions have held that AIDS is protected as a handicap under law not only because of the physical limitations it imposes, but also because the prejudice surrounding AIDS exacts a social death which precedes the actual physical one. This is the essence of discrimination: formulating opinions about others not based on their individual merits but, rather, on the membership in a group with assumed characteristics." Once again the camera's focus moves back and forth between the two men's faces, and we read volumes in their expressions. It's a very human moment that sends cold chills down the spine: there's no way Miller can refuse to take the case after that declaration of "the essence of discrimination," which is the real heart of the film's message and its power.

Other issues are raised in *Philadelphia* as well: how to present Andrew's deteriorating physical condition without morbidly sensationalizing it; how to handle his relationship to his family and his lover; how to deal with the question of AIDS activism; how to honestly confront the questions of dying, grief, and mourning.

Tom Hanks' performance, for which he won both a Golden Globe and an Oscar as Best Actor, is central to the issue of presentation. He plays Andrew as neither overly gay nor overly sick, but he does so without denigrating the character's homosexuality or denying his condition. Instead he plays the character with a quiet but unassuming strength, and it's that strength that carries him through the trial and the crisis. His deteriorating physical condition is honestly alluded to, too, but never overstated.

Unlike some AIDS patients, Andrew has an unusually supportive family: a sister that encourages him to hold her baby, a father who's not afraid to kiss and embrace him, a strong and spunky mother (Joanne Woodward, no less) who declares that she never raised her kids to ride at the back of the bus. To complain, as some critics and activists have, that this is a misrepresentation of how families respond to AIDS and homosexuality seems unfair: a lot of prejudice and discrimination does exist among families of PWAs, but a lot of love and acceptance also exists. To deny that would be to stack the deck as well, and to overlook an equally true and valid picture of AIDS.

Some viewers have particularly bemoaned the fact that Andrew and Miguel don't have any love scenes. Indeed, it would have been nice to see a kiss, a love scene (and Banderas has certainly done that and more with other men in some of his roles with gay Spanish director Pedro Almodóvar). But they do get to dance together, dressed like naval officers at a costume party, and the relationship has a wonderful naturalness about it that is both believable and refreshing, touching and tender.

Screenwriter Ron Nyswaner has answered the Antonio Banderas question rather neatly: Asked why the two characters didn't kiss in the film, he responded:

> Most of the scenes between Tom and Antonio take place during medical crises in the emergency room of a hospital and in a courtroom during a civil trial. I've never had the opportunity to kiss my boyfriend in the emergency room of a hospital or in a crowded courtroom, although we have made it our New Year's resolution to kiss in both those locations as soon as possible.[3]

Though Andrew is not a political activist himself, he at least has friends who are involved in the movement. Furthermore, Demme sought out activists from the Philadelphia area and invited them to participate in location scenes outside the courtroom, bringing their own signs and yelling their own slogans to counter those of the homophobes written into the script. Another precinct heard from, in other words: a mainstream film which finally acknowledges that community action groups like ACT UP (the AIDS Coalition To Unleash Power, the most vocal and active AIDS action group) actually exist.

Concerning death and grieving: again Demme and Nyswaner face the issue head on, neither avoiding nor romanticizing it. Andrew dies, as most people with full-blown AIDS do, sooner or later. But he dies with a certain amount of dignity and self-respect, surrounded by friends and family who care about him, and after he's won his court case. And the last scene is not a hospital death-bed scene, but Andrew's wake: a happy time of celebration, with Miguel's parents having flown in from Spain or Latin America (it's never clear exactly where Miguel comes from) to lend their support to their son and his lover's friends and family. It's a small but very special touch, the kind Demme and Nyswaner have managed so well throughout.

That Jonathan Demme should be the director of the first big Hollywood film about AIDS may come as a surprise to those gay activists who attacked him for what they considered anti-gay stereotyping in his earlier Oscar-winning thriller, *The Silence of the Lambs*, in which a transvestite psychopath preys on women and gays.[4] Demme has always insisted that the psychopath character was not gay, but the strong complaints from the gay and lesbian community clearly had an impact on his conscientious handling of *Philadelphia*. Moreover, he has been particularly honest in interviews about his own consciousness-raising on the issue of AIDS: "I respect the fear of AIDS out there because I had that," he told an interviewer in February 1993. "Until you know someone with AIDS, you're afraid of it, and this movie gets at that."[5]

The PWA whom Demme was referring to was a painter and activist named Juan Botas, a classmate and close friend of Demme's wife Joanne Howard. Demme consulted regularly with Botas on early versions of the Philadelphia script and also helped Botas produce a film of his own, *One Foot on a Banana Peel, the Other Foot in the Grave*, a documentary of his AIDS support group (see Chapter 3). When Botas died during the filming in August 1992, Demme's production company took over the project and brought it to completion.

In spite of his success in Hollywood, Demme has maintained strong ties with New York, where his offices are based and where he frequently gambles on independent film projects with downtown artists, musicians, and theater personalities. Along with his full-scale Hollywood productions like *Silence of the Lambs*, *Married to the Mob*, and *Swing Shift*, he has also made *Stop*

Making Sense with musician David Byrne, *Swimming to Cambodia* with Wooster Group actor and monologist Spalding Gray, plus several music videos. He's currently producing a film version of Ron Vawter's AIDS duet, *Roy Cohn/Jack Smith* (see Chapter 18). Demme uses a number of Botas's paintings in Andrew and Miguel's apartment in *Philadelphia*, and the scene where the two finally get to dance together includes a host of New York downtown originals, from the late Michael Callen to Quentin Crisp and Lola Pashalinski and Black-Eyed Susan, former regulars with Charles Ludlam's Ridiculous Theatrical Company. Vawter, who plays one of the members of the Andrew's firm (and gives one of the key testimonies in his favor in the trial), also sneaks in a second cameo appearance in the film, coming to the costume ball wearing his Jack Smith harem drag. (The film is full of such casting touches, like important minor roles for performance artists Karen Finley and Anna Deavere Smith, plus having former soft-core porn star Charles Napier play the trial judge.)

Demme's music world connections helped him snare an impressive array of talents for the soundtrack of *Philadelphia*, including original compositions by Bruce Springsteen and Neil Young, which frame the film by opening and closing it with lyrics keenly attuned to the inherent ironies of the city-metaphor Demme sought to explore. Springsteen speaks of wasting away, walking the streets endlessly, lying awake, and fading away; Young echoes a similar loneliness of not wanting to be blamed, abandoned, alone, wishing for love and light instead.[6]

In the press kit for *Philadelphia*, Banderas is quoted as saying: "If 15 years in the future we see that we did nothing to fight AIDS and the discrimination leveled against those suffering from the disease—I mean no movies, paintings, plays—then we will not be able to say that we are artists."[7] Andrew echoes a similar note of conscience when Joe puts him on the witness stand near the end of the film, "What I love most about the law is that every now and again—not that often, but occasionally—you get to be part of justice being done. It really is quite a thrill when that happens." Art—even movies—can do that, too, and despite what W. C. Fields once quipped to the contrary, maybe being in Philadelphia is not so bad after all.

Another Philadelphia Story

hy Philadelphia? people have wondered, thinking it an odd setting and title for a movie about AIDS. Yet for me the connection was staggering. It's not exactly where the story begins for Peter and me, but it is certainly a major interlude.

Most cities and towns—at least those I have known—have a quality, almost a symbolic resonance all their own. It has something to do with history, with architecture and layout, with the people who live there. But mostly it's a kind of personality of place, something that goes far beyond geography or demographics.

Philadelphia has a decency and a self-respect that few cities today seem to have. It stands for something: the Liberty Bell and Constitution Hall are part of that, but so are the Rodin museum, the World Aid Concert (pop music did have some conscience, even before AIDS), the baked apples every Tuesday at the restaurant at the corner of Third and Market. Something about values that are more human values than just "family values": a city of brotherly love where brotherhood clearly extends beyond familiar ties or macho camaraderie. Something about tolerance and acceptance.

Philadelphia wasn't all peace and harmony during the almost three years I spent there. It had crimes and craziness, like any other urban area. It had hate and fear, even the hate and fear that led to the horror of the MOVE bombings, where a bungling mayor managed to burn down 60 houses trying to get rid of some "dangerous" radicals. Peter and I could see the flames from our balcony, and what magnified the disbelief was not that this was happening, but that it could happen in Philadelphia.

Still, in general, the streets were clean. Homeless people were treated with respect and concern. Races and ethnic groups had a long history of living in harmony—certainly as far as we could see, after two decades of dealing with the filth and tensions of New York City.

We came to Philadelphia with a lot of hope. It had been a bad year. Peter had had an operation for a swollen lymph node: it was non-malignant, but we were both quietly frightened. Peter was out of work. His mother had died suddenly, depriving him of one of his strongest emotional supports. I had been out of town constantly, working part-time in Philadelphia and returning to New York only on weekends.

When I was offered a full-time job in Philadelphia, I jumped at the chance, hardly waiting to see what Peter felt about the move. It would be best for him, I decided (as I always tended to decide, for both of us): it would offer us a new beginning, in an environment which would be healthy, safe. We could start over.

Part of that was true. We were happy in Philadelphia. We had a beautiful apartment, downtown near all the bars and cultural activities, and our rent was less than half what it would have been anywhere in New York City, let alone Manhattan. We made new friends, and we could visit New York easily whenever we wanted. Peter found a job, then another one, which he actually liked. Even after I left my job, following an angry blow-up with my boss, and found another job back in New York, we decided to stay: I commuted from Philadelphia to New York five days a week for almost a year. I wouldn't have had it any other way.

Then the swollen glands came back. Dental problems. Low-grade fevers and night sweats. Peter began to lose weight. We went first to a doctor recommended by a friend, then to the local gay clinic. Long batteries of inconclusive tests in the days before HIV was proclaimed to be the cause of AIDS. At last the doctors listed Peter's condition as AIDS Related Complex (ARC), a kind of grab-bag diagnosis which seemed to mean he had all the signs but hadn't qualified by having one of the two approved opportunistic infections yet.

The fevers and night sweats increased. Peter worked nights, when he could. I went to the bars: Philadelphia has great gay bars, especially the piano bars; they seemed friendlier and less cliquish than those in New York. Everything seemed so much better when I sang at the top of my lungs all night long and ordered another beer. If I drank enough I could still fantasize that everything was going to be OK, that we would find a way out of this slow-building nightmare.

Maybe, I thought, we should go away again. Not move, but take a vacation, to someplace warm and happy. I called travel agents, got brochures. We decided (or, again, was it I who decided?) on Cancun.

Cancun only continued and intensified the nightmare. The hotel accommodations were wretched. We switched hotels, and things were only slightly better. We went to a bullfight and were horrified at the brutality, not even redeemed by style. We went to Chichén Itzá and took lots of pictures. When we got back to Cancun itself, we both had dysentery. The dysentery got worse, especially for Peter. We came home early.

Peter was really sick. We were really scared. He wanted to go back to New York, where he could be closer to his family: his father, his brother, his two sisters. This time he decided, although now almost all of our decisions were being made by this thing, this intruder, this mysterious new disease.

We left Philadelphia, which we had loved, where we had been happy, but where love and happiness—and even decency and tolerance—had not been enough.

But when Jonathan Demme named his AIDS movie "Philadelphia," I knew exactly what he meant.

3

Hollywood Silence vs. Independent Voices

n October 1988, some three years after Rock Hudson's AIDS-related death, veteran *TV Guide* observer Mary Murphy wrote a frank account challenging Hollywood's hypocrisy about homosexuality and AIDS, noting: "The community that prides itself on being tolerant of alternative life styles, the community that is so publicly supportive [through AIDS benefits, etc.], is privately becoming more repressive." Only television coverage (which she saw as similarly dominated by the homophobic—and frequently closeted gay— studio executives) was worse: "Indeed, of all the arts, TV is the least tolerant of gays."[1]

When actor Brad Davis died in September 1991, his widow delivered a scathing indictment of Hollywood's hypocrisy, which Davis had written just before he died and which was picked up by newspapers from coast to coast: "I make my money in an industry that professes to care very much about the fight against AIDS—that gives umpteen benefits and charity affairs with proceeds going to research and care. But in actual fact, if an actor is even rumored to have HIV he gets no support on an individual basis. He does not work." Davis therefore felt he had to keep his illness a secret, always fearing that "somehow the gossip mill would get hold of me and that would be that: I'd be one more pariah in Hollywood who would never get a job."[2]

At least until *Philadelphia*, things had improved little in terms of studio-produced works about either homosexuals or AIDS. Television has greeted the subject with saber-rattling documentaries about the "threat" to the "general populace," and most dramatic portrayals (with a few notable exceptions) have opted to depict all people with AIDS as innocent victims of some outsider's guilt or indiscretion. Even when gays with AIDS were incorporated into a plot, the focus was generally directed not at their own situations but on the reactions of their families.

Even *Philadelphia* was treated with kid gloves by its studio, TriStar Pictures, which consistently refused to acknowledge it as a film about gays or AIDS and did its best to steer clear of gay or AIDS-aware reporters. (*Village Voice* columnist Michael Musto's sardonic account of his treatment at a star party after a screening is a notable case in point,[3] but many other reporters had similar experiences with the press department and other TriStar executives.) The company's insipid newspaper ad campaign for the film featured nothing more than bland profiles of Hanks and Washington, with quotes from some reviews, never once mentioning the words "gay" or "AIDS" (though this was in sharp contrast, for some inexplicable reason, to the TV trailers, which mention AIDS prominently while capitalizing on the courtroom dramatics of the film in a well-edited montage of intercut scenes).

Hollywood has, however, made a number of films that seem to be haunted by AIDS, turning its closeted concern into oblique but hardly subliminal references. Critics were quick to note the AIDS implications when the Fifties sci-fi classic *The Fly* was remade in 1986 by idiosyncratic horror master David Cronenberg. In the update, Jeff Goldblum plays the scientist who becomes diseased and infected after a botched teleportation experiment: there was a fly in the transport device and their genes got mixed. But unlike the scientist in the original film, who ends up with a mere fly head and arm, Goldblum turns into a creature that slowly transmogrifies from human to fly-creature, disintegrating from scene to scene and becoming more and more isolated and despairing as his deformity grows—an especially unsettling but powerful AIDS-like metaphor. Similarly, when Francis Ford Coppola made his version of *Bram Stoker's Dracula*, the parallels were bothersomely chilling: the vampire contamination being, of course, spread by blood—and predatory sex.

Almost no one was fooled by the cop-out of Joel Schumacher's *Dying Young*, where a handsome, wealthy, but rather eccentric young man

(Campbell Scott) succumbs to leukemia, while his caretaker (Julia Roberts) falls in love with him. Though the film lacked the conviction of even acknowledging that it was really about AIDS (and oddly so: the director admitted that he decided to do the film after a friend had died of AIDS,[4] and Scott, the son of George C. Scott and Colleen Dewhurst, had already played a gay character in another AIDS movie, *Longtime Companion*), it was credited by Hollywood as proving that a film about AIDS could not be successful at the box office.

Probably the most touching example of AIDS as oblique reference is the gentle Disney animation feature, *Beauty and the Beast*, a film project largely conceived by lyricist Howard Ashman (who also wrote the lyrics and screenplay for *The Littlest Mermaid* and *Little Shop of Horrors*) just before he died of AIDS. Drawing on the popular fairy tale about a handsome prince trapped in an ugly body, Ashman brings a particular poignancy to the anger and despair of the character who is condemned to live out his life as a giant dog-bear "Beast" unless he can find someone to love him before the last petal drops off a magical rose. Wonderfully executed by its animators, the film is full of touching moments which become even more poignant when the viewer knows the circumstances under which Ashman was working: he, like the Beast, was racing against the clock; he, too, had been transformed into something "other." But this Beast is too kind, from the start, to be really ugly or frightening, and he quite easily and rightfully wins the love of the film's Belle. At the end, when a second transformation takes place, one feels a strong sense of hope and justice, which is only slightly undercut by the irony of Ashman's own fatal illness.[5]

If Hollywood has been cowardly or overly obtuse about AIDS, independent and foreign filmmakers have dealt more directly with the subject, though there has not been any great groundswell of works about AIDS there, either, and such works have had much less distribution and attention than major studio movies.

In *Buddies* (New Line Cinema, 1985), Arthur J. Bressan, Jr., made one of the first independent features about AIDS, focusing on the relationship between a gay activist hospitalized with PCP (*Pneumycistis carinii* pneumonia, one of the most common conditions leading to a diagnosis of AIDS) and his caregiver, or "buddy," David (David Schachter). David has had no experience with AIDS prior to volunteering to help Robert (Geoff Edholm): he arrives at the hospital wearing a surgical mask and robe and rubber gloves, offering a box of candy; Robert quickly educates him, both about AIDS and about gay politics.[6]

Though both David and Robert have lovers, they remain off-screen presences. Robert's lover Edward has abandoned him; David's simply belongs to another world, not related to his caregiving and consciousness-raising. The focus remains on the transformational aspect of living with AIDS and caring for someone with AIDS, as David and Robert help each other towards a greater sense of identity and acceptance. The sexual subtext of that relationship is very potent (Bressan, who has since died of AIDS himself, was best known prior to this as a maker of gay erotic films), but the film, though in no way anti-erotic, chooses interestingly not to consummate the attraction that both men obviously feel for each other.

Near the end, David comes out in a newspaper interview as being both gay and an AIDS buddy; when he arrives at the hospital to show Robert the article, Robert has died. The final scene shows David outside the White House, holding a sign protesting government inaction on AIDS—the sign Robert would have carried, he had indicated earlier, if he could be given "24 hours of good health" before he died. David has become a fighter, a resister, an active participant in the struggle, taking up where Robert left off.

Made for New Zealand television in 1986, *A Death in the Family*, directed by Stewart Main and Peter Wells, is a documentary-like dramatization of the actual death of a young man named Andrew, surrounded by his adopted family: the gay and straight friends who stick with him and care for him through his illness. In his analysis of the film as good gay melodrama, Canadian critic Thomas Waugh has pointed out the special reverence with which Andrew is treated in the last sixteen days of his life:

> Andrew's body is constantly maintained in sensuous tactile contact with his grieving friends. Comfort is implicitly shared back and forth through caresses, touching, looks, and smiles. The bathing scene, a traditional format for the erotic representation of the body, is particularly eloquent in this regard, luxuriating in the textures of skin and fabric, in the light reflected in the movement of water, and above all in the simple child-like pleasure registered on Andrew's face.[7]

Even after his death, Waugh continues: "Andrew's corpse continues to be an erotic icon, like the bodies of martyrs in the Baroque painterly traditions evoked continuously by the filmmakers' composition and lighting." Such tenderness and romanticized sentiment stands in stark contrast to some controversial photographic representations of PWAs (see Chapter 14). But Main and Wells have their own distinct message to present, even hinting at a budding romantic liaison between two of the caretakers/mourners. There is, they seem to say, and there must be, life (and even sex) after others die, even if they die of AIDS.

Bill Sherwood's *Parting Glances* (Cinecon, 1986) was hailed as a breakthrough independent gay film at the time of its release. Interestingly, the subject of AIDS is presented as a subplot, not the main dramatic turning point of the action. Many gay critics have pointed out the necessity of such an approach, so that gays (and PWAs) become a real part of the total movie landscape: background characters, next-door neighbors, old boyfriends and girlfriends—not just the leading players in the foreground.

In *Parting Glances*, a secondary character has AIDS, though the main focus of the film is on two lovers, Michael and Robert, and the tension on their relationship due to Robert's imminent departure to take a new job in Africa. The character with AIDS, Nick (Steve Buscemi), is the ex-lover of Michael (Richard Ganoung), and it is partial testimony to the power of AIDS as subject matter that most critics have found the relationship between Michael and Nick far more interesting than that between Michael and Robert (John Bolger). Nick, a rock musician, faces his disease with a balance of bitterness and stoicism. As one observer has written: "Nick, while looking gaunt enough, shows no visible signs of the disease. He clearly understands the seriousness of his situation, but he is at times able to laugh in the face of death.... If nothing else, *Parting Glances* argues that the anguish of AIDS need not preclude the joy of life. Nick is too busy trying to live to worry very much about death. His friends seem to worry more about him than he worries about himself." [8] By refusing to accept the role of victim, Nick ends up teaching the two well characters a good deal about both life and relating.

P.J. Castelleneta's *Together Alone* (FrameLine, 1990) is a talky, two-person film about gay identity and HIV status. Filmed artily in stark black and white, it begins with a pickup in a gay bar, the camera following the two guys home, one on his bike, the other in a car. After the lights go out, then come back on, there's a long exchange of opinions and ideas between Bryan (Todd Stites) and Brian (Terry Curry), who, back in the bar, originally had told Bryan (the one with a "Y") that his name was Bill. This denial of his own name is not appreciated by the other Bryan.

As the two have just engaged in unsafe sex, the question of HIV status also comes up rather quickly. Bryan is negative, but now worried: he has never had anal sex before. Brian, on the other hand, states, "I never got tested. If I get AIDS, I'll deal with it then. I'll deal with it if I have to, not before." Much talk then ensues about control and responsibility, as we find out more and more about these two polar-opposite sex partners: Bryan, the one with the bike and the apartment, is the over-cautious, passive, slightly wimpy one: blond, flip, self-effacing, politically aware. He has never had a relationship which lasted longer than six months, though he did have a desperate crush on his college roommate. Brian, the laissez-faire hedonist brunet, is the active bisexual one—the more philosophical and romantic of the two, considerably less political, but worried that people may think of him as "too smooth, too shallow, too much the party personality." He too is haunted by an experience from his past, like Bryan's unconsummated love for his college roommate: in Brian's case there was a girl whom he desperately wanted to marry, especially after getting her pregnant, but who ditched him when she found out about his side attraction to guys.

With so many differences—and Bryan's reference to yin and yang ("They complement and contain each other, and no line drawn through the circle will ever be all black or all white")—naturally we're set up for Brian's announcement: "I think you have to admit it, Bryan, there's something between us."

Later when Bryan finds out that Brian is both married and "just in town for the week," he has good reason for animosity, but by then things have gotten very sticky emotionally in this one-night stand. The two have even discovered that they both had the same dream after having sex, something about flying and feathers, then diving deep into dark waters.

The film concludes with an open-ended exchange that leaves the "who will call whom" responsibility up to Bryan. "Maybe I will, and maybe I won't," he shrugs. Castelleneta seems clearly to be positing the yin and yang of the AIDS era gay personality: Bryan and Brian as two halves of the same whole. Maybe they'll get together. Maybe not. One can't help but wish it weren't such a chilly proposition, for characters and audience alike.

When New York playwright Craig Lucas wrote *Longtime Companion*, it was the closest thing American movies had had to a Hollywood movie prior to *Philadelphia*, though the project was rejected by every major studio and ended up being financed by public television (PBS's "American Playhouse") in 1990. It was directed by Lucas's longtime collaborator, Norman Rene.

The film tells the story of a group of friends, living in New York City and summering on Fire Island, by examining one day in their lives during scenes set in each of nine years, from 1981 to 1989. It is thus a progressive tale of the toll of AIDS on one particular group of friends, and all the complex responses are there: horror, anger, pain, grief, nostalgia for the past, and, ultimately, transformation and conscience.

Lucas's script in no way pretends that his characters are representative of a whole spectrum of people with AIDS: works of art hardly tend to be equal opportunity employers or to follow quota systems. As one analyst of the film, John M. Clum has pointed out:

> The young men we see live in roomy, expensive Manhattan apart-ments and Fire Island beach houses. They are either rich or, through their beauty, charm, and availability, friends of the rich. The men work in advertising or show business. One writes episodes of a soap opera in which another stars. These men see the new "gay cancer" as something that couldn't touch them. It must be attacking men who are sleazier, more promiscuous, dirtier than they would ever be.[9]

The irony—and whole point of the film, of course—is that they aren't immune to the plague: there is no "they" and "us," between the gay characters in the film and other gays, or indeed between gays (and people with AIDS) and the audience. The film was subsequently both attacked and defended for its presentation of affluent, well-adjusted homosexuals: "For once, a film is inhabited by beautiful, well-adjusted gay people for whom homosexuality is not a problem. It is a cosmetically perfect fantasy world—gay men deserve to see that once in a while—but it is also just that fantasy, that gay version of the American dream, that AIDS has destroyed."[10]

This nostalgia materializes in a fantasy sequence near the end of the film. Three of the characters (one gay couple and a straight woman who's the sister of one) have gotten together on Fire Island to remember the friends they've lost during the eight-year time-frame of the film. As they reminisce, all their dead friends come back and join them for one last party on the beach, ending things on a bittersweet but touching note of irony.[11]

In general, screen documentaries about AIDS have lacked the polish and impact of such TV projects (detailed in Chapter 7) as *Common Threads, Absolutely Positive, Tongues Untied*, or *Silverlake Life*. Mark Hustis's *Sex Is...*, as its title implies, clearly has other fish to fry, though it purports to be a documentary about gay life before, during, and since the advent of AIDS, intercutting interviews of 14 men with flashes of hard-core porn. Kermit Cole's *Living Proof: HIV and the Pursuit of Happiness* documents a photography project of the same name attempting to show positive images of people who are HIV positive, but in its attempt to show only the non-negative side of the epidemic, it ends up ringing false (not even acknowledging, for example, that the founder of the project, George DiSipio, died of the epidemic during the filming).

Juan Botas's *One Foot on a Banana Peel, the Other Foot in the Grave*, on the other hand, succeeds honestly where the other two documentaries fail: it remains insistently straightforward about the disease, unburdened by any ulterior motive to prove some sort of other agenda about sex or positive representation. Botas went to Jonathan Demme and other members of Demme's production company, Clinica Estecica, and told them he'd like to make a film about "the Dolly Madison room," an outpatient clinic where AIDS patients could get daily IV medications without being hospitalized. During the course of the documentary, ten patients (including Botas himself) are interviewed, along with the clinic's founder, Dr. Paul Bellman, and two health care workers; together they form a spunky alliance against AIDS and the rest of the world. Botas felt that "important kinds of dialogue were happening in that room," involving "humor, heroism, insight, soap opera—a lot of different things."

The document has an extraordinary raw power to it. Both the camerawork and editing are unabashedly rough, and the sound is occasionally hard to understand: life went on at the clinic while the interviews were taking place, so there are ringing telephones, other people talking, and assorted background noises throughout.

The force driving the film (and, one feels, of the Dolly Madison Room itself) was Botas: as artist and patient, interviewer and interviewee, his spirit and personality are everywhere evident. The documentary covers only four months of time, from May 12, 1992, to mid-August of that year, when Botas was hospitalized. As they wait for news of Botas's condition, the others who come to the clinic try to talk about how they feel about his absence and, later, his death (the film was finished by its editor, Lucas

Platt). The answers are not easy. "This is the down side of the Dolly Madison Room," another PWA, Daniel Chapman, says after Juan is hospitalized. "There are little counterpoints of joviality that make you able to bear it. Being able to work through it is ultimately the up side. But then there's this down side." The final credits include more sad notes, as well: four other citizens of the Dolly Madison Room have also died, as of late 1993. But it is a great tribute to Botas as a canny first-time filmmaker that he managed to capture both sides of the picture—both up and down—so honestly and well.

Four of the features in *Boys' Shorts* (FrameLine, 1993), a collection of short films which was billed in its New York theatrical run as an example of the "new queer cinema," deal directly with AIDS. The other two examine gay-bashing and gay self-defense, a reaction to stigmatism that owes much to the new consciousness of AIDS activism.

The opening sequence, "Resonance," by Australians Stephen Cummins and Simon Hunt, is a black-and-white ode to empowerment, using dance and poetry ("Lined up in your sights / I live beyond your reach / My steps resonate") to pose an alternative to both queer-bashing skinheads and abusive heterosexual boyfriends.

Laurie Lynd's "R.S.V.P." is a small gem of a film, telling a tale of loss and grieving through subtle visual references underpinned with messages on a telephone answering machine ("Hello, this is Andrew and Sid, we're not here now, leave a message." "Hello, Sid, I hope Winnipeg was OK. The service is on Friday. Bobby's going to sing.") and a radio broadcast of a write-in musical request show ("This is Jessye Norman in a selection from Berlioz' *Les Nuits d'Été*, which is requested by Andrew Selman of Toronto, who regrets he was not able to hear it in her recent concert. Andrew requests the CD version, which we have just received. Now on 'R.S.V.P.,' Jessye Norman in "Le Spectre de la Rose."). A man we assume is Sid, who has just walked in with a load of groceries, fumbles nervously trying to record the selection from the radio, then calls Winnipeg, to tell Andrew's sister and parents to listen to the broadcast as well. As the song soars, the scene shifts, not only between Toronto and Winnipeg, but also to an AIDS activist office and bookstore (where Andrew's obituary is being posted on a bulletin board already overcrowded with such notices), to a dentist's office, to a restaurant/bar (where a black waitress listens for a while, then changes the station, looking for a music less mournful), to the halls of the high school where another notice has been posted, onto which two teenage boys, whispering "Selman, the English teacher," have just scrawled the word "FAGGOT"). The camera returns to Sid who is looking around the apartment at all the memory-objects left behind: pills in a refrigerator, clothes, a favorite sweater, a wall of photos representing his life with Andrew and their cat, named George (presumably after George Eliot, whose words form an epigram at the start of the film: "So I shall join / the choir invisible / Whose music is / the gladness of the world."). Words, images, sounds of grief merge together softly, a near-perfect elegy to loss and to life.

Marlon Riggs' "Anthem" is black and proud and angry, using poetry and rap and fast visual cutting to celebrate gay black identity. "Freaky, free…. Flaunt it like a man," proclaims the voice-over at one point. "*Pervert* the language," it advocates at another. Two men kiss. Images flash by of an American flag, the black liberation banner, the SILENCE = DEATH button (see Chapter 13), a bottle of Vaseline, a cockring, a cross, an African spear.

In Christopher Newly's ironically titled "Relax," a young gay man waits desperately for the results of his HIV test, which the doctor tells him will not be ready for ten days. He tries sunbathing with a friend, sexual fantasy, cruising in a dark alley, but nothing helps the stress (even a scene where his kinky trick pours motor oil all over his body—obviously a variant of safe sex, though one of questionable sanitary value in other respects). At the end, he gets the result: "Syphilis, negative. HIV, negative." But as soon as his perplexed hero starts to celebrate (relax), director Newly pulls a fast one on him: the final scene replays, with exactly the opposite result(s). Blackout.

In Michael Mayson's "Billy Turner's Secret," there's not much suspense regarding what Billy Turner's secret is: he's gay, and he's trying to hide it from his straight, sexy, homophobic roommate Rufus and the rest of his black Brooklyn friends and neighbors. The story unfolds as conventional narrative (none of the allusiveness of "R.S.V.P." here): good story, good plot developement, good characters (also including Rufus's girlfriend and her sassy younger sister, Billy's boyfriend, and a very spunky queen who's a friend of the girlfriend). Billy finally comes out and Rufus gets his comeuppance, first being knocked out by Billy then being decimated on a basketball court by the queen he keeps insulting. But there's one final secret (or at least surprise) in store when the credits roll, though perhaps the viewer should have gotten the hint when the screen went black the two times that Rufus was knocked out: Rufus, the character, is played by Michael Mayson, the director.

Mark Christopher's "Dead Boys' Club" opens with a shy guy named Toby in a blue baseball cap standing at a bus stop, where he's being cruised by a Christopher Street clone in cut-offs. The guy gives him his name and telephone number, but Toby tosses it in a trash can and heads on to meet his cousin, who is helping a friend sort through the belongings of someone who has obviously died of AIDS. One of them gives Toby the dead man's dancing shoes, which appear to be haunted by years of cruise bars, sex clubs, and disco dancing (sort of like the finale to *Longtime Companion*). As soon as Toby dons the shoes, he hears Thelma Huston belt out "Don't Leave Me This Way," his shyness vanishes, and he can have his pick of anyone on the street, the bar, or the gym. He meets up with Dick again, goes home with him, wakes up, gets out of bed, and promptly steps on the open tube of KY lubricant and finds an unopened condom beside the bed. Switching shoes with Dick, he rushes out into the morning light (just as Dick rolls over and reveals an *opened* condom package underneath his body: they had had safe sex after all). Although Dick returns the shoes, Toby then throws them out the window, convinced he's gotten rid of them at last. But in the next scene, he's walking down the street and sees that a street vendor has them for sale, along with old record albums by Sixties rock groups like Spirit and It's a Beautiful Day. He stops to glance through the albums, and another young guy (in a baseball cap just like him), shyly casts a furtive glance at Toby. The guy looks away, embarrassed, then he spots the magic dancing shoes.

The beat goes on.

In Gregg Araki's films, no one remembers Thelma Huston or It's a Beautiful Day; everyone wears baseball caps or post-punk minimalist garb and listens to alternative or industrial bands like Braindead Sound Machine, Psychic TV, and Drance. In *Totally F***ed Up*, shown at the 1993 New York Film Festival, a mixed bag of young nihilists, mostly gay and lesbian, spend most of their time stoned and horizontal, either in beds or just sprawled out on the floor, lamenting the lack of meaning or relationships in the age of AIDS and homophobia. Their plight is deeply disturbing—and Araki makes no attempt to either glamorize it or moralize about it—all the more so because it is so honestly laid out. These characters have nothing to be nostalgic about, no magic disco shoes to slip into, nothing, really, to be hopeful about.

Araki's previous feature, *The Living End*, has more liveliness, but is hardly less bleak. In it, two young gay men who have just learned they are HIV positive, take off on a cross-country spree, following the general attitude of the opening graffiti image of the film: "FUCK THE WORLD." Though structured tongue-in-cheek after the traditional road movie, these good-time boys have more than hedonism on their mind, believing (rightly or wrongly) that they have a death sentence hanging over their head from the word go.

Araki has described the genesis of *The Living End* (originally entitled *Fuck the World*) as follows:

> It came from a very dark, personal place—those feelings of dread and insecurity, which characterized the mid-late 80s AIDS crisis pervaded the consciousness of my whole generation. Even though I am HIV-negative, the specter of the virus loomed overhead like a radioactive cloud. Suddenly sex, love, trust, desire—which are troublesome enough in themselves for gays and straights—were even more emotionally treacherous. What would I do if I tested positive? How would I feel? What would my reaction be? Being something of a hopeless romantic, I found the concept of "till death do us part" more and more thematically and metaphorically pertinent.[12]

Araki's films hold a bleak sense of despair, yet there's something gentle and wistful about them. Almost a tenderness, almost a kind of hope:

> In the back of my mind, I was sort of hoping that by the time THE LIVING END was finally released, the AIDS holocaust would be over and the movie would be something of an anachronism. Unfortunately, given our presentday sociocultural climate of rightwing oppression and rampant gaybashing, it seems even more relevant now than when it was written over three years ago. And while it may appear angry and confrontational, THE LIVING END to me has always been a love story calling for tolerance and compassion. If it manages to open at least a few minds, it will have served its purpose in my eyes.[13]

A number of films have broached the equally bleak subject of plague as a metaphor for AIDS and the despair and discrimination that often accompany it. Meredith Monk's *Book of Days* and Vincent Ward's Australian feature *The Navigator* both eerily contrast a medieval pestilence (the Black Death) with the present; AIDS is strongly implicit in both films, which tend more toward dream-like surrealism and poetry than straightforward narrative, and both have a compelling sense of sadness and urgency, and a feeling that little progress has been made in the centuries which have passed since the Black Death, either in terms of combatting disease or the corresponding social conditions and attitudes which accompany it.

Argentine director Luis Puenzo (*The Official Story*) filmed a 1992 version of Albert Camus' *The Plague*, starring William Hurt as Rieux, the doctor who helps a French seaport town struggle through a strange and devastating outbreak of bubonic plague. Puenzo and director David Pittman chose to downplay any correlation to AIDS, keeping the movie a metaphor for the epidemic of fascism (a limited reading of the Camus novel often favored in academic circles). At any rate, people stayed away in droves wherever the film was shown, and the movie never opened in the U.S.

Other than the recent, award-winning French film *Savage Nights* (see Chapter 4), not too many foreign films about AIDS have made it to the United States, even to the gay film festivals in major cities like New York, Los Angeles, and San Francisco. Third world directors in Africa and Asia seem as unready to confront the epidemic as are their Hollywood and European peers, with a few exceptions.

One such exception is the iconoclastic gay German director, Rosa von Praunheim. His name, like his sensibility, is adopted: everything Rosa does is a bit of a shock to staid mainstream sensibilities of propriety and style. He makes primarily documentaries, including a number that have dealt directly with AIDS, in both Europe and the United States. *Silence = Death*, which takes its title from one of the most popular slogans of the AIDS activist group ACT UP, opens with a performance artist (Emilio Cubeiro) faking rectal suicide with a pistol ("I want to die the way I lived") and also features interviews with poet Allen Ginsberg and artists Keith Haring and David Wojnarowicz. *Positive* is a second documentary spotlighting outspoken playwright and activist Larry Kramer, film director Phil Zwickler, and singer activist Michael Callen. But von Praunheim is most notorious for his first AIDS film, a pseudo-documentary employing high camp and barbed satire, *A Virus Knows No Morals*. At the time of its release in this country in 1987, no one was using humor or camp to deal with the subject of AIDS, and some of the audiences who saw the film at the New York Shakespeare Festival

Public Theater's film division stormed out in an angry huff. No one really escapes getting lambasted in the film, from government and medical villains to AIDS activists (and even the director himself, who makes a cameo appearance as the sleazy proprietor of a gay bath house).

Another German director, Jochen Hick, made his 1992 film *Via Appia* in Brazil, following a German airline steward through the back streets of Rio as he tries to track down a male prostitute who has scrawled "Welcome to the AIDS Club" on the mirror of a hotel room the night they tricked. The search, which proceeds with growing desperation as the steward worries about whether he has been infected or not, is not above pandering to the audience's wish to see Brazilian hustlers strutting their stuff on the streets and beaches of Rio. But the hero's dilemma is unsettling, even though the director seems uncomfortably close to implying that the situation is the character's "own fault."

Peter's Friends, by British director Kevin Branagh (*Henry V, A Midsummer Night's Dream*), offers a similar problem of attitude on the part of its well-meaning characters. The film is a nice little British chamber piece. To call it an AIDS film unfortunately gives away the plot gimmick, sort of like revealing the Jaye Davidson secret in *The Crying Game*. In *Peter's Friends*, Branagh and his wife, Emma Thompson, star in a story that centers around a reunion of old college chums at the country estate of Peter (Stephen Fry), who has never married, for reasons that become more and more apparent as the plot unfolds. His final disclosure of his HIV status, though it quickly sobers up Branagh from a horrid drunk scene, is both sentimental and misleading. Everyone rushes to sympathize, and there's even a reconciliation with the crusty old cook, who'd been ready to leave the estate after Peter's father's death, but now, apparently, will stay on to care-take and care-give. But like a number of earnest, liberal attempts to show solidarity with PWAs and to increase awareness of the epidemic, the film unfortunately perpetuates one of the major myths about AIDS: that testing positive for the HIV virus means not only that one is doomed to get the virus (which is often not the case) but that one is doomed, period.

In general, almost all these films mentioned so far, including *Philadelphia*, have opted to tell the story of AIDS in straightforward, conventional narratives—certainly a worthwhile and, in some cases, effective approach. But considering the radical challenge that AIDS presents to life and art, surprisingly few of these works use similar radical techniques—the unique-

ly visual tools of framing, perspective, and montage at film's disposal
which make it so effective a medium.

The best of these works cinematically—like the "R.S.V.P." segment of
Boys' Shorts, Gregg Araki's films, or Meredith Monk's *Book of Days*—are
usually the most subtle and obscure in terms of direct narrative references
to AIDS. It is as if most of the other filmmakers distrusted relying on cinematic style alone to tell their tales, preferring theatrical or TV-documen-
tary-like devices instead. The directors in the next chapter exhibit a very
different attitude, offering films that break down barriers of technique as
well as content, and their works are among the most powerful yet presented in any medium about AIDS.

4

Three Iconoclasts: Derek Jarman, Cyril Collard, & John Greyson

ccasionally a film comes along, either inside or outside the AIDS community, that challenges all the old conventions, offering a unique perspective on its subject matter and questioning the very nature of filmmaking itself. Derek Jarman's *Blue*, Cyril Collard's *Savage Nights*, and John Greyson's *Zero Patience* all do this, pushing beyond previous ideas of cinematic form and discourse and, at the same time, making the viewer see their subject matter—AIDS—in a completely new way. Jarman and Greyson have been longtime rebels and innovators in the worlds of film and video. *Savage Nights* was Collard's first and only feature film, but Collard had spent most of his life in various aspects of movie-making and *Savage Nights* shows a canny knowledge of the cinematic vocabulary. It also stunned moviegoers with the idiosyncratic and perhaps amoral approach it takes to AIDS, in presenting a bisexual AIDS-infected anti-hero (played by Collard himself) who continues to have sex with both male and female partners with what seems to be little remorse.

Both Collard and Jarman have since died of AIDS, so the temptation is strong to see their film statements as completely autobiographical. At any rate, both films examine the thin line between fact and fiction, imagination and reality, which is always such fertile ground for cinematic exploration. And all three directors refuse to simply let their AIDS story unfold in a conventional narrative way: each instead gives his film a look and style that is as unique as its subject matter.

Derek Jarman's *Blue* is noteworthy in that it is the first on-film statement by an internationally known movie director about his own experience of AIDS: the very structure of the film, in fact, reflects Jarman's condition. Diagnosed some time ago as infected with CMV (cytomegalovirus), the British director, known primarily for his lush, homoerotic imagery in works like *Sebastiane, Caravaggio,* and *Edward II*, had been slowly and painfully going blind for two years when he made *Blue*. He died in February, 1994, the winter after the film was shown to acclaim both in London, where Jarman lived and worked, and at the prestigious New York Film Festival.

To help the moviegoer appreciate the extent to which loss of sight affects a visual artist, Jarman made a film in which the screen, from start to finish, is a even expanse of blue: there are no images, no moving actors or actions, only this resonant, reverberating blue. Against this *carte bleu*, the director placed voices and music, memories of happier times, and details of his deteriorating physical condition. The result is an extraordinarily moving presentation of the conflicting meanings of AIDS in his own life: an uncensored compendium of both the prose and poetry of the epidemic, from the mundane to the sublime.

But both anger and melancholy converge in *Blue*, along with lots of irony. The film has been released on CD rather than videotape, capturing the aural nature of the project: its words, its voices, its musical backgrounds. But the impact of the looking deeply into the solid expanse of blue filling an entire movie screen is missing, though the CD jewel box and booklet emulate the device. The CD case has no title on it (other than on the spine), nor does the enclosed booklet. Both instead are solid blue, but not quite the shade of blue on the screen of the film, and not the same shade as each other, one being printed on paper, the other on plastic.

Blue unfolds on several levels, sonically and verbally, beginning with the ringing of what sound like Tibetan prayer bells. Three narrators join Jarman's own voice as readers or characters: Tilda Swinton (a regular in Jarman's films who also starred in Sally Potter's *Orlando*), John Quentin, and Nigel Terry. Of the three male voices heard, one is soft and poetic, one querulous and sarcastic, one somewhere in between, rather matter-of-fact. We aren't told for sure which is Jarman himself. The voices mesh, actually, into a kind of tapestry of sound, an effect that seems intentional.

The word "AIDS" is not used until ten minutes or so into the film, but there is no doubt, from the beginning, what the film is about. An opening poetic reverie about a boy named Blue (the title word shifts throughout: sometimes it's a character, sometimes a color, sometimes a symbolic concept, sometimes an emotional state) quickly gives way to a jolting opening scene in which the narrator is sitting in a cafe talking about the war in Bosnia when a woman remarks to him that he has his clothes "on back to front and inside out." Jarman immediately philosophizes, "What need of so much news from abroad while all that concerns either life or death is all transacting and at work within me?"[1]

The next scene places the speaker at St. Bartholomew's Hospital where the doctor "could detect lesions in my retina" and the nightmare begins: that condition which has taken so many friends from him is now his own burden. A storm rages and he hears "the voices of dead friends...David. Howard. Graham. Terry. Paul." His disease progresses, and the doctor diagnoses CMV, thus ending six years of fear and uncertainty. Now the speaker must face not only physical deterioration but the symbolic and emotional weight of near blindness as well: "If I lose half my sight will my vision he halved?"

Jarman's description of the physical ravages of the disease are almost brutally clinical, like the journals of New York artist David Wojnarowicz[2] or the late autobiographical novels of French writer Hervé Guibert,[3] as they faced their own slow deaths from AIDS. Jarman speaks with a flat, matter-of-fact tone:

> The virus rages fierce. I have no friends now who are not dead or dying. Like a blue frost it caught them. At work, at the cinema, on marches and beaches. In churches on their knees, running, flying, silent or shouting protest.

> It started with sweats in the night and swollen glands. Then the black cancers spread across their faces—as they fought for breath, TB and pneumonia hammered at the lungs, and Toxo at the brain. Reflexes scrambled—sweat poured through hair matted like lianas in the tropical forest. Voices slurred—and then were lost forever.

At times the objectivity gives way to anger: "I shall not win the battle against the virus—in spite of slogans like 'Living with AIDS.' The virus was appropriated by the well—so we have to live with AIDS while they spread the quilt for the moths of Ithaca across the wine dark sea." The anger shifts from political to spiritual in his next remark: "The Guatama Buddha instructs me to walk away from illness. But he wasn't attached to a drip."

Then comes a fantasy in which Blue (now again a character) is in a labyrinth "built from crystals and mirrors which in the sunlight cause terrible blindness." Blue must move carefully and remain absolutely silent, as Jarman also seems to poetically describe his own fragile, labyrinth-like condition: "The archaeology of sound has only just been perfected and the systematic cataloging of words has until recently been undertaken in a haphazard way. Blue watched as a word or phrase materialised in scintillating sparks, a poetry of fire which cast everything into darkness with the brightness of his reflections." Then the speaker wonders, "How did my friends cross the cobalt river? With what did they pay the ferryman?" He recalls the specifics of their deteriorations: "David ran home panicked on the train from Waterloo, brought back exhausted and unconscious to die that night. Terry who mumbled incoherently into his incontinent tears.... Howard turned slowly to stone, petrified day by day, his mind imprisoned in a concrete fortress until all we could hear were his groans on the telephone circling the globe."

Switching from prose to poetry once more in the text, the speaker adds: "We all contemplated suicide / We hoped for euthanasia / We were lulled into believing / Morphine dispelled pain / Rather than making it tangible / Like a mad Disney cartoon / Transforming itself into / Every conceivable nightmare."

In the eeriest moment of the film, the speaker recites a laundry list of the side effects of the drug DHPG:

> Low white blood cell count, increased risk of infection, low platelet count which may increase the risk of bleeding, low red blood cell count (anaemia), fever, rash, abnormal liver function, chills, swelling of the body (oedema), infections, malaise, irregular heart beat, high blood pressure (hypertension), low blood pressure (hypotension), abnormal thoughts or dreams, loss of balance (ataxia), coma, confusion, dizziness, headache, nervousness, damage to nerves (peristhecia), psychosis, sleepiness (somnolence), shaking, nausea, vomiting, loss of appetite (anorexia), diarrhoea, bleeding from the stomach or intestine (intestinal haemorrhage), abdominal pain, increased number of one type of white blood cell, low blood sugar, shortness of breath, hair loss (alopecia), itching (pruritus), hives, blood in the urine, abnormal kidney function, increased blood urea, redness (inflammation), pain or irritation (phlebitis).

As his condition deteriorates, the speaker faces a progression of frustrations and indignities, from stinging eyedrops to bitter pills (30 a day now) and white flashes. He begins to worry about his caregiver ("I must try and cheer up H.B. as he has had a hell of a fortnight.") He thinks about buying a new pair of shoes but decides, "The shoes I am wearing at the moment should be sufficient to walk me out of life." Memories rush in, accompanied by poetic images of his little boy Blue "His blue jeans / Around his ankles," holding on tight to this erotic vision as his own sight grows dimmer and dimmer and he acknowledges time and life are running out "like sparks through the stubble."

"I place a delphinium, Blue, on your grave."

The original French title of Cyril Collard's *Savage Nights* alludes to its technique as well as its content: *Les Nuits Fauves* was both a play on the idea of wild or savage nights and a reference to fauvism, a movement in French painting in the early years of the twentieth century known for its use of bright, primary colors and "bold, often distorted forms."[4] The leading character of the film, a handsome film technician named Jean (played by Collard himself) drives around Paris is a glistening red sports car. Most of the scenes are shot in hot white sunlight or equally bright neon artificial light. Even Jean's anonymous sexual assignations under a bridge are bathed in tones of cool blues and purples. The costumes and decors are mostly bold and trendy, in wild primary colors the fauvists would have loved, reminiscent of such expert Technicolor stylists as Douglas Sirk and Rainer Werner Fassbinder.

The main action of the film takes place in Paris, where Jean bounces back and forth between a new girlfriend and a new boyfriend, plus various quickie encounters with faceless men in the dark in semi-public places. Though he has been diagnosed HIV positive and is beginning to show some symptoms of AIDS, he seems to not quite believe his condition most of the time—and he certainly doesn't accept it. At the moments when he does acknowledge the facts, to himself or others, he seems to be trying to drown his fear and anger in more and more passion and lust. The attitude takes its toll, not so much on his own physical well-being (which continues to hold up remarkably well) but on the mental and emotional states of the two people who love him: Laura (Romane Bohringer) and Samy (Carlos Lopez). When he first has unprotected sex with Laura, he doesn't even tell her of his condition. He later casually drops the bombshell in a scene where the camera stays riveted on both characters, seen facing each other from opposite sides of the frame; the camera never blinks, and neither character can escape either it or the information that has just been revealed. Jean's tantalizing seduction of Samy, a Gypsy by birth and a rugby player by trade, is hardly more conscientious, though at one point Jean does rather half-heartedly tell Samy to use a condom (as he later advises Laura as well), though all three now seem to have given in to what they perceive as the hopelessness of the situation, as if it were now too late to worry.

Both Laura and Samy crack under this wild promiscuous swirl, being played off not only against each other but against other casual sex partners as well. Laura ends up having a complete breakdown and being hospitalized; Samy turns to sadomasochism and joins a skinhead gang that preys on foreigners (like himself) and queers.

In a kind of last-minute display of nobility, Jean visits Laura in her institution, to see how she's doing, and orchestrates a scene between Samy and his musician kid brother Paco, a powerful moment which indicates maybe Samy might get his life back on track (as indeed Laura does, thanks partly to Jean). When the skinheads try to beat up a customer outside a gay bar, Jean intervenes, cutting his hand with a glass and threatening the bullies with his AIDS-contaminated blood.

Two scenes outside Paris frame the film: the opening scene, in Morocco, has Jean confront a mysterious non-Arab woman (Maria Schneider) during a music festival. She gives him a key and tells him to loosen his grip on life (misreported by one New York critic as "Lose your grip on life") and to learn from his disease. It's a lesson that it takes Jean the entire film to learn. But at the end, the character faces the setting sun on the western coast of Portugal and acknowledges that though AIDS may kill him and will now always be a part of his life, it is not *all* of his life. It seems doubtful that he will go back to Paris and continue to live and love and infect more partners in the same selfish way, for there's been a kind of reversal, a major shift in attitude: the sun, which is supposed to be setting (after all it's the west coast of Portugal) begins to rise in the sky instead, filling the screen with white hot light, washing out the fauvist savagery at last.

Collard himself died of AIDS three days before *Les Nuit Fauves* won four Césars (the French equivalent of the Oscars), including best debut film and best picture. Up until his death, the author/director remained obstinately true to his vision: "AIDS, like tuberculosis in Thomas Mann's *The Magic Mountain*, is just a backdrop," he's quoted as saying in the production notes to the film.[5] "Jean's struggle with the illness is also a struggle with stupid-ity, with all sorts of racism, with tyranny.... Jean acts as though nothing were different in his daily life. He continues to drink, laugh and drive fast. In his own way, he is shattering the taboos. He doesn't let himself get locked into the status of being HIV positive, like some people for whom the illness becomes a sort of identity card."

Far from seeing AIDS as a prison, he seems to see it as a key, like that given him by the Maria Schneider character in the prologue: "I believe that AIDS is a kind of language, that it has 'something to tell us.' It brings to the forefront all of the dysfunctions and aberrations of our society....The threat of death gives meaning to everything that had no meaning for Jean. Artistic creation can be used to that end. I believe in the idea that an artist must be engaged in his times. I made this film with the purpose of opening up toward others."

John Greyson's *Zero Patience* is a wild and wicked take on AIDS, completely different from any of the films previously discussed, not so much because of what it says or does (which are outrageous enough) but because Greyson is a true original, somehow at once political and apolitical, campy and serious, highly literate yet extremely visual. One has to look pretty far afield for comparisons: Pedro Almodóvar perhaps, or New York's late Charles Ludlam and his Ridiculous Theatrical Company.

The title of *Zero Patience* is a play on Randy Shilts' problematic conceit in his study of the early history of the AIDS crisis, *And the Band Played On: People, Politics, and the Epidemic*:[6] namely, that "Patient Zero," a Canadian airline steward named Gaetan Dugas, was *the* person primarily responsible for bringing AIDS to North America and spreading it to a "cluster" of tricks (and in turn their sex partners) in Canada, New York City, Los Angeles, and San Francisco. The film sets out to rescue poor Zero's name and reputation and to question two other alleged "causes" of AIDS: the African Green Monkey (a theory now widely discredited) and the HIV virus (the theory of the moment, which Greyson also brazenly challenges).

The first scene features a cute young schoolboy, of undetermined exotic multicultural lineage, recounting to his classmates the tale of Scheherazade, the dancing girl who has to satisfy her sultan nightly—not in the usual way, but by telling an intriguing story. If she manages to get through 1001 nights that way (*The Arabian Nights*, in other words), she can go free.

Cut to scene two, where a Murphy Brown-soundalike TV reporter voice-over introduces us to Richard Francis Burton (the British explorer and translator of classic erotica, including, not coincidentally, *The Arabian Nights*—not the Welsh actor who was one of the several husbands of Elizabeth Taylor). This Burton, contrary to popular opinion, is apparently still alive and well (and looking quite young and trim in fact), working as chief taxidermist at the Natural History Museum in Toronto. He is preparing an exhibit on "Plagues of the World" and has just gotten the bad news that the museum can't spring for the $60,000 tab to buy him the Plague Rat of Düsseldorf. "But that rat was to be our Book of Kells, our Shroud of Turin, our King Tut death mask!" he storms. Tut, tut, his boss, Dr. Placebo, informs him: it can't be helped.

Suddenly the screen explodes into Esther Williams-style swimming pool aquatics and male diver gymnastics: a high camp production number, in other words, right here in the middle of a movie about AIDS. Enter Patient Zero, walking through scenes of singing, dancing, swimming, diving, and hot tub splendor, while Burton at the same time puzzles over how to save his "Hall of Contagion" exhibit now that he can't get the rat. Finally Zero figures out that no one can see him ("I'm a fucking ghost"), just as Burton hits on the idea of making the late villain, Patient Zero himself, his Düsseldorf plague rat, the *pièce de résistance* centerpiece for his exhibit. He immediately approaches Dr. Placebo, who at first scowls a bit. "A promiscuous, irresponsible homosexual Canadian?" he harrumphs. "That's hardly a very good role model." Burton smiles, "But he's French Canadian," and old Placebo grins from ear to ear. They quickly agree that this will top even the stuffed African Green Monkey, which had been the focus of the AIDS exhibit in the Hall of Contagion up until then.

Zero continues to roam his old haunts, looking for someone who can see him, while Burton videotapes interviews with Zero's old friends and family, which he then re-edits to "prove" Zero's guilt. One of these women friends happens to be a member of Canada's version of ACT UP, so a whole sub-plot (to take over the project) begins to simmer. Meanwhile Burton proceeds with his plans for an elaborate MTV-type presentation, with red lasers, a 20-foot hologram, and "towers of video monitors" to tell Zero's sad and dastardly tale. Dr. Placebo thinks they can probably interest Gilbert N. Sullivan Pharmaceuticals in sponsoring the show—especially if they can coopt the radicals into being part of the show (good press, you know, old boy). The company also figures the opening of the exhibit will be the perfect venue for introducing their latest overpriced drug for AIDS-related cytomegalovirus (CMV), named (for the occasion) Zed-P-Zero.

It's inevitable that Zero and Burton meet, of course, and since Burton is the only one who can see Zero, the two are destined to become boyfriends (as much as a recent ghost and someone who was supposed to die about a hundred years ago can become boyfriends, that is). Zero visits the Hall of Contagion, with its wax Typhoid Mary and an animated painting of a Dutch plague ship with naked sailors jumping off of it. He also meets the other two scapegoats: the African Green Monkey, who comes to life as a spunky lesbian, and Miss HIV, played by the late Michael Callen in drag.

There are wild song-and-dance scenes throughout—a trio of naked guys singing in blue spotlights in a bathhouse shower room, for example, and even one truly tasteless bit with some singing sphincters (they can animate anything these days, after those California raisins started singing)—and Zero keeps reappearing wearing the same gray T-shirt with different writing on it (all having to do with eyes or blindness—a reference to the CMV drug—such as "Love Is Blind," "An Eye for an Eye," "Eye of the Storm," "Cry Me a River," and "Seeing Is Believing"). Meanwhile a secondary character, the teacher of the cute kid in the opening classroom scene (remember? Scheherazade, singing for her life) develops CMV, can't afford the drug, and is visited by the kid (who later told a very bad AIDS joke one day in class and needs to apologize) in the hospital. And, of course, the grand opening of the expanded exhibit is transformed, gloriously, by a radical takeover of the museum and the exhibit.

What does it all come down to? A challenge to the whole Cause-and-Cure Syndrome—that PWAs should be blamed for their own disease, and that capitalist profiteers should then be able to rip off the same people with AIDS by selling overpriced, dangerous, and questionably effective cures. As Burton finally realizes (having begun to acquire a slight bit of conscience near the end of the film), "From the start, AIDS was not only an epidemic of medicine, but an epidemic of blame." *Zero Patience* has no patience for either epidemic, and does its best at least to correct the latter, by spinning its madcap tale over and over again, "just like Scheherazade."

Just because Greyson happens to be a very funny guy doesn't mean that his activist or filmmaking credentials aren't impeccable. He has been making films and videos about the epidemic since 1986 and is the co-founder of the Toronto Living With AIDS Project, which has produced over a dozen video documentaries about various aspects of AIDS activism and has compiled a number of collections of short videos for general distribution. He started making documentary films and videos in 1981 and has made works about Nicaragua, farm workers in Ontario, and apartheid, as well as what he calls "a trilogy on queer sexuality and imperialism" and studies of gay-bashing, gay life in the former Soviet Union, and AIDS. When an interviewer stumbles to find a word to describe his style, he quickly supplies one: "Perverse?" He respects the work done by more conventional documentary makers, but acknowledges that he finds such an approach a "little too simple-minded. My own works are a bit more self-questioning and self-reflective." [7]

Greyson first had the idea for *Zero Patience* in 1987, when Randy Shilts' book first appeared: "That was birth of the Patient Zero myth. Even then, there were all sorts of reasons to question it. Scientists were already testing stored blood samples, including one from a boy who died in 1959, that showed retrospectively and posthumously, that he had died of AIDS. So to say that a Canadian flight attendant had brought AIDS into North America was absurd. Even the scientist who did the cluster study—which was simply meant to show sexual transmission of the disease—denounced Shilts' interpretation of it."

Greyson's early works on AIDS include the deliriously funny *The ADS Epidemic*, where he points out that a main danger of AIDS (for gays especially) is not so much a spreading of germs as a spreading of "ADS": lies, innuendoes, and half-truths, in both the popular press and the advertising media. What the ads are really selling, moreover, is "Acquired Dread of Sex," especially gay sex, a prissy attitude that Greyson has linked elsewhere with the attitude foisted on the general public in "closety classics that metaphorically conflate disease with desire" (like *Death in Venice* and *The Picture of Dorian Gray*).[8] To drive his point home, the video features a Tadzio-lookalike (from Visconti's film version of the Thomas Mann novella) with the on-screen message: "This is not a Death in Venice / It's a cheap unholy menace." As gay theorist Douglas Crimp has written about the video:

> The plague in Greyson's version of the tale is ADS, acquired dread of sex—something you can get from, among other things, watching TV. Tadzio is a pleasure-loving blonde who discovers that condoms are "his very favorite thing to wear," and Aschenbach is a middle-class bigot who, observing the sexy shenanigans of Tadzio and his boyfriend, succumbs to acquired dread of sex. Made for a thirty-six-monitor video wall in the Square One shopping mall in Mississauga, a

suburb of Toronto, The ADS Epidemic, like [public service announce-
ments on TV] is directed at adolescents and appropriates a format
they're used to, but in this case the message is both pro-sex and made
for the kids most seriously at risk—sexually active gay boys.[9]

When the Los Angeles artists' space LACE asked Greyson to contribute
to an exhibit entitled *Against Nature*, based on contemporary AIDS-aware
response to the Huysmans novel of *fin-de-siècle* decadence, he sent them a
deliriously funny "fake video script" for the catalogue, exploring the
whole question of relationship of camp sensibility and gay activism in relationship to the AIDS crisis.

In the script itself, we meet several familiar friends: Aschenbach (who is
"dressed from head to toe in a white suit and boating hat, just like Dirk
Bogarde in that Visconti film. After adjusting his pillow and pince-nez, he
petulantly turns the page of his book. Mahler plays mournfully in the background."[10]), Sir Richard Burton (likewise a dandy, and with a particular
penchant for "studying" sexual perversions in this case), and the African
Green Monkey:

> GREEN MONKEY (sounding like Alistair Cooke): Good evening.
> Tonight on *The Wonderful World of Human Nature*, we examine the
> bizarre and often misunderstood habits of the *dandy*. This sub-group
> of the Homosexual species used to proliferate in 19th-century
> European artistic milieux, but its numbers have sharply decreased in
> the last few decades with the ascendancy of the more aggressive
> clone. The dandy can be identified by its eccentric clothing, its
> erratic wrist movements, and its predilection for Parma violets in
> lieu of a cravat.

Aschenbach quickly agrees to participate in the documentary:

> What a divine concept! An entire show devoted to our languid
> reveries, our elegiac, our plaintive sighs of capitulation in the face of
> mortality! We decorative dandies have been marginalized too long
> by those puerile politicos, those righteous gay libbers, those dykes
> and feminists who *on principle* disdain both soufflés and sequins! It's
> time to reclaim our rightful place as the arbiters of aesthetic tran-
> scendence!

Burton is about to decline appearing on the show, for equally fatuous
reasons, but the Green Monkey and Aschenbach convince him to join in,
and Burton and Aschenbach decide to meet at the Natural History

Museum in New York for the exhibit on the history of epidemics (Greyson has not yet made Burton the culprit for masterminding the show). We're now left entirely with Greyson's dishy stage directions for the ensuing scene—clearly the antics of a very visual and funny director at work with very serious material:

> They reach AIDS: It's a rear-projected slide show of photos of PWAs from Miami, Brazil, and New Jersey: men in hospitals, wrapped in IV tubes instead of leather straps, with lesions instead of bruises. The new S/M. Real kinky. A grade-school class in search of the African dioramas accidentally enters the exhibit. A little boy glances, freezes. In a split second, without the aid of captions, he can "read" the image. Nine years old and he has mastered the visual semiotics of a purple splotch on a forearm. It takes him two seconds. "AIDS!" he screams. The others, the same age, freeze, glance and get it. They too can read. They scream "AIDS!" They stampede their terror cut with giggles: a herd of unstuffed little animals fleeing from visual contagion, half-convinced the KS lesions could leap from the projected image onto their pre-pubescent bodies.

The ADS epidemic is indeed alive and well, and they've got it. Greyson then indicates a couple of quick cuts, one from a Cecil B. DeMille Bible epic, another from *Star Trek*, to drive his message home. He then takes Aschenbach and Burton to a cliff overlooking a gay nude beach near San Francisco, then offers four alternative conclusions to the video script. The most outlandish involves Aschenbach, Burton, the naked sailors from the Dutch plague ship, and members of AIDS ACTION NOW! all joining forces to take over the CBC broadcast of the documentary and replace it with a pirate transmission ("Shocked viewers are treated to an hour of anarchic antics," as "BURTON and ASCHENBACH continue their debate with the cast and crew from AIDS ACTION NOW!, while the sailors perform impromptu demonstrations of safer-sex techniques.")

Greyson's mock scenario is the epitome of serious camp, a form of outspoken outrageousness that found its zenith in the zany theatrical transvestitism of the late sixties and early seventies and continued to flourish underground in the gay underground of New York's black and Latino communities as the "voguing" drag balls of the eighties and nineties (so well chronicled in Jenny Livingston's film documentary, *Paris Is Burning*[11]). Perhaps not coincidentally, both these communities (the theatrical world of

Charles Ludlam, Jackie Curtis, Ethyl Eichelberger, and others;[12] and the drag balls) were devastated by AIDS. But just as transvestites played a major role in the Stonewall Rebellion that gave birth to gay liberation, camp transvestite humor helped lay the groundwork for the politics of AIDS activism of groups like ACT UP that intentionally offend and upset a large portion of the general public—but certainly don't go unnoticed. Greyson clearly believes that politics and camp are not such strange bedfellows after all, as both attempt to shock awake the conscience of a public that continues to ignore an increasingly desperate situation. Even noisy or rude information about AIDS is preferable to the alternative, where indeed "SILENCE = DEATH."

Greyson also realizes that popular culture—especially that of younger viewers—no longer recognizes the old-fashioned divisions of high and low art, or indeed of camp sensibility and political sensibility. Both dandies and activists, agitprop[13] and elegies must have their day. There are 1001 nights after all—some of them savage and fauve or a deep expanse of blue—and an endless array of stories to tell, especially when the film or video medium is allowed to soar on its own, not imitating theater or literature, but finding new and daring visual references to explore the many questions of AIDS.

INTERLUDE

Halloween, 1981

eter always called it our "best year." I was working for the *Daily News*, editing a free-wheeling hodgepodge page called "Tonight in Manhattan," suggesting to readers various activities that they could do any night of the week: concerts, movies, operas, plays, literary readings, restaurants, clubs. I could—and did—write about anything I wanted, which meant we could—and did—go anywhere we chose. The other critics at the paper hated it; Peter and I loved it. It was, indeed, our "best year."

The free ride ended when the afternoon edition of the paper folded. I found another job fairly quickly, on a small quarterly magazine, with people I liked and respected. But it was a far cry from the party days of the year before.

We were living in Greenwich Village, in a dumpy basement apartment, so that Halloween we decided to go to the annual Halloween parade which was practically right outside our door. We also decided to go in drag. I wore a horrid lavender Afro that I'd picked up for a party the year before, and a tacky purple and white taffeta dress; Peter took the whole game much more seriously, having learned the art of dressing up well as a child, double-cross-dressing with his twin sister Patti each Halloween. This time he got to work applying real makeup and slinking into a form-fitting leopard-skin dress.

We went to the parade—blocks and blocks of costumed celebrants, with each outfit more outrageous than the next. This parade is quintessentially New York: the one night of the year when everyone in the city (young and old, gay and straight, male and female, uptown and downtown) can become a Greenwich Village bohemian, a character in the play, a fantasy jumping off the stage, off the canvas or the movie screen, and scampering down the streets of this Village of the world.

The parade is not just a gay event, but it is one of the classic moments where the gay sensibility shines, and everyone is welcome to come into the ghetto and join the party. And it's the one night when drag is the order of the day (and night). Maybe people don't spend the entire year and half their annual salary planning their costumes, like the denizens of the *favella* in Rio making outfits for Carnival, but some of the masterful inventions clearly exhibit months of wild, creative fantasy at work.

I've always felt that drag is both a theatrical device and a political statement, as disturbing as the latter prospect may understandably appear to some feminists. But what could be more challenging to the patriarchy and the Establishment than such a brazen disruption of the very stereotypes of "proper" masculinity (and femininity) that drag draws on? Even the cheapest forms of masquerade—like that by the sailors in *South Pacific*—momentarily liberates the participants (and the viewers) from the restricted and restrictive codes of behavior they have been taught since birth. Maybe there's some misogyny mixed in—some serious misconceptions of what women really are and do—when men (especially heterosexual men) perform drag. But at least the real challenge is there, not to the femininity being misrepresented, but to the masculinity being questioned and transcended. There lies the real liberation. And since all art is about representation of the truth, ultimately, such a basic challenge to one of the fundamental truths of our being (our sexual identity) is—or certainly should be—a basic component of any real radical art.

Peter and I left the parade after a while and took a cab to s.n.a.f.u., an offbeat little punk rock cabaret run by Lewis Friedman, a longtime friend who once managed the ultimate torch-diva cabaret of the early Seventies, Reno Sweeney. It was a wild Halloween party night at s.n.a.f.u., with performers like the inimitable Ethyl Eichelberger (who once gave me an original Peter Hujar photo to run with a review and never asked for it back, so that it ended up in our guest bathroom) all doing short sets, and a critic and his boyfriend in drag simply got lost in the crowd. Again there were the wonderful theatricalized challenges to the status quo: to images of male and female, gay and straight, propriety and impropriety, order and chaos (or, as the participants might insist, rigidity and freedom). It was a wild, wonderful show: sexy, madcap, tasteless, campy, ballsy, and groundbreaking—especially during the moments when a diva as canny as Eichelberger was in charge.

Remembering the night—its statement of freedom, of flaunting authority, of stretching the boundaries of art and life to the very limits— some twelve-and-a-half years later, I feel a deep nostalgia and loss: Peter is dead, and Lewis, and Ethyl, and Peter Hujar, and God knows how many more people we saw or said hello to that night—all to AIDS, the real chaos that was waiting just around the corner, to try to co-opt and destroy this freedom by killing off its chief prophets.

In the TV docudrama, *And the Band Played On*, there is a scene where a character looks out at a Halloween parade in San Francisco a year or so later and declares, "The party's over." I think Ethyl, and Charles Ludlam, and Jackie Curtis, and Jack Smith, and all the Radical Transvestite Theatrical Fringe, dead or alive, would join Peter and me in challenging that lie. Halloween didn't bring us AIDS. It may have appeared at the party, like in Edgar Allan Poe's "Masque of the Red Death," but the party didn't create it and the partiers are certainly not to blame. To give up, to give in to Death, would be to acknowledge its victory, which denies the purpose for which Halloween, the holiday, was created in the first place: to challenge and counterpoint the somber and sanctimonious embrace of dying and the afterlife represented by All Souls Day, which Halloween night directly precedes, just as Mardi Gras precedes Lent.

The party's not over. AIDS has only raised the stakes and mobilized the opposition.

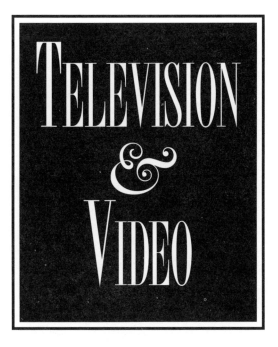

5

Bringing the Battle Home: And the Band Played On & A Time of AIDS

he image which John Greyson so tantalizingly posits at the end of his "fake video script" is every guerrilla videomaker's dream: "pirates" (a nice sexy/revolutionary gay image) taking over a prime-time television network to broadcast their alternative message. The fantasy plays upon the dual nature of the video medium: the basic technology is rather cheap and accessible, so that anyone with a home camcorder could conceivably create his or her own statement (about AIDS or anything else); but the big business of television (even articulate, liberal "public" television) is so complex and profit-motivated that those same personal or political statements are rarely actually seen or heard. Nonetheless, the power of broadcast television remains phenomenal: no other medium takes words and moving images directly into people's living rooms, kitchens, and bedrooms; no other medium has so much potential to influence attitudes, for better or worse.

It's small wonder that AIDS activists have turned so frequently to video to relay their message—or that so few of these statements have made their way onto commercially supported broadcast television. Even cable television has been skittish about AIDS—and especially government-challenging AIDS activism—though in the fall of 1993 both Home Box Office and The Discovery Channel took a chance with fairly controversial programming in the area: HBO's original docudrama based on Randy Shilts' *And the Band Played On* and the four-part documentary, *A*

Time of AIDS, narrated by Adam Baldwin, which Discovery publicized heavily though it was not actually produced by the channel. Cable may lack the clout of network TV, but getting the word out to even this somewhat more limited audience is a giant step forward. In fact, after HBO's lead, NBC aired *And the Band Played On* as a "Monday Night Movie" the following March, though in a rather truncated version.

Both the docudrama and the documentary cover basically the same territory: the history of AIDS in the United States and the rest of the world, from the first reports of a mysterious new disease (or group of diseases) which began puzzling doctors and researchers in 1981. Both programs also present a rather well-balanced view of the epidemic: not just AIDS hysteria and AIDS angst, but AIDS anger and activism as well. Both also challenge the inaction of the U. S. government and much of the medical community when faced with the deadly challenge.

Randy Shilts' *And the Band Played On* had a particularly long and rocky road to travel before it first aired on HBO on September 11, 1993, having gone through three directors and 20 screenplays. The third director, Roger Spottiswoode (following Joel Schumacher and Robert Pearce, who both walked off the project), was reportedly highly perturbed at HBO's final reediting of the docudrama without his approval. Pressure came from both sides: gay activists (including Shilts himself), who felt there was an "underrepresentation of positive images of gay people and too many negative stereotypes,"[1] and from studio executives, who seemed to think the images were *too* positive (or at least too explicit). At one point, there was even talk of refusing to let the character Bill Kraus (played by British actor Ian McKellen) embrace and kiss his lover Kico (B. D. Wong) after returning from a business trip.[2] (That scene did finally make both the HBO and NBC versions, the latter coming just about a month after ABC finally allowed Roseanne Arnold and Mariel Hemingway to share a kiss on 'Roseanne," after initially trying to pull the scene.)

The other pressure exerted on the director and editor is a bit more problematic. Shilts seems to have exercised far more censorial acumen on the screenplay than on his own writing in the book,[3] being suddenly overwhelmed with a fit of political correctness. Among the "negative stereotypes" he reportedly wanted cut from the final production were scenes about gay bathhouses, the use of amyl nitrate ("poppers"), and (most ludicrous of all) the participation of transvestites in a gay Halloween parade. All the references seem to have made it into the final version, though it's hard to judge how much they were toned down. (One would also have to assume that the choice was made not to include any images of the gay world's other notorious subgroup, the S&M leather crowd.)

What is surprising, as John J. O'Connor points out in his review of the TV film, is "that the film still manages to pack a considerable wallop,"[4] and "adds up to tough and uncommonly courageous television" in spite of all the tinkering. It unfolds like the medical thriller that it is, following the desperate race of hard-working low-level government scientists to discover the explanation for a mysterious new epidemic—while their superiors and other government functionaries meet their concern with blatant indifference, as do politicians, blood bank executives, and even certain members of the gay community (who particularly resist the attempt to shut down gay bathhouses, even after there seems to be clear proof that the disease is being spread by sexual contact).

The film begins with a harrowing scene in which a young researcher named Don Francis (Matthew Modine) arrives at a makeshift hospital in a remote village in central Africa to find piles of corpses—men, women, and children, staff and patients alike, all dead. A dying woman, covered with blood, reaches out to him, and a young boy—seemingly the sole survivor—demands: "Why? Why this happen? You doctor, why don't you know?" Across the bottom of the screen, words are typed tickertape-style (like a "severe storm warning" report) informing the viewer that this was "not AIDS," but another epidemic known as Ebola Fever. Still the stage has been set for a mysterious disease that is about to break out; the scene puts AIDS into the context of other devastating, plague-like epidemics in human history, something that is all too often ignored in press coverage of the condition as if it were a uniquely modern scourge of humankind (or, worse, of certain "guilty" subgroups of contemporary society).

Several brief scenes from around the world detail the first reported cases: in Copenhagen in 1977 a woman dies of *Pneumocystis carinii* pneumonia (PCP)—"not possible," the Danish doctor insists; in Paris in 1978, another patient succumbs to "toxoplasmosis, a cat disease"; a man in a Los Angeles hospital has "no T-cells at all." The testimonies mount, as we meet Francis again, now working for the Center for Disease Control in Atlanta, the government agency that is supposed to keep track of such things, to make sense of them so that they can, indeed, be "controlled."

It becomes apparent that most of the early people infected are gay men. All sorts of theories are explored, some more serious than others: "Do they all use the same kitty litter?" "Is it related to poppers?" Gay activist Bill Kraus tries to mobilize gay men in San Francisco, with the help of savvy health worker Selma Dritz (played with considerable spunk and flair by Lily Tomlin). One early problem in trying to educate the general public about the disease, Kraus points out, is that "the only people interested in reading about gay men dying are gay men and the ones who wish they would all die." Richard Gere (who was instrumental in getting a number of actors like Tomlin, Steve Martin, and Angelica Huston to play small cameo roles) appears as a gay choreographer (patterned after Michael Bennett, one of the early casualties of the epidemic), the one who looks out the window at San Francisco's gay Halloween parade and intones: "The party's over."

The film continues to follow the parallel mobilizations of the medical community and of gay AIDS activists over the next few years. A villain appears in the person of Dr. Robert Gallo (in a deliciously nasty portrayal by Alan Alda, in the best playing-against-type ploy since sugary Shirley Jones played a whore in *Elmer Gantry*), the government scientist who was so eager for glory that he apparently claimed to have discovered the retrovirus (later named HIV) that most observers believe was actually isolated by a team of French scientists (who sent Gallo a sample of their culture so that he could "compare it" with the one he had claimed to have already discovered: when the two viruses were later tested, they were found to be, as the film states "*exactly* the same, not just similar, but exactly the same," though Gallo still maintains himself innocent and was not found guilty of any "actual misconduct" by a government investigation into his behavior just prior to the the HBO showing of the docudrama. Virtually all of the section critical of Gallo was dropped from the NBC version, which gutted the program of one of its chief dramatic devices.

Since Shilts' book ends in 1987, the film does not deal with later developments in either research or AIDS activism. To make an ending, Spottiswoode and screenwriter Arnold Schulman invented a confrontation that never really happened: they place Francis at the deathbed of Kraus (whose last speech indicates he's less afraid of dying than of "what will happen to the people who live," like his lover Kico); actually Francis and Kraus never met. But showing the two men embracing in that last scene makes a symbolic statement: Francis, who pulled away in fear from the woman with Ebola Fever in Africa in the opening scene, can now accept and even welcome the touch of a man dying of AIDS, without fear or discrimination.

At the end of the HBO version film, the names of people thought to have died of AIDS-related illnesses roll by on the screen as Elton John sings "The Last Song" on the soundtrack. There are a lot of them: Rock Hudson, Ryan White, Perry Ellis, Rudolf Nureyev, Arthur Ashe, Liberace, Freddie Mercury, and many more. Friends of some of the people listed (like Steve Rubell) were not too happy that their names were used in this particular context. (This portion, too, got the ax at NBC.)

O'Connor made the following interesting observation about these final credits in his *Times* review of the docudrama: "Accompanied by a soppy song, the piece is calculatingly misty and undeniably moving. But the anger of Mr. Shilts' book and of this movie deserves something more, something like an uncompromisingly ferocious jeremiad from the playwright Larry Kramer. Still, flaws and all, this HBO production has guts, and that's more than can be said for much of the rest of the television industry."[5]

If gay activists of the ACT UP variety seem to play more of a role behind the scene than on-screen in *And the Band Played On*, that choice was made in the name of historical accuracy. The group AIDS Coalition to Unleash Power was not formed until after Shilts' book had already been published. Created to resemble a New England town meeting, where everyone gets to have his or her say, ACT UP was started in New York City in mid-1987, primarily as the idea of playwright and activist Larry Kramer. It now has chapters around the world and has done more than any other group to raise world consciousness about AIDS.

ACT UP gets considerable coverage and respect in the TV documentary *A Time of AIDS*, directed by Jenny Barraclough and Katherine Carpenter and written by George Carey and Stacey DiLorenzo. Leading activists like Peter Staley, Rodger McFarlane, Cleve Jones, Martin Delaney, and Michael Callen are prominently featured in interview and news footage, doing and saying their thing, right along with several of the real-life medical researchers portrayed in *Band*: Marcus Conant, James Curran, Mary Guinan, Dritz, Gallo, Francis, and many more.

The first segment of the four, "The Zero Factor," examines both the epidemic and the gay "Belle Époque" (as one interviewee describes it) that was its setting. The real Patient Zero does appear, but more as an irresponsible contributor to the problem than as its cause.

What Dritz calls "the whodunit of the century" (a slightly skewed metaphor) gets further examination in the second part of the series, "Hunting the Virus." Gallo enters the scenario, and if anything, he's even more dislikable in person than in Alda's impersonation. The segment continues the examination of AIDS abroad as well as in the United States: in France, in England, and in Africa, in particular.

"Fighting for Our Life," the third section, begins with Rock Hudson's death: Gay Men's Health Crisis co-founder Rodger McFarlane recalls, "I remember being astounded that it took Rock Hudson to galvanize America's attention. It had *never* crossed my mind that something so seemingly trivial as a movie star tragedy would capture the national attention. I guess in this culture of fame and wealth, it took a movie star getting sick to get America to take it seriously." In this section we also meet some of the heterosexual heroes of the epidemic: the Ray family of Florida with three young hemophiliac sons (whose Baptist minister told them not to come back to his church and whose house was later burned to the ground, in all probability by some of their fundamentalist Christian neighbors); C. Everett Koop, the AIDS-sensitive no-nonsense Surgeon General that Ronald Reagan apparently appointed by mistake; and young Joey DiPaola, a kid from Staten Island whose mother was told by his doctor to keep quiet about his condition because "AIDS is not an acceptable disease. It has a stigma on it." Cleve Jones, who generated the idea of the AIDS Memorial Quilt, is also quoted questioning even the Quilt's power to change the conscience of America: "And all of this has been inadequate . . . all of it has been insufficient to move the leaders of our country to responsible action. I'm proud of the Quilt. It is a beautiful thing. And it's a monstrosity."

In the final segment, "The End of the Beginning," there are more deaths (Ryan White, in 1990), more heroes, more countries heard from (the news is particularly bad in Thailand and India), more risk groups (women and teens, especially), and more despair ("Sixty-six acres of the quilt," says Rodger McFarlane. "It's a fool's paradise to think this thing is under control.").

6

From An Early Frost to Today: Dramatizing AIDS on TV

n 1985, NBC television presented a made-for-TV movie entitled *An Early Frost*, written by Daniel Lipman and Ron Cohen, and directed by John Erman. Without apology or much fanfare, it told the story of a young gay man with AIDS, focusing on his relationship to his family. Even now, almost a decade later, the work holds its own remarkably well with most films and TV treatments that have been done since. The chief criticism leveled against the drama by gay activists is that it focused its primary attention on the family's reaction (which irritated AIDS activists like movie critic Vito Russo,[1] though this, surely, is part of the AIDS story that needs—and deserves—to be told), rather than telling just the man's own story or detailing his relationship with his lover.

Like Andrew Beckett in *Philadelphia*, Michael Pierson (Aidan Quinn) is a lawyer, both a workaholic and a closet homosexual. Unlike Andrew, who's out to his family, Michael hides his homosexuality from his family as well as his employers. He has a lover, Peter (D. W. Moffett), but his family knows nothing about their relationship. Once Michael is forced to reveal both his sexuality and his condition, the responses by family members (mother, father, grandmother, sister) are much more problematic—but perhaps more realistic—that the unquestioning support that *Philadelphia*'s Andrew gets from his atypical family: Michael's sister (Sydney Walsh) won't let him be around her because she's pregnant (out of an unwarranted fear that he will somehow contaminate the unborn child); his father (Ben Gazzara) flies into a rage (more because his son is gay than because he's ill) and refuses to speak to him; his mother (Gena Rowlands) stews and agonizes but at least tries to educate herself about the disease (although one always gets the feeling, from the pained expression on her face, that she is constantly wondering why this is happening to her). Only the grandmother (Sylvia Sidney) is really open and matter-of-fact: When Michael at first shies away from embracing her, she insists: "It's a disease, not a disgrace—come on, give your grandma a kiss."

The drama is full of helpful information about the epidemic and the condition, especially considering that it was made in 1985. Paula A. Treichler, a medical scholar who's also a leading critic on contemporary depictions of AIDS, gays, and women (she coined the phrase "the epidemic of signification"[2] to describe the proliferating misrepresentation of AIDS in the media), has written a very even-handed analysis of how an attempt was made to incorporate the most up-to-date medical data of the day into the drama, right up until the time it aired: "Despite its critics both left and right, *An Early Frost* became the gold standard for the representation of AIDS on television, a standard most critics predicted would not be sustained."[3] The teleplay underscores the message (still necessary even a decade later) that AIDS cannot be spread by casual contact. When two nurses refuse to bring Michael his food tray in the hospital, his doctor glares at them, picks up the tray, and carries it inside, announcing (more for the benefit of the nurses than Michael): "You can't get AIDS just by being around someone who has it. It's only transmissible though intimate sexual contact or blood." The doctor's descriptions to Michael and Peter of Michael's pneumonia are also reasoned, precise, and comprehensible to the ordinary viewer, as is his insistence: "It's not a gay disease, Michael. It never was. The virus doesn't know or care what your sexual preference is. Gay men have been the first to get it in this country but there have been others—hemophiliacs, intravenous drug users—and it hasn't stopped there."

Treichler wishes that the television drama had gone even further, stating that the script "makes little reference to AIDS as a national health care crisis, and renders the rage and political mobilization of activist groups invisible, indeed incomprehensible." Perhaps the larger and more necessary agenda would be to find the balance between meaning and entertainment. The way television, like film, has often done this is through melodrama and humor. Though not much of the latter was deemed allowable in 1985, what was left—in this medium which at that time was dominated by prime-time soap operas like "Dynasty" and "Dallas"—was melodrama. In this context, it's worthwhile to return to Thomas Waugh's study of that form and its relationship to gay identity:

> The melodrama—the woman's film, the weepie, the tear-jerker, the soap opera—has been traditionally opposed to the male genres of effective action and rationality in the outside world, from the western to the whodunit, and, until the feminist renovation of the discipline of film studies, was unjustly stigmatized by film historians for this reason. Gay critics have often followed this pattern, batting about pejorative terms like "sentimental," "maudlin," and "Rodgers-and-Hammerstein" to dismiss one of the special if not essential forms of gay popular culture. They follow, as Richard Dyer has pointed out, our culture's put-down of forms too closely allied to bodily responses, like horror, arousal, belly-laughs, and weeping.[4]

A number of scenes of *An Early Frost* fit significantly into this melodrama mode, which in no way undercuts or devalues their importance to the work as a whole. The melodramatic moments includes Michael's attempted suicide (from which he is rescued by his father), the ensuing confrontation scene between the two, and the father's rage when two ambulance workers come and refuse to transmit the sick Michael to the hospital. Such moments of manly communication between a father and son are rarely attempted in TV or film, and it's interesting that it is the advent of AIDS that has brought them about.

Another melodramatic touch involves Michael's relationship with the effeminate Victor, whom he meets during one of his hospitalizations. The character of Victor (for which actor John Glover received an Emmy nomination) is everything that Michael is not: out-of-the-closet, self-effacing, wickedly funny, even though he is dangerously and very visibly ill (Kaposi's sarcoma, PCP, and toxoplasmosis have all taken their toll). He also appears to be completely alone: no family, no lover, no friends, no home—having even been kicked out of his apartment by his landlord. Yet it is this spunky outsider who, more than anyone in the film, helps Michael to come to terms with both his sexuality and his diagnosis. When Michael returns one day to visit, he finds Victor's bed empty and realizes he has died: Michael (and the viewer) thus has to confront that AIDS scenario as well, even though his own future in the struggle with the condition is left ambiguous at the end of the film.

There are more tears and an even more copious supply of gay camp humor, in *Our Sons*, which aired on the ABC network in May 1991. It was written by William Hanley (whose New York Stage credits include *Slow Dance on the Killing Ground* and *Mrs. Dally Has a Lover*) and directed by John Erman (who had the same duties for *An Early Frost*). It featured a first-rate cast led by Julie Andrews and Ann-Margret as the mothers of two gay men, one of whom is dying of AIDS. The focus is again on the mothers and *their* reaction to the fact their sons are gay, at risk, or dying. But the television audience—which is weaned on such melodrama—also happens to include a increasing number of mothers or other family members in similar situations. Ignoring their stories would be curiously unfair as well.

Treichler points out two very interesting facts about *Our Sons* in relation to *An Early Frost*: how much more sophisticated the television audience has become about the medical details of AIDS in six years, and how the camp and wisecracking character (the "outsider" Victor in *An Early Frost*) is now allowed to be a main character Donald (Zeljko Ivanek), whose first line in the film, spoken after his lover James (Hugh Grant) gets him admitted to the hospital, is a camp reference to *The Wizard of Oz*: "Toto, I have a feeling we're not in Kansas anymore."

James's mother Audrey (Andrews) turns out to be a workaholic businesswoman who vaguely acknowledges her son's relationship with Donald without really thinking about it too much. But when Donald gets seriously ill, her denial begins to wear thin. James then asks her to undertake a kind of heroic quest—to find Donald's mother, Luanne (Ann-Margret), who lives in a small town in Arkansas and has not seen or spoken to Donald since she threw him out of her life for being gay eleven years before. Audrey must then try to bring Luanne to the West Coast for a final reunion with her now dying son.

Most of the film details her trip to Arkansas, where she finds Luanne working as a waitress and living in a trailer. Audrey convinces Luanne to make the trip, but the latter refuses to fly, so the quest turns into a kind of female-buddy road movie as the two seemingly very different women drive cross-country together and talk, talk, talk, coming in the end to realize that maybe they're not so different after all. Neither wins the other over to her side of the discussion, but both articulate their feelings and questions, and out of the dialogue comes a great deal of positive soul-searching. The reunion between Luanne and Donald remains fumbling and bittersweet. The differences are too great to be overcome in one soul-searching deathbed scene. Even after Donald dies, Luanne's gesture of reconciliation—offering James a picture of a sand castle that Donald had drawn as a child—can only take place through Audrey as intermediary. And it is the seemingly liberal, free-wheeling Audrey, not the still rigidly conservative Luanne, who comes to a genuine acceptance of her son's homosexuality in the course of the film's development.

Though the drama—perhaps intentionally—raises more questions than it answers, Treichler points out how important the medium of television can be to exploring such open questions about AIDS: ". . . perhaps the privacy of the home is precisely where some people would prefer to learn about AIDS—not in a public theater where they might be seen, might be identified as homosexual, might share the space with homosexuals or people with AIDS, and where they can't just change the channel if they don't like it."[5] Both *An Early Frost* and *Our Sons* thus point to the potential good that such television narratives can have (they can be "taken up and used in more diverse and progressive ways than their makers or critics may have imagined"), but they also leave a number of open questions about AIDS, its treatment, and the irrational discrimination which often accompanies it. What they do achieve is to raise the issue for the wide general audience which watches television: a demographic that includes many people who, either due to isolation or by choice, have little or no foreknowledge about AIDS. Making the epidemic understandable, recognizable, and familiar to such an audience is a tremendous task, in and of itself.

Two TV adaptations of works by significant gay playwrights also emphasize the interaction between gay and straight characters in dealing with an AIDS-related death. Terrence McNally's *Andre's Mother*, which aired on PBS's "American Playhouse" in March 1990 (and was adapted from a brief, 3-page stage vignette that McNally had written for a benefit at Manhattan Theatre Club in 1988), deals with the relationship between a homophobic mother and the lover of her dead son. Harvey Fierstein's *Tidy Endings*, which aired on HBO in 1988, was an expansion of part of his trilogy of one-act plays, *Safe Sex*, which had a brief run on Broadway the previous year; it centers on a confrontation between the wife and male lover of a man who has died of AIDS.

In *Andre's Mother*, the setting is a memorial service for a New York actor. Andre's lover Cal (Richard Thomas) and his mother (Sada Thompson) have come to Central Park to release a balloon in his memory. The scene has great poignancy, not because the two reconcile, celebrating and *releasing* Andre's memory (as the ceremony indicates), but because they do not reconcile. The mother is finally able to let go the string of the balloon from her tight hand, but she is completely unable to let go of the feelings she has about her son's sexuality or his illness. This, too, is part of the picture of AIDS; this, too, is an uneasy story that needs telling, if only to preclude its proliferation in life.

Cal's own family, his father (Richard Venture) and sister (Haviland Morris), offer comfort to him, just as they accepted his relationship with Andre in life. But the teleplay is, after all, entitled *Andre's Mother*, and its focus is, in this case, on a woman who has victimized herself because of what McNally has described as her "inability to connect even in the most primary relationships."[6]

Fierstien's *Tidy Endings* offers a more hopeful rapprochement between the worlds of the sick and the well, the gay and the straight. In it, Arthur (Fierstein himself) and Marion (Stockard Channing) slug it out verbally when they meet to "tidy up the affairs" of the late Collin Redding, who was Arthur's lover and Marion's ex-husband. Using dialogue to air out all sorts of fears, prejudices, and angers (similar to the scene in his best-known play, *Torch Song Trilogy*, between a homophobic Jewish mother and her son, whose lover has just been killed by a gay-basher), Fierstein succeeds in both educating and entertaining.

In two British teledramas, *Intimate Contact* (1987) and *Sweet As You Are* (1988), the focus is on married heterosexual men who contract AIDS, one through a prostitute on a business trip to New York, the other through an extramarital affair with a college student (the positioning of "promiscuous" young college students and American prostitutes as "outsider" risk groups by the British is telling here, reminiscent of early condom ads in Britain, which pretended that the country's gay population didn't even exist[7]).

Intimate Contact, written by Alma Cullen and directed by Waris Hussein, features Claire Bloom as Ruth, a wife whose whole world changes when her husband Clive (Daniel Massey) is diagnosed after the dalliance with the Manhattan hooker. The movie examines the rampant prejudice they experience: the daughter (Abigail Cruttenden) is taunted by class-mates until she drops out of school; the son (David Phelan), a rising Tory politician, cuts all ties with both parents; friends and business asso-ciates all vanish. Even further indignities confront the family: "In an especially appalling scene, Clive shows up for a luncheon meeting only to have all his workmates leave him sitting alone at the table. The local vicar is a sanctimonious cad who hints that AIDS may be a form of divine judgment. Ruth's golf club members stab her in the back and caution others not to drink out of Ruth's glass; eventually they ask her to resign from the club."[8]

Intimate Contact turns out to be extremely catholic in its consideration of the demographics of the epidemic: the plot line also involves a hemo-philiac (similarly ostracized at school) and a gay couple, as well as two characters who don't have AIDS (a recovering alcoholic and a former IV drug user) who help Clive and Ruth face both society's stigma and their own struggles for stronger self-identity.

In *Sweet As You Are*, Liam Neeson and Miranda Richardson play a young couple whose marriage begins to collapse after the husband, a col-lege lecturer, tests positive after a fling with one of his students. Though the script dips dangerously close to implying that the real issue here is not AIDS (or mistreatment and misrepresentation of people with AIDS), but mere marital infidelity, one critic has pointed out that the TV film "traces the disquieting effect AIDS has on the lives of quiet, ordinary people and shows how in their ordinariness they have depths of strength on which they can rely in the face of the pandemic."[9]

Most American TV movies, on the other hand, have tended to be "Disease of the Week" type treatments, and the emphasis has been pri-marily on "innocent victims" of AIDS: children with hemophilia and women, who contract the disease "somewhere else" rather than in such guilt-associated activities as IV drug use or homosexuality. These dra-mas include *The Ryan White Story*, *The Joey DiPaolo Story*, and *Something to Live For* (the story of Alison Gertz, a straight woman who become an AIDS activist after contracting the disease). All are perfectly valid accounts of PWAs and the discrimination their families suffered at the hands of smug, insensitive neighbors, schoolmates, and others, but they tend to whitewash the overall picture of AIDS as an epidemic which has primarily hit the gay, black, and Latino communities, often poor and inner city dwellers, not the suburban white kids who happen to be (so the networks seem to think) more "salable" to TV audiences.

TV has also included AIDS as a theme on a number of prime-time series, including (and this list is undoubtedly incomplete) "St. Elsewhere," "thirtysomething," "Cagney & Lacey," "Designing Women," "Roseanne," "Trapper John, MD," "Lifestories," "L.A. Law," "Miami Vice," "Midnight Caller," "Law and Order," "The Commish," "Brothers," "The Trials of Rosie O'Neill," and "Life Goes On." Various approaches have been taken, some more predictable than others. The cop shows tend to focus on bias crimes against persons with AIDS, though the controversial "Midnight Caller" faced the dilemma of a heterosexual murderer-with-AIDS who uses the virus as his weapon. The lawyer dramas have tended to deal with the question of euthanasia for people with AIDS or the legal rights of their partners. The medical shows have examined medical questions (though "St. Elsewhere" also dealt rather powerfully with AIDS discrimination and homophobia in the medical profession itself).

Probably the most full-fledged treatment of AIDS on a prime-time series came in "Life Goes On," a show notable for tackling other big questions. The Thatcher family, on which the series centers, both is and isn't your typical American nuclear family: it has a husband and wife, two daughters, a son, a new baby, and a "wonder dog named Arnold." But one son has Down's syndrome and one daughter is in love with a guy who has AIDS, so the "family values" explored are far from rigidly conventional.

Chad Lowe, the actor who played the PWA Jesse McKenna in the series, did so with real sensitivity and depth. His thin wiry frame allowed him to play the character convincingly both when he was very ill and when he was stabilized, functioning. His relationship with the Thatchers' younger daughter Becca underwent realistic ups and downs over two seasons as Jesse (who had acquired AIDS from a prostitute) struggles with his condition while continuing to go to high school, then to college, where he studies painting. All the while, the question of his love for Becca remains central: how do they deal with the dilemma of whether or not—and how—to consummate their relationship? And how do other members of the Thatcher household feel about all this? The convention through which these questions are raised may be soap opera, melodrama, but the questions are raised.

At one point Jesse takes a part-time job at an AIDS service center and takes Becca there to show her a bigger picture of the disease: the different kinds of people who have the condition, including gays. The scenes in the center serve to raise consciousness considerably (not just of Becca but of the viewing audience) about AIDS in the same way that scenes in a group home for Down's syndrome patients broaden the discourse on that theme.

When the show was canceled, the final segment answers the soap opera cliffhanger: Will Becca and Jesse Ever Get Married?—but does so somewhat duplicitously: Becca meets up again with Jesse in college and does marry him, bringing him home during a college break and reintroducing him (with considerable dramatic buildup) to the rest of the Thatchers. The next scene is a flash-forward to Becca telling her young son, several years later, about Jesse, who has since died of his condition: "Jesse taught me not to be afraid of death, and I taught him not to be afraid of life." Whose child is it? Did Jesse and Becca risk having one of their own, against all conventional medical wisdom? Did they adopt? Or is the the product a second marriage, with the old high school boyfriend who lost out to Jesse in an earlier bid for Becca's heart and asked her then, rather horribly, "If I had some fatal disease, would you fall in love with me, too?"

So Becca and the viewers manage to have it both ways. Jesse is gone, at rest, and nobody has to watch him die. But at least, as Lowe, the actor who played him, stated on the ABC AIDS special, "In a New Light," broadcast in late 1993, the show may have helped make a younger generation of viewers more aware: "AIDS is our Depression, AIDS is our Vietnam, AIDS in our World War. And I think it's brought my generation to a higher sense of consciousness." Even though "the flip side of that courage and dignity is still an enormous sense of fear."

7

Common Threads &

Other AIDS Documents

ommon Threads, a TV documentary which tells the stories of five persons whose panels are part of the NAMES Project AIDS Memorial Quilt, begins, like an actual quilt, with patches, small fragments of material that are the building blocks of a larger tapestry. Rather than being swatches of colored cloth, however, the patches which introduce the film are snapshots—those contemporary signifiers of casual, commonplace identity. We see a moving collage of faces and forms of ordinary-looking men and women, young and old, gay and straight, sick and well, together or alone, with pets or possessions, with families, lovers, or friends. Snapshots both personalize and universalize the stories they tell, whether they show individuals or groups. Here they are the beginnings of "stories from the Quilt" that make up the memorial itself and the film document that celebrates it, directed by Robert Epstein and Jeffrey Friedman.

Epstein and Friedman offer five stories, representative of the scope of the epidemic: three gay men, one black male IV-drug user, and one hemophiliac boy, a rather balanced demographic in 1989, the year it was made (when the proportion of women, sexually active teens, and babies born with AIDS had not reached the frightening ratio it has in the five years since that time).

Each of the five panel subjects is remembered by a friend or family member. Tom Waddell, Olympic decathlete and co-founder of the Gay Games, is memorialized by a lesbian friend, Sara Lewinstein, with whom he had a child; Robert Perryman, a recovering drug addict, is recalled by his wife, Sallie; Jeffrey Sevcik, a young gay man, is decribed by his lover, film historian and AIDS activist Vito Russo; David Mandell, Jr., a young hemophiliac, by his parents, Suzi and David Mandell; and David C. Campbell, by his fellow military officer and lover, Tracy Torrey.

As the five parallel stories unfold, the directors intercut them with images of quilt panels and a voice-over countdown of the number of deaths, year by year. By the summer of 1989, when the documentary was being made, the toll had passed the 100,000 mark, "more than all lives lost in the Vietnam War."

Certain moments stand out from the tapestry of the whole: Russo, ever the movie critic and fan, vividly describes Sevcik's favorite movie, based on Carson McCullers' classic novel of the child-as-outsider, *Member of the Wedding*. "Jeffrey always identified with the Frankie character, played by the young Julie Harris," Russo recalls. "He always felt he didn't really belong, that he didn't know what to do with his life."

Mrs. Mandell recalls her son's reaction when "authorities" tried to keep the young hemophiliac isolated from his schoolmates: "We have the right to do what everyone else does. We have the right to run around and play. We didn't come from a different planet. We're still the same human beings that they are."

Lewinstein describes the unreasonable resistance she got from her own family when they found out that Waddell, the father of her daughter, was diagnosed: "Don't go near him. Don't let the baby go near him. You can catch it in a tear, you know."

Speaking of his own diagnosis, Torrey (who is obviously quite ill in the film and died before its completion), says: "I didn't shed a tear. All of my tears had been shed the year after David [his lover] died.... When the other shoe finally fell, it was just—comforting, I guess, more than anything, to know where I was heading." He chose to make his own quilt panel, in exactly the same pattern and style that he made for Campbell; the two panels consist solely of each man's name and military rank, against a deep maroon background.

Mrs. Perryman, likewise, is positive about being HIV-positive: "I'm not going to let worrying about being sick *make* me sick."

Mrs. Mandell recalls going with her husband to a community center for gay men and lesbians in their Midwest hometown to find out about how to make a quilt panel in David's name. They were a little uncomfortable at first, she admits, but within a few minutes both began to feel at home as they got involved, she helping sort patches for a quilt, her husband stuffing envelopes for a mailing. "For the first time since my son's death, it was OK to laugh," Mrs. Mandell recalls. "I was thinking of all the different things I wanted to put on David's panel—satins and bright colors and things that flew—all the possibilities—everything that would say to somebody, 'This was David.'"

Common Threads is part of an exceptionally fine crop of documentaries that have been produced by the AIDS community, both for broadcast and for other venues ranging from home video to community viewing situations. Groups such as AIDS Community Television, Testing the Limits, and DIVA TV in New York and John Greyson's Toronto Living With AIDS Project in Canada have pioneered the production and distribution of such works, and a few of these documents have made it to more commercial or public television outlets as well. But since some of the best videotapes made by such groups have sought to challenge authority directly and to present an alternative vision of the truths of AIDS, their success at reaching a general public has been limited. (Also deserving mention, of course, are the numerous video education projects directed at the communities at risk. Greg Bordowicz's safe sex videos for the Gay Men's Health Crisis in New York are a first-rate example of this.) Many of these more radical political or sexual works were shown as part of a 24-hour marathon of AIDS documentaries aired by New York City cable station CUNY on World AIDS Day, December 1, 1993.

Another docementary of note is Robert Hilferty's 1991 *Stop the Church*, detailing the demonstration led by members of ACT UP and WHAM (the Women's Health Action Mobilization) at St. Patrick's Cathedral in New York City December 1989. Though PBS broadcasting stations had originally scheduled it for the "P.O.V. (Point of View)" series— which often handles similarly controversial subjects through the disclaimer of its title—but stations apparently got feet and backed off. (A few PBS stations around the country later did carry the segment, but not as part of "P.O.V.")

A more traditional documentary approach was taken by *Absolutely Positive*, which was widely shown on PBS. It was directed by Peter Adair, who 15 years earlier teamed up with Epstein (*Common Threads*) and Veronica Selver (his editor on this project) to produce the first major gay and lesbian identity documentary, *Word Is Out* (1977). Like that groundbreaking project, *Absolutely Positive* simply lets ordinary people tell the far-from-ordinary stories of their lives. The "characters" are introduced in short scenes that establish who they are, where they come from, and how their story fits into the overall picture being drawn; then each character returns, over and over again, in short segments to comment on a particular aspect of the overall question being explored. By the end, they seem to be old friends.

Absolutely Positive, however, has one surprise in store: one of the characters is Adair himself—the objective observer as subject. This challenges the old credo of documentary "distancing," a technique that belies the fact that almost all documentaries have their own agenda, their own message, anyway, in the manner in which they are filmed, written, and edited. And in this case, the question being explored is particularly complex: the impact of HIV-positive status on the lives of people who are otherwise "well." Since Adair himself is in that category, he decided not to exclude himself, but to simply let his story be one of eleven others, which may allow him even more objectivity in the long run.

Adair, in fact, starts with his own story first. The camera looks over his shoulder, where he is typing on a laptop computer the very words we hear as voice-over commentary on the screen. What he really wants to know is something very basic: "How are people handling the news?" In *Word Is Out*, the news had been the empowering act of self-identity: facing it, proclaiming it, may have been scary, but it was essentially good news. Testing seropositive to the HIV virus is hardly good news, no matter how you look at it. But is there a way that it can empower, can be "absolutely positive," as well?

This power can sometimes be seen in others more easily than in oneself: One of the interviewees (who is later diagnosed as positive himself) describes how, early in the epidemic, he was introduced to someone with AIDS and felt obliged, out of common courtesy, to shake his hand: "I put my hand in my pocket, and as soon as we got to a restaurant, I ran to wash it. But I felt so sad and so guilty, that here was someone who was in a place of needing so much compassion and understanding, and all I wanted to do was run away, I didn't even want to touch him." At the same time, he remembers how he thought: "This guy is so beautiful and so powerful—the way he put his hand out to everybody."

The need for such empowerment is made clear early in the film with the story of a young Asian boy named Johnny: when he discovered the gay community of San Francisco, "the virus was already there." Like the characters in a Gregg Araki film, he has never known gay life, or self-identity, before AIDS. He only had unsafe sex once or twice, he says, and "Now I've got it." It was, he shrugs, "like getting an F on a report card." Before making the documentary, he has told almost no one, neither his friends or family.

But there is a gentle strength that Johnny seems to have acquired that comes through each time he speaks. That strength is shared by the other interviewees as well, including several non-gay interviewees: Doris Butler, a black woman who acquired the virus through IV drug use with her husband ("We had a bit of history that we thought was behind us") and passed it on to her baby; a salt-of-the-earth working class couple, Margery and Delmar Middleton, who trace the infection to a blood transfusion Delmar had gotten in the late seventies and who at first tried to drink themselves to death (so they wouldn't have to die of AIDS); a redheaded mother who got the virus from shooting up ("we used to talk about it all the time, how we ought to use bleach on our needles and all that, and we never did"); and a charismatic young Latino, Juan Alejandro, who thinks he was infected by his first wife and gently describes the misdirected homophobia he encountered on an army base in Germany after his diagnosis became public.

The gays interviewed by Adair also represent a cross-section, two good-looking, all-American hunks; black filmmaker Marlon Riggs; a spunky lesbian whose substance-abusing life is turned around by her diagnosis; and a campy male nurse who continues to minister to full-blown AIDS patients while dealing with "the quintessential bad news" in his own life.

The hardest question is directed by Adair, not to one of the people he's interviewing, but to himself (and the viewer): "Is there a balance between denial and obsession?" Not all people who are HIV positive will develop full-blown AIDS. If they have no symptoms, should they simply go about their lives as if nothing were wrong, or should they begin medicating themselves in hopes of preventing the virus from progressing into AIDS? Can that very fear become an obsession, destroying their emotional health? Or is being positive a "manageable illness"? What about alternative therapies? Adair himself takes AZT and follows certain prescriptions of holistic medicine, "but I just can't get my hopes up over Chinese cucumbers." Others turn to "crystals, Louise Hay, oils, and healing groups," he acknowledges, neither promoting nor denouncing such choices. ("Even the spiritual path can be a tight shoe," the gay man who earlier had been afraid to shake the hand of someone with AIDS states. "My new goal is to just be human.")

In a final note of irony, Adair admits that "if they found a cure tomorrow, I think I would be a bit depressed," having gotten so used to living with the virus.

"But, I'd get over it though," he admits.

Marlon T. Riggs, the black filmmaker included among the interviewees in *Absolutely Positive*, has made a number of major statements of his own about the impact of the virus on the black gay male community. *Non, Je Ne Regrette Rien (No Regrets)*, presented as part of the "Fear of Disclosure" video project originated by artist David Wojnarowicz and videomaker Phil Zwickler, mixes images, onscreen words, recited poetry, and vocal music to bombard the viewer with fragments of his triple-identity message: be black and proud, be gay and proud, and be equally open and proud about your HIV status.

When the men interviewed begin to speak, we see only parts of them (eyes, a nose, lips, hands) through small openings in a black screen. Only as they become more adamant about their identities do the images fill the whole screen. "I'm not going to be ashamed," says Haitian-born Assoto Saint. "It's a *virus*. People are not made to feel ashamed when they have cancer or a heart attack." As he continues to speak, the image and words of Magic Johnson flash on the screen. "We now have celebrities apologizing for being infected with this disease," says Saint. "And there is some real problem with that for me, because no one's choosing to live with this disease. It's circumstance."

The film then questions media representations of the disease among blacks, from discriminatory sex personals ("HIV-negative, seeks same") to obituaries (among the deaths Riggs implies were misrepresented by most of the press were those of the Rev. James Cleveland, designers Willi Smith and Patrick Kelly, choreographer Alvin Ailey, and newscaster Max Robinson).

Against the onscreen words and image of tennis star Arthur Ashe in his public acknowledgment that he had AIDS ("There was a silent and generous conspiracy to assist me"), Riggs contrasts an angry statement spoken aloud by one of his subjects that such "privacy" helps no one: "People are most deeply affected by the personal. There is enormous power in talking about the 'I,' the 'me.'"

Such apolitical silence is also the subject of Riggs' other best-known work, *Tongues Untied*, which caused a stir when a number of PBS stations refused to run it because of what they deemed its (gay) erotic content. In the opening segment, poet Essex Hemphill is shown reciting an ode to silence, with counter-comments inserted with Riggs' standard words-on-the-screen technique:

> Silence is my shield
> [It crushes]
> Silence is my cloak
> [It smothers]
> Silence is my sword
> [It cuts both ways]
> Silence is the deadliest weapon.[1]

Riggs is again especially tough on homophobia and AIDS discrimination in the black community, citing an Eddie Murphy comedy special and a Spike Lee film as evidence, along with remarks by "black preachers, black academicians, black literati, and black leftists." Near the end, as obituaries appear on screen, the poet again speaks of waiting "for my own quiet implosion." [2] (Marlon Riggs died in late April 1994)

AIDS affects far more than the storyline or the political agenda of art being made; it often directly impacts on the very form of art itself, as it does in Jarman's *Blue* and two video documents made by men who realized they were dying and wanted to share that experience with others, *The Broadcast Tapes of Dr. Peter* and *Silverlake Life: The View from Here*.

The former is a TV documentary made for Canadian television covering the last two years of the life of Dr. Peter Jepson-Young of Vancouver. It originally contained over 110 episodes, and the weekly segments followed Dr. Jepson-Young's decline with taste and objective clarity. The programs were filmed and directed by David Paperny, who later edited an 80-minute version for HBO. This HBO version ends with a memorial service for Jepson-Young, attended by people from all over Canada who had watched the weekly diary. The doctor's unassuming honesty in the face of death is a keynote of the work, as is his gentle humor. At the memorial service the mourners are asked to join Jepson-Young, on video, leading them in a kind of church-like responsive reading of a manifesto about "accepting and absorbing" disease and death. His lover reminds the crowd of the obvious truth: "Peter gave us [PWAs everywhere] an indentifiable face."

Silverlake Life: The View from Here is another video diary started by film- and videomaker Tom Joslin and completed by Peter Friedman after Joslin's death. Joslin knew he was dying and decided to record that event—and the months leading up to it—assisted, both in life and on the project, by his lover of twenty-two years, Mark Massi. Friedman, once a film student of Joslin, joined the project after Joslin had died, primarily to edit the footage and shape it into the form it now has. Friedman also incorporated portions of Joslin's earlier coming-out documentary, *Autobiography of a Close Friend*, featuring interviews with Joslin, his lover, and Joslin's family (mother, father, brother, sister-in-law) about his sexual identity, just as the later work documents the same subjects discussing Joslin's living and dying with AIDS.

The work is devastating. The filmmaker/subject (who also did much of the initial editing himself, using equipment at his bedside) did not spare himself (or the viewer) the more painful details: we see his KS lesions (and those of his lover), we see him waste away into a virtual skeleton, we see him dead and being placed into a body bag. The earlier scenes are upsetting enough to watch ("It's so tough, the simplest five-minute task," he tells the camera at one point, when he feels weak during a trip to the grocery store and has go to lie down in his car in the parking lot. "You have to come to the car and put the seat back and rest. What a way to live, what a way to die."); the final scenes are almost unbearable, as treatment (both medical and homeopathic) give way to mental confusion and further and further physical deterioration.

The end result is an eloquent celebration of two men's brave journey together, supported by friends and family, united by something even stronger than the declarations of love by which they nourish each other. At the end Massi is left alone, understandably angry and sarcastic, fumbling to pour Joslin's ashes from a leaking plastic bag into an urn. "You're all over the place, Tom," he tries to joke.

This, too, then is a story of AIDS, its very form and structure dictated by its content. Grief is seldom tidy, but we sweep it up, try to contain it, and do the best we can—perhaps nowhere more importantly than in that art that we make in anticipation of our own death or in memory of those we love.

8

Rock & Roll Television

he music video revolution coincided with the AIDS epidemic; like AIDS it has drastically changed the way a younger generation looks at art and life. Gone are the days of well-constructed dramas, leisurely novels, slow-moving cinematic mood pieces. Such "old-fashioned" storytelling no longer speaks to a generation weaned on MTV and confronted with AIDS and so many other shattering personal and political dilemmas.

Older art forms continue to exist, of course; it's just that younger viewers and observers today have little patience with such presentations, preferring the fast-edit, cut-to-the-chase (or the bedroom), sex-and-action pyrotechnics of music video. The message may be muddled (as it is to those of us old-timers who try to follow the "plot" of most music videos), but the presentation is high-tech, high-fashion, and high-concept, and anything that doesn't meet those challenges is likely to get lost in the shuffle.

These facts of life have not been lost on those wishing to bring the message of AIDS to this generation, one thought to be particularly at risk according to recent surveys. Television—particularly music-related television, and not just the MTV cable channel, which is probably the best know example—is seen as a key way to reach these younger viewers, using programming that ignores standard drama and documentary devices and addresses issues like AIDS through music itself, said to be *the* language of Generation X.

There is a presumption even in this programming, however, that this generation is as homophobic as its elders—an assumption hardly borne out by personal observation or statistics I've seen. But much AIDS awareness music video programming avoids any acknowledgment of the impact the epidemic has had on the gay community—or the active political response of that community—even when it acknowledges (usually rather circumspectly) the toll the epidemic has taken in the music community itself.

David A. Keeps, an editor at the magazine *Details*, zeroed in on the problem in a Sunday piece for the *New York Times*:

> Forced together, pop and AIDS compromise each other, forming a contradictory alliance between an industry that markets sex as fun and a disease that links sex with death. It's a coalition that walks the razor's edge between art and commerce, consciousness-raising and trivialization, sincerity and sanctimony.... Much of pop music ... defines itself in the vocabulary of adolescent heterosexuality. Operating in an oftentimes homophobic culture many musicians— particularly the men of rap and heavy metal—fear that associating themselves with AIDS will call into question their own sexual preferences. Or worse, their HIV status.[1]

Jon Pareles, the regular pop music critic at the same paper, wrote similarly after Bruce Springsteen's "Streets of Philadelphia" had won an Oscar as Best Original Song—without ever actually mentioning the word AIDS (like the print ads for the movie):

> Rock has been skittish about AIDS for obvious reasons. From its propulsive rhythms to its innumerable stories of love and lust, much popular music is associated with pleasure; its made for dancing and romancing. Music's time-honored use as social lubricant is incompatible with thoughts of a lingering, incurable, sexually transmitted disease; nothing stops a party faster. In particular, the association of AIDS with homosexuality has been worrying to male rock stars whose exuberant heterosexuality is part of a bankable image. Heavy-metal singers with shoulder-length hair and glittering spandex costumes apparently feared that paying attention to AIDS would make them seem effeminate.[2]

As with the question of Hollywood homophobia, music industry homophobia is often at its worst among closeted gay executives in the industry itself: willing to shell out big dollars for AIDS benefits, but totally unwilling to acknowledge the presence of the virus within their own fraternity.

Witness, for example, the Freddie Mercury benefit concert, where virtually no mention was made onstage of either the virus that killed him or Mercury's sexual orientation. Even such first-rate presentations as ABC's "In a New Light" specials in 1992 and 1993 and the various state-of-the-art Red Hot album and video productions have tended to tread softly on the question of gay sexuality as a major part of the picture of AIDS.

While such programming may gloss over the impact of AIDS on the gay community, the makers often try to soften that omission by paying lip service to broad-minded tolerance. Mingled among the quick sound bites on "In a New Light" from celebrities like John Stamos, Geraldo Rivera, Paula Abdul, and "Dear Abby" in the program are several statements from people actually living with the virus, like a young gay Latino named Hector Zamosa, who notes one of the more difficult aspects of his condition: "Not having sex with another person will protect me physically, but it will not protect me emotionally." And singer Michael Callen, who lived openly and publicly with full-blown AIDS for twelve years, insists: "There is life after diagnosis. And for many of us, a better life than before.... I am singing more joyously than I have sung at any point in my life because the clock is really ticking for me." Then he sings his powerful anthem: "Love don't need a reason / Love don't always rhyme. / And love is all we have for now / What we don't have is time." [3]

Several performers recall how close the disease has hit to them. "I don't know how you spare someone the loss of a friend," said choreographer Debbie Allen. "I've gone through it so many times. I'm going through it now." One of the singers from the group Expose describes losing "three people of my generation on the street where I grew up, and this was just this little *cul de sac*: twelve houses."

Elton John's "The Last Song" talks movingly of male bonding, of finding depths of compassion the speaker didn't realize were there, and Patti Austin's "We're All in This Together" powerfully strikes the evening's most direct and powerful chord, moving from fear and denial ("It only happens to them, I said, there's nothing for me to worry about") to courage and community ("We're all in this together, there's no one we can do without"). As Austin's song winds down, the camera catches several panels of the quilt behind her, one of which reads: "For those who have died with their music in them, to those who never had the chance to sing."

Pat Benatar declares, "This is a time when people can really show what they're made of. It should be now. It should be for this." Melissa Ethridge sings her coming-out song, "Silent Legacy," which is as applicable to HIV status as to sexual identity, from her album, *Yes, I Am*, whose title says it all. Silence helps only the oppressor: "Refuse to hand it down," Ethridge sings. "The legacy stops here."

In 1989, John Carlin, a young entertainment lawyer and art critic for the New York downtown weekly *Paper*, came up with the idea of producing *Red Hot + Blue*, an album of old Cole Porter songs by pop music stars in contemporary arrangements as "a kind of Trojan Horse way of getting the AIDS epidemic noticed in popular culture."[4] Carlin says the Cole Porter connection especially intrigued him: "Here was an artist who wrote these terribly sophisticated lyrics that my grandmother knew. And he was also a gay artist, so that gave added significance to many of the lyrics of his songs." Carlin made some phone calls and got singers David Byrne and Neneh Cherry (who went on to do a version of "I've Got You Under My Skin" with a rap about clean needles and drug addiction) to join the project.

When Leigh Blake came aboard as co-producer, delivering a number of British groups and singers as well ("The British artists were more willing to go a step further" with the subject matter, Carlin recalls), things started to click. Sometimes the producers suggested songs to the artists; sometimes the artists had their own ideas. The collection contains a number of superstar homages: Sinead O'Connor as Marilyn Monroe in "You Do Something to Me," Lisa Stansfield doing a gesture- and intonation-perfect early Streisand takeoff in "Down in the Depths (On the 90th Floor)"; Debbie Harry and Iggy Pop, of all people, romping through "Well, Did You Evah" as Grace Kelly and Bing Crosby in *High Society*. A couple of men singers get to torch it up as well: Jimmy Somerville in "From This Moment On," Tom Waits in "It's All Right

With Me," and Bono from U2 in "Night and Day." And k.d. lang's "So in Love" from *Kiss Me Kate* has practically become a definitive classic already, in its own right.

Many of Porter's lyrics hold a surprising relevance to the subject matter of AIDS, but it's the video versions—the little MTV-type mini-movies—that really bring the subject matter to the fore: Somerville's "From This Moment On" features a gay male couple in various embraces, plus images of that embrace being threatened (barbed wire over a Piéta pose); "Too Darn Hot" includes footage of an ACT UP demo; Sinead O'Connor's "You Do Something To Me" has a dance floor full of same-sex couples; "So In Love" has Lang as a caregiver in yellow gloves, doing a load of laundry (presumably of someone sick with AIDS—there's also the hint of a hospital room at another point) as the lyrics take on an eerie counterpoint "So taunt me and hurt me / Deceive me, desert me / I'm yours till I die / So in love with you am I." Similarly, Annie Lennox's "Every Time We Say Goodbye," with home movies of a young brother and sister frolicking in happier days, seems to refer to a personal loss experienced by the singer herself.

Intercut with the songs are various celebrity clips (such as fashion designer Jean-Paul Gaultier describing condoms as a new accessory), public service ads, and various "art breaks" by David Wojnarowicz, Sue Coe, Keith Haring, and others. All of the artists involved (including the filmmakers who did the clips, such as Jonathan Demme, Jim Jarmusch, Ed Lachman, and Wim Wenders) donated their services, and all profits were donated to AIDS organizations worldwide.

A shorter edited version of the *Red Hot + Blue* tape was presented on ABC. Carlin himself helped edit out some of the content: "I knew we needed more of a Cole Porter approach for them, and less of an AIDS show." The network axed most of the condom ads, art breaks ("They kept Keith Haring, but no Sue Coe or David Wojnarowicz"), and gay-identified material ("But we got the k.d. lang in, which is really subtle anyway, and the Sinead O'Connor, with the gay and lesbian couples dancing. Maybe they didn't notice.") The network also added some celebrity hosts to the show, primarily Richard Gere who, according to Carlin, "rejected the ABC script and wrote his own. I think it was one of the first times condoms and needles were mentioned on a network entertainment show in reference to AIDS. So these were small steps in the right direction."

Carlin and Blake then went on to target a younger audience with their next two Red Hot projects, *Red Hot + Dance* and *No Alternative*, the latter featuring a wide variety of alternative or underground "new music" sounds. The former includes three original songs by George Michael, whom Carlin describes as key to the project (as Byrne had been to *Red Hot + Blue*), plus studio remixes of a number of other selections by such artists as Madonna, Lisa Stansfield, and ELF, spotlighting the remix producers rather than the original artists in the liner notes. None of the selections seems to address the issue of AIDS (except perhaps Michael's "Do You Really Want to Know?," which could conceivably refer to HIV status). Carlin explains this by saying that "Generation X is tired of tribute albums and packaged concept material," which also holds true to an extent for *No Alternative*, though he feels "on each of these albums there are one or two cuts where the artists go beyond the music and address the issue ... maybe not directly, but symbolically."

Even an organization as savvy as Red Hot Productions shows an occasional lapse of taste, however: the liner notes to *Red Hot + Dance* make an irritating attempt to distance the listener from any hint of gay association with the mindboggling heterosexist disclaimer: "Don't believe the hype [sic]. The first cases of AIDS were diagnosed in the United States. Worldwide the majority of people with AIDS were infected through heterosexual sex. Worldwide gay men make up less than 50% of people diagnosed with HIV."[5]

Some of the bands included in the *No Alternative* special similarly bend over backwards to avoid the stigma that *they* might be HIV positive or gay. Billy Corgan, the engaging young lead singer of Smashing Pumpkins, deems it necessary to issue a disclaimer: "I don't subscribe to the politics around AIDS. I don't subscribe to the politics around anything." Yet, ironically, the Pumpkins song, "Glynis," is one of the few on the compilation actually about someone with AIDS, the woman singer in Red Red Meat who died of the disease. "What affected me more was the way people talked about her dying and moralized about her passing," said Corgan.

On the other hand, other selections address questions of sexuality quite directly. Mark Eitzel's "All Your Jeans Were Too Tight" for American Music Club is an open eulogy to a male friend whom the speaker remembers accompanying on Tuesdays and Thursdays to "The Stud's well drink special / A well cheap as the tide / Like the one that swallowed you up." The Stud was the name of popular gay bars in both New York (in the late sixties and early seventies) and San Francisco; other references to the friend (who left the speaker his clothes but "all the jeans were too tight") are full of gay signals about liking Barbra Streisand and the soundtrack from *Diva*, tanning salons, tatoos, and earrings. The song ends with "And I hope you know that I really loved you / and we had a good time didn't we?"[6]

The Urge Overkill video is shot in an AIDS hospice. Avoiding the quick-cut, disruptive style of most MTV rock videos, it presents gentle images of caretaking (washing, holding, touching) as well as the less aesthetic side of hospital care (needles, IV tubes, people close to dying). The lyrics of "Take a Walk" powerfully echo the commitment and conscience of the images. "I don't fight anymore / Sometimes my fists close up in rage," states the intro. Then the main refrain: "Take a walk / Outside yourself / Get to know the person / Behind the face. / Is it someone / You can really love?" [7]

Patti Smith delivers a moving tribute to her close friend, the photographer Robert Mapplethorpe, who died of AIDS: "I don't really have anything I can say except—well, nothin'. I just want us to take a minute—it's a hot night and we're probably uncomfortable, but we're here and let's take a minute to think about our friends."

Red Hot's other projects include *Red Hot + Country*, featuring an array of country stars singing tributes to musical influences on their careers, and a collection of jazz and hip-hop selections. The organization also has future plans for a project called *Red Hot + Film*, producing six short one-hour films relating to the epidemic by directors including John Scheslinger (*Darling, Midnight Cowboy*) and Gus Van Sant (*My Private Idaho, Even Cowgirls Get the Blues*).

The country effort was spearheaded by Kathy Mattea, who appeared at the Country Music Awards in 1993 wearing three red ribbons, for three friends who had died of AIDS. Billy Ray Cyrus and Mary Chapin Carpenter have also been highly supportive; Carpenter sings a song written by her guitarist, John Jennings, about a friend and fellow musician, Willie Short, who died of the disease. Current stars like Garth Brooks, Marty Stuart, Marc Chesnutt, Patty Loveless, and Brooks & Dunn are participating, as well as such relative old-timers as Dolly Parton, Earl Scruggs, Doc Watson, Carl Perkins, Willie Nelson, and Johnny Cash (singing Bob Dylan's right-on-target "Forever Young").

Red Hot's associate producer for the country project, Brian Hanna, points out that the active cooperation of the country music community is especially encouraging considering the fact that "This can really still make a difference. AIDS is just beginning to make inroads into rural areas, and these artists can take the existing lack of urgency there and turn it around, helping people understand that what they can still do matters—that prevention can make a difference. That's something that listeners are really going to hear from these artists, and it can be tremendously effective."[8]

On all the Red Hot projects, Carlin says, it has been his purpose to "use music to help modify people's behavior. I wanted to make records that people would buy: pop culture with a conscience. I've always been a big fan of popular culture—using the arts to effect change. When I was an art critic, I was very influenced by the works of David Wojnarowicz and Sue Coe. I was very interested in how art can relate to politics, how it can force people to not be so simplistic, to look at things they wanted to avoid. Perhaps the radicalism of the nineties can take the grief of the eighties and turn it around to make a world we can live in."

In late April 1994, MTV's sister station on cable, VH-1, aired an hour-long program called *sex, drugs, rock + roll: aids and music*. It was hosted by performance artist Ann Magnuson and took a no-nonsense look at the rock music industry's long silence on the epidemic. Carlin was interviewed, as was the late Bob Caviano, founder of an AIDS awareness organization within the music industry called Lifebeat. Madonna was singled out for her long support of AIDS causes (she gave one of the first big benefit concerts, at Madison Square Garden, in 1987) The heterosexism of a number of rap and heavy metal artists was attacked, but even those genres had their spokespersons on the program, standing up for awareness and non-discrimination: Rob Halford of Judas Priest, and rappers Salt-n-Pepa and M.C. Lyte (no male rappers appeared, interestingly). There were tributes to Queen lead singer Freddie Mercury and Ricky Wilson of the B-52's, both of whom died of AIDS.

Pop music still could, and should, do a great deal more than it is currently doing to get the message out about AIDS, for pop music is a special universal language to which the young around the world respond.

That young audience may well be far more open to information and tolerance than the heterosexists who control the industry realize. Projects like those under the umbrella of the Red Hot Organization are important steps in the right direction, as is the new consciousness finally emerging at industry trendsetters like MTV, who seem to be finally acknowledging that a large portion of the younger generation is either gay or gay-friendly, and no longer willing to put up with the homophobia, sexism, and racism of their elders—including those elders who run the music industry.

But old ideas will die hard in an industry which has long ripped off women, minorities, and the disenfranchised in general (both as musicians and as a record-buying public). And the fact that AIDS has not yet taken as brutal a toll inside the world of pop music—or heavy metal or rap—as it has in some other arts may make the growth of conscience there slower than elsewhere. But the related epidemics of drug use and teen suicides are equally sobering factors, which make it all the more important for musicians, like other artists, to stand up and be counted—and to sing and make music out of their own direct experience, their own view of the world—a world that is no longer just an endless party of sex, drugs, and rock 'n' roll.

INTERLUDE

Pete's Mix

never really paid much attention to it until after Peter died. I noticed it there by the tape deck the last year he was so sick, but I don't remember him ever asking me to put it on and play it for him. I might have brought it to him that first time in the hospital, when I tried to cart in all sorts of things he might want to read or listen to, trying to make him more comfortable, while he did nothing but stare blankly at the TV and attempt to comprehend the diagnosis that now, with Pneumocystis pneumonia, he really had AIDS. "Full-blown," as they say. Full-blown.

I don't remember when or how he made the tape, whether he did it off the radio or from records and CDs. Maybe he'd gotten some help from his friend Michael, who had given us a similar tape that Peter labeled "Micheal's Disco Tape" (Peter was dyslexic and always spelled Michael's name wrong). At any rate, he made it, recording his favorite songs, and wrote "Pete's Mix" on the label. Neither he nor I, nor anyone else I know ever called him Pete. But there it was. A kind of recording engineer persona all his own.

It's a bit eerie to listen to the tape today, strangely upsetting and comforting at the same time. Music has the power to soothe or heal, but also to excite and disturb the very feelings that need to be calmed. And the music we love most— or that those close to us love most—may be the most dangerous of all.

The happy times are here, the good memories. Knowing Peter, I'm sure he chose the selections that brought him only the best feelings and remembrances. But remembering even the good times sometimes hurts. And the other images are never far below the surface: looks of pain and fear in the eyes of someone you love, washing their soiled clothes through your own tears, fighting with nurses and hospital aides who are only doing their job, going home alone and half-sleeping, terrified the phone will ring. Then bringing him home, on your own birthday, pretending it's a party, a celebration. Watching him grow sicker and more skeletal, frightened, and confused. Carrying him from the bed to the bathroom.

Shuffling back and forth between hospitals and home-care, until you no longer remember which is which. Afraid to fall asleep at night for fear that his breathing will stop.

"Bring Him Home" is a song from *Les Misérables*, the Broadway show that was our last big "night out" together, between hospitalization number one and number two. Dinner and a show, I had decided: just what he needed—to go out and celebrate being home, being better, just like the good old days. He suffered through it: another mistake, like Cancun, I realized too late, another mistake. Get him home, get him home.

"Bring Him Home" would be on my tape, of course, not "Pete's Mix." But that's OK. Both responses are valid, part of the larger mix.

Rewinding Peter's musical diary, I try to remember which Bonnie Tyler song he picked: "We Need a Hero" or "Total Eclipse of the Heart."

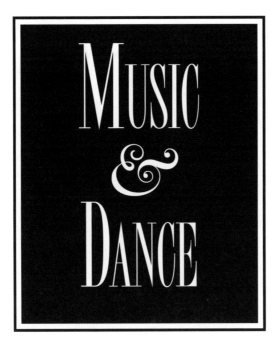

MUSIC & DANCE

9

Anthems & Mourning Songs

usic and dance, being abstract art forms, have a particular power to touch the heart, the emotions. Music can have lyrics, of course, but they are closer to poetry than prose or rhetoric. Both music and dance can at times be literal, plot-oriented, intellect-driven, but the more essential examples of these forms zero in on something more like pure poetry or sculpture.

This may be why music and dance have a particular power to heal, especially in this age of AIDS, and why they bring such comfort to the living, whether their makers are sick or well, participants or observers in the struggle with death.

A number of composers and choreographers have created anthems or memorials, some of which will be discussed here and in the following chapters. But there are other songs and dances which help heal the sick and the well, the anxious and accepting, in ways more subtle and oblique. Each person makes his or her own choice of these selected moments, these personal epiphanies and catharses.

Music critic Barry Walters has eloquently zeroed in on how pop music in particular achieves this: "We play pop to soothe the losses, fill the void, remind us of what we've repressed, flush away sorrow and drown in it. We use pop to both forget and remember."[1] He discusses putting on an old A-Ha record, "Manhattan Skyline," and playing it repeatedly after hearing "Another friend is sick again":

> It unnerves me, lifts me up, makes me furious and comforts me to think that some forgotten pop star of the other side of the globe feels as I do, even though he's contemplating the loss of his Nordic sweetheart and I'm dreading the loss of one more friend to a virus that doesn't stop taking and taking. *I don't wanna cry again. I don't wanna say goodbye. Don't ever wanna cry again.* But I do, time after time.

Walters then positions his personal grief into a larger framework, one heartbreakingly apt to not only AIDS but other brutal killers of the young today:

> We are not at war, yet people in their twenties and thirties often grieve more friends who have died—from AIDS, drugs, cancer, gunshots, suicide—than their parents do. Many of our mentors are gone, the musicians and artists and dancers and designers and teachers and doctors, the leaders who inspired us to live, gone. And if death hasn't touched us in any direct way, we're nevertheless bombarded with signs, symptoms, that the earth itself is on its way out.

The songs we relate to in this crisis are intensely personal, often having little to do with the listener's political or critical agenda. Walters lists a number of pop songs or albums that, intentionally or not, have a particular resonance in the AIDS crisis: U2's "One," R.E.M.'s "Losing My Religion," Whitney Houston's "I Will Always Love You," Boy George's "The Crying Game," Bob Mould's "The Slim" for the group Sugar, the CD by the British folk duo Dead Can Dance. (Others that could also be listed would be Salt-n-Pepa's "Let's Talk About AIDS"; Cyndi Lauper's "Boy Blue"; Madonna's "In This Life"; Jimmy Somerville's "Read My Lips"; and Prince's "Signs of the Times"— where a friend is dying of a "big disease with a little name". Walters also suggests a close reading of R.E.M.'s entire *Automatic for the People* album.) Some of these songs and albums are more direct than others; some merely allude to the pain and loss that are so universal.

Other people, of course, find the same experience in classical music, especially opera, as with the Maria Callas scene from *Philadelphia* or the Jessye Norman aria in the "R.S.V.P." section of *Boys' Shorts*. For a friend of mine, it's Kiri Te Kanawa doing Strauss's *Four Last Songs*. For me, it can be anything from Janis Joplin to "Bring Him Home" or "Empty

Chairs at Empty Tables" from *Les Misérables*, Arvo Pärt's "Cantus in Memory of Benjamin Britten," or the Hungarian woman keening on Kronos Quartet's *Black Angels* CD. I'm sure people grieve to the blues, to gospel, to country, to disco, to jazz. There's probably even grief to be found in heavy metal or rap, depending on the griever.

Such trips into grieving can be traps, of course—a kind of morass in which the listener gets stuck. I can't decide whether Walters thinks it's a good thing when he writes: "A means to carry the lives of the dead inside us, mourning has become a way of life for those of us lucky enough to survive what others have not." Mourning always has this bittersweet quality to it, threatening self-indulgence or self-pity instead of transformation. It needs some sort of counterbalance—some silliness, some lightness, some laughter even—in the mix. Perhaps the seemingly nonsensical name of the group Dead Can Dance does have some meaning after all, as a way out of our grief.

A number of songs have appeared in the past decade which have been interpreted as anthems for the epidemic. Michael Callen's "Love Don't Need a Reason" from his *Purple Heart* album is such a work: whenever he performed it, as at the March on Washington for gay and lesbian rights in 1993, whole audiences were united. As much as his presence will be missed, the song and its power will live on—as, indeed, will many of his songs, including those recorded but unreleased at the time of his death.

An earlier anthem was "That's What Friends Are For," released by Arista Records in October 1985 and featuring Dionne Warwick backed by Stevie Wonder, Elton John, and Gladys Knight. It was written by Burt Bacharach and Carole Bayer Sager and stressed caretaking and understanding. It has a slightly saccharine, middle-of-the-road quality to it, but anthems and mourning songs don't have to be cutting-edge or sophisticated: they usually aren't, in fact.

The most recent AIDS anthem is Liza Minnelli's "The Day After That," from the Broadway show *Kiss of the Spider Woman*, which Columbia released as a CD single in English, Spanish, and French on World AIDS Day, December 1, 1993. Though the song is sung by a left-wing political radical in the play, even on Broadway it rang out as a call-to-arms which could equally well apply to the gay and AIDS activist causes. In contrast to the illusion-obsessed gay character in the play (who spins out old movie plots by fantasizing a Maria Montez-like actress best known for playing the Spider Woman: onstage Chita Rivera wriggles in a gigantic web and clearly represents Death), the singer of the song favors realistic struggle and political commitment. But the song unites both the impossible dream and the reality of struggle. There are references to "candles in our hand" and "the war we've got to win" which seem to reach far beyond the prison cell onstage, promising victory "if not tomorrow/then the day after that."[2] Like the other anthems just mentioned, it offers hope, courage, sustenance to those facing the often bleak realities of the condition itself.

Jim Fouratt booked and managed Danceteria, New York's leading dance club of the early eighties, and continues to be a new music promoter and a leading spokesperson for underdog opinion in the gay rights movement (as anyone knows who has watched him do battle for hours with a host of attackers on a gay computer bulletin board). Fouratt, never a stranger to controversy, thinks it may be time to move beyond mourning in our art and music. "Every gay man is not going to die of AIDS," he notes. "All the gay art that we've had recently—and some of it has been great—is about dying. It's skewed towards death. But that's only part of the story."[3] Personal mourning goes on, of course: Fouratt was a close friend of Michael Callen and was back in New York for his memorial service. But he points out that Callen celebrated survival, not dying, in his music and writing.[4]

Yet Fouratt is also disturbed at the flip side of mourning, what he calls the "celebrating of a new gay sexual radicalism" (including safe sex orgies), a trend that he's observing more and more, especially among younger gays. "Transgressive behavior is a response to death, but it's not the only response. Transgressive sexual acts are being seen as self-defining what it means to be queer among young gay men, and that's sad." Fouratt recently lambasted such attitudes, which had been championed in an article by *L.A. Weekly* writer Doug Sadownik, in an open letter in *Spunk*, another L.A. underground paper. "I sent a copy to Michael, and he warned me, 'If you publish this, they're going to crucify you, because you are publishing it where they live.'"

Referring to ideas the French philosopher Michel Foucault (who himself died of AIDS though he never acknowledged having the disease publicly), Fouratt adds, "To give them credit, Foucault and the post-

modernists did bring desire to the forefront, but I wish Foucault had
been able to accept his humanness as well as his lustfulness. Identity politics are fine: It's very important to know who you are, but to identify
with what we have in common as humans is even more vital, and identity politics often goes against that."

Mourning is in a sense the most apolitical of acts: it is intensely personal, something we do in strict privacy. As Walters says: "The songs
we cling to in private to kill the pain or give it its due, those songs
aren't ordinarily acknowledged because our relationship to them isn't
public discourse." Such moments are not to be talked about (not because
they're secret, but because they can't really be put into words), not to be
shared (not out of selfishness, but because no one else has quite the same
context for understanding the situation). They have to be faced alone,
pondered in the heart. Being thus contained, these rituals have a particular power to change us rather than destroy us, to make some kind of
sense out of the inexplicable loss.

10

Dance: At the Vanishing Point

ance is, by its very nature, the most ephemeral of art forms. It always exists, as critic Marcia B. Siegel has written, at the vanishing point. No other art form—even theater—is quite so dependent on being experienced live. Theater, after all, can be written down, transcribed, filmed, or videotaped, with much of its immediacy preserved intact. Dance never "lives" on a screen or a page in anything other than two-dimensional moving pictures (in the case of film and video) or frozen moments (still photography).

Because the form itself is so ephemeral, the losses to AIDS that the dance world has experienced are even more devastating. What is lost can never be replaced or duplicated: that is always true in dance. But when performers or choreographers just beginning to bloom are cut down in their prime, there is an even deeper loss. And in an art so dependent on form, grace, and bodily beauty, AIDS has been especially brutal, attacking, as it does, the very tools of the dancer's trade: the face, the body, even agility itself.

The epidemic has been particularly cruel to dance, contrary to a rather astounding statement to the contrary by five leading choreographers at the time of the *Dancing for Life* benefit in 1987.[1] . The "AIDS Obituaries" folder in the Dance Collection, New York Public Library for the Performing Arts lists, among others, William Carter, Clark Tippet, and Charles Ward (of American Ballet Theatre); Tim Wengerd (of Martha Graham); Paul Russell (of Dance Theater of Harlem); Art Bauman and Jeff Duncan (two of the three founders of the premier Off-Off-Broadway dance showcase, Dance Theatre Workshop); performance artist John Bernd; drag ballerina Tony Bassae, a.k.a. Tamara Karpova; Demian Acquavella and Arnie Zane (of the Arnie Zane/Bill T. Jones Dance Co.); dance critics Barry Laine, Charles Barber, and Charles Jurrist; modern dance dynamos Louis Falco and Juan Antonio; Glenn White, Gregory Huffman, Burton Taylor, and Edward Stierle (Joffrey Ballet); Broadway hoofer Nicholas Dante; James Michael Karr and Christopher Gillis (Paul Taylor Dance Co.); and Emile Ardolino (who helped create the legendary "Dance in America" series for Public Television, then went on to Hollywood to direct *Dirty Dancing, Sister Act*, and the TV version of *Gypsy*).

The folder does not include all the scores of lesser stars: the corps dancers and chorus boys, the dressers, the costumers, the set designers, the press agents, the booking agents, or any of the other behind-the-scene casualties of the dance world. Many of us, indeed, have folders with far more dance world names in them than that: For one thing, those collected by the library include only obituaries where the official cause of death was linked to AIDS. Frequently family members or professional associates sought to camouflage the truth, as did Rudolf Nureyev himself, whose longtime diagnosis (though hardly a secret in the dance world itself) became public knowledge only after his death (and thus made it into the folder, no thanks to Nureyev's own intentions).

Moreover, when queried by TV interviewer Joanna Simon, in a special segment of PBS's "MacNeil Lehrer Report" in July 1987, New York City Ballet's director Peter Martins flatly denied being aware of "any problem" in his company; Mikhail Baryshnikov of American Ballet Theatre was more forthright, indicating that it was a "private matter" for those affected in his troupe.[2] In general the dance world has walked this thin line between "outing" and circumspect denial.

A number of dancers and choreographers, on the other hand, have openly acknowledged their struggle with the disease and have made their confrontation with AIDS the subject of performance or original choreography. Ian Horvath, a dynamic soloist with both the Joffrey Ballet and American Ballet Theatre before becoming director of the

Cleveland Ballet, acknowledged his battle with AIDS early on: rather than shying away in horror, ballet fans in the Midwestern city rallied to his side, greeting his public honesty with warmth, sympathetic under-standing—and, importantly, continued financial support.

Among the first works created about AIDS were Gerald Arpino's "Round of Angels" for the Joffrey Ballet. In it, Arpino memorialized a friend, Jim Howell, who had been one of the earliest casualties of the epidemic. "We know now that Jim died of AIDS, though we didn't know what to call it at the time. It was 1982 and AIDS hadn't even been named yet. But he had pneumocystosis and Kaposi's sarcoma."[3]

The death of such a close friend affected the usually ebullient choreo-grapher deeply: "As Jim was leaving, he became more handsome. The actual acceptance of this other dimension was a revelation to me. And out of that came 'Round of Angels.' That became my tribute to the spirit of his being. It was also my salvation. I thought the end of the world had come. It was the first terrible experience I had had in my life. I had never lost my best friend, a close associate. I would sit alone after Jim died and listen to the Mahler. I hadn't really planned to make a piece, but then in the studio, it just happened and it took me out of that abyss." The work, which premiered on January 5, 1983, is a lush, ethereal work, bathed in white light, full of touching and feeling: a good-bye and a round of angels, as the title implies.

Another important early work about AIDS was Lar Lubovitch's "Concert Six Twenty-Two," set to a Mozart clarinet concerto. It was a kind of centerpiece at the *Dancing for Life* benefit that Lubovitch helped put together in 1987 and has been danced by his own company and American Ballet Theatre. It is a tender love duet for two men, filled with Lubovitch's signature choreographic juxtapositions: boyishness and tenderness, perkiness and languor. The men embrace, lift, watch, sup-port each other in an exchange that is both sad and sexy, moving from moments of shared strength to others which seem to imply failing ener-gy, a cry for help, a rush to assist each other. There's an extraordinary tableau at the end, with the dancers side by side, their inner arms arced above their heads, hands joined, and their outer arms crossing in front of their torsos, with hands there joined as well. Then arm in arm, they walk upstage and separate, one going off to the left, the other to the right. The reference to AIDS is subtle—more a statement of tenderness, support, caretaking—but dance is always, at its best, subtle and abstract. And the Lubovitch piece is unique in the amount of touching and tenderness it permits two men to express, making it as much a work about positive gay identity as about AIDS, as much about solidarity and unity as it is about the challenge that has both threatened and reinforced that solidarity. (Though "Concerto Six Twenty-Two" continues to be performed, it has gotten increasingly less sensual over the years. As Wendell Ricketts put it in a recent issue of *Dance Ink*, "Since its earliest performances . . . the tender, mannered love duet has been systematically dehomosexualized, described in coded phrases that have helped make homosexuality disappear—not just as the duet's only possible subtext, but as any sort of legitimate subtext at all."[4])

Susan Marshall's "Standing Duet" was choreographed in 1992 for company member Arthur Armijo, who had just been diagnosed with AIDS but kept dancing as long as he could in high-energy pieces exactly like this one. Like the Lubovitch work, it is a duet for two men (one Armijo himself) and has a feisty muscularity mixed with tenderness and touching. Beginning with fisticuffs and roughhousing, the mood switches abruptly when Armijo's "character" begins to run out of energy. He sits down, his head drops, then he rises again. He takes Andrew Boynton's hand and puts it on his heart. He collapses slowly, to the ground, then struggles back up; Boynton lifts, carries, supports him.

In "D-Man in the Waters," which Bill T. Jones made for company member Demian Acquavella after the company's co-founder Arnie Zane died of AIDS, Jones at one point carried Acquavella onstage and set him down, where Demian (the D-Man of the title) then danced mostly with his arms. As Acquavella (who died in June, 1990, after living with his diagnosis almost three years) told an interviewer for the AIDS Oral History project in the Dance Collection, New York Public Library for the Performing Arts: "Some people wrote a bad review. They said that they thought Bill was taking advantage of me and using me as a ploy to make his dance a better dance. But I didn't agree with that. I think he did me a favor. I was honored."[5]

Christopher Gillis kept choreographing in his head even from his sick-bed. About six months earlier, he also made a piece for his sister Margie entitled "Landscape," which Deborah Jowitt recalled was "as if he were choreographing her mourning while he was still there to help her bear it." (In the same article, Jowitt went on to describe Marshall's

piece for Armijo as "dedicated to him and prefiguring his passage." She
adds, with a particularly apt poignancy, "I hope these rituals comforted
the men they honored; they helped the rest of us, even as they ripped at
our hearts."[6])

In a memorial service for Gillis in the large open space at St. Marks
in the Bouwerie Church, another late work by Christopher Gillis, "Farewell," was performed (a sad duet for a man and woman in street clothes
arguing, fighting, saying good-bye). His sister Margie danced one of her
own dances, "Slipstream," another swirling, swooping piece in a wonderful aqua dress, with her hair dancing along with her. In the middle
there is a section of tight, taut anger; then her hands go to her heart and
it all spins out, releases. Then came "Vers Champs Élysées," reinforcing
for all who had seen it at *A Demand Performance* what a powerful, major
work it is, full of healing and hope.

Earlier, among other readings and performances, the Paul Taylor
dancers did Christopher Gillis' "Icarus," from 1991, a group piece mostly for men, about flying too close to the sun and falling (like the title's
namesake) and facing death somewhere between defeat and glory. And
someone quoted Renoir, speaking of how he painted with brushes tied to
his hands when the agony of his rheumatism became too great: "The
pain passes, but the beauty will remain."

Not all of the dances being made by persons with AIDS are about
death and dying, of course, and not all of the AIDS dances being made
are being choreographed by persons with AIDS. But AIDS has allowed
choreographers and performers to address a number of issues more
directly than at any time previously: issues of mortality, sexuality, and
sexual identity, of course; but also issues of anger, frustration, discrimination, addiction, and despair—and hope, spirituality, recovery, and
acceptance—that the existing forms of dance (ballet, modern, or postmodern) previously touched on only rarely with any real depth of feeling
or intelligence. The great dance of the twentieth century has been mostly about abstract form (George Balanchine), clever conceptualism
(Merce Cunningham), mythopoetics and psychology (Martha Graham),
regional or ethnic celebration (Agnes DeMille and Alvin Ailey), or the
very nature of movement itself, in all its mystery and ordinariness
(Laura Dean) or style and quirkiness (Twyla Tharp). Most of this relies
either on prettiness and sentimentality on the one hand, or icy aesthetics

and repression of *all* feeling on the other, to sell its wares. Social issues and controversy (other than a bit of nudity here and there) have been anathema to twentieth-century dance in this country (though the same has not been true in Europe or the Soviet Union).

AIDS may help change that, as it is changing all the arts, forcing them to a new awareness and conscience. And now that a kind of wake-up call has been sounded, not only artists with AIDS are responding. Lance Gries and Stephen Petronio, both of whom cut their teeth on the rugged postmodernism of Trisha Brown, are now using Brown's neo-Spartan style in their own individual ways to challenge the age-old sexual stereotypes of dance. At the same time, there's room for the almost opposite approach of Terry Creach and Steve Koester, who dance together like Fred Astaire and Ginger Rogers, somewhere between camp and High Romance, challenging the macho dance concept that male dancing is just about lifting and muscle power. Performers like John Kelly, Tim Miller, and Tere O'Connor (whom a friend once described as "fiercely faggotty") have focused their arch sense of humor and out-front gay sensibility on that gray area between performance art and dance. Black choreographers, including Garth Fagan, Ishmael Houston-Jones, and David Rousseve, are making major new statements (as is Bill T. Jones) about race as well as sexuality and mortality.

AIDS exists as metaphor, as subtle underpinning, in many other works as well. When Gary Chryst, a former Joffrey star, spoke to Jennifer Dunning of the *New York Times* about an 11-minute solo work called "Dammerüng" that he had performed at the American Dance Festival in the summer of 1993, his words were telling: "We started [rehearsing] on Jan. 2. A very close friend of mine had just died, of AIDS, on Dec. 30. I was thinking a lot about him and about doing something for him."[7] Then Nureyev, also a close friend, died January 6.

The solo, which Dunning describes as "an encounter with a gentle Death" that "at times looks like a meeting centuries later between a weary but enduring Bottom and an exhausted Titania," was choreographed by dance/theater director Martha Clarke specifically for Chryst, who has found himself, very interestingly, in Jiri Kylian's Netherlands Dance Theater III, a dance troupe "for older dancers" (though Chryst is only in his mid-40s).

The idea of a troupe for "older dancers" is a shock in a world that often puts its performers out to graze at the first sign of aging; the idea of allowing a sick or weakened performer (as Bill T. Jones did with Demian Acquavella) onstage—and finding something appropriate for that dancer to do—is even more daring. One of the cruelest aspects of AIDS is that careers are often terminated several years before death: people with AIDS (or HIV diagnoses) are told to think positive, to think survival, while their whole reason for surviving suddenly seems to be denied to them. Occasionally dancers with AIDS find other outlets (painting, writing): how much more healing it might be if they could find a way to dance, or choreograph, fully acknowledging their condition but working within it.

Edward Stierle of the Joffrey may be the classic example of the dancer who would not give up. When he learned he was HIV positive in 1989, he not only refused to slow down, but actually increased his high-energy drive as a dancer, not only in pretty-boy cavalier roles (which he was born to play) but in deeper, more emotionally taxing roles like the lead in Gerald Arpino's "Clowns" and the marionette in "Petrouchka" (two of Chryst's old roles, coincidentally).

Arpino recalls Stierle coming to him when he was first diagnosed and telling him the news. "He thought it would affect his role in the company, but I said, 'No way.' But I added that I would like to schedule rehearsals so that he could maintain and build his strength. It was inspiring to see him in rehearsal, to see that great love and determination. It was a real ascension in a way. In rehearsals he would dance as if he were in another dimension, as if it were the last time he was going to dance, each rehearsal. You just had to hold the tears back at times. You could see that he was fighting, with his great spirit. He was one of the most unusual young men I've ever encountered during his illness."[8]

Stierle also began to choreograph. His first ballet, "Lacrymosa," was created for the Joffrey II company, the main troupe's training ground for young dancers. It was so well received that Stierle reworked it for the main company, at about the time that the company's founder, Robert Joffrey, died in 1988.

In an interview for Mississippi Public Television, Stierle described how he went back to Joffrey II director, Richard Englund, and told him that he wanted to make the ballet longer because "it's not about Mr. Joffrey's death: it's about us."[9] He elaborated: "I observed the people around me, how they were feeling, how they were dealing with his death, the tragedy of the loss. These feelings that we're all confronted with about death, especially going into the 1990s. Young people are being confronted with issues concerning death so young. I wanted to say something, not only about the person who died, but about the people who are left."

When his own health problems became known, Stierle later admitted that in fact "Lacrymosa" was as much about confronting his own possible death as about Joffrey's[10]—and, even more, about the grieving entailed in both those processes: "'Lacrymosa' is a ballet about the stages of grief, about what one goes through when they lose someone. Choreography, dance, is a way of taking the audience in and showing them your feelings through movement, and ultimately moving them to another place."[11]

Stierle told Englund that he "didn't want to stop the ballet with grief, I wanted to continue it with acceptance, the acceptance of death—how someone feels, but how they must move on in their life, that they can't be stuck. And that is what the Joffrey Ballet is doing now in this period, we're regrouping and moving on."

If these words seem extraordinary for a dancer (or anyone) to speak in his early twenties, consider what Stierle said two years later, knowing he himself was dying, as he finished he second ballet, "Empyrean Dreams," for the company: "[AIDS] changed my life dramatically, but it didn't ruin it," he told Janice Berman of *Newsday*. "I didn't just crumble. In actuality, I started living more."[12]

Concerning the condition that was killing him, he said: "This is a tiny part of me. It bothers me that people make it so big. They give it so much power." Arpino recalls Stierle coming to rehearsals for "Empyrean Dreams" with an oxygen mask. "But his illness did not deter from his exacting nature," Arpino recalls. "Not at all! Art has no place for kindness in that way."[13]

This new ballet was set in architectural ruins, inspired by a trip to the Temple of Dionysus near the Acropolis in Athens. Against this backdrop of death and ruined buildings, he places living, vibrant dancers: "These people are in this destroyed place, and they are rebuilding it with their spirit," Stierle explained to Berman.[14]

The night of the premiere of "Empyrean Dreams," the choreographer was brought from his hospital bed to the New York State Theater, where he was greeted with a standing ovation at the curtain call. Two days later he died.

(When Robert Joffrey, head of the Joffrey Ballet, himself died in 1988, several sources reported that the cause had been AIDS. Three Quilt panels have been made for Joffrey. Yet those closest to the company, including people who have no vested interest in protecting Joffrey or the company from such a rumor, state plainly that the cause of death was liver disease. Arpino, who co-founded the company with Joffrey and is now its artistic director, openly addresses the issue: "As the doctor's report says, Bob died of a liver ailment, and that is the truth. It was a similar way that his father died. I know people have said he died of AIDS, and I'm not going to go around challenging them. What would be the point?. If Bob had died of AIDS, I'd be the first one to say it. Because I don't think it's dishonorable to die of AIDS. My best friend Jim Howell died of AIDS, Eddie died of AIDS. There's no dishonor to it, there's no stigma to dying of AIDS."[15])

Arnie Zane and Bill T. Jones met in college, became friends and partners, and went on to found one of the most successful postmodern dance companies in the country. Zane was short and of a mixed Lithuanian/Jewish/Italian/Brazilian heritage; Jones was tall and black and American. As Zane told Lesley Farlow of the Dance Collection's Oral History Project in December 1987: "I think that was really quite the beauty of what we were doing. We didn't realize we were so different. This was not a calculated partnership. We had become friends, and we had both become involved in dance."[16] Whatever the differences, the onstage combination worked: "Our relationship was *so magical*. These two men—it was so unlikely. And actually we showed up different traits in each other that would not have shown up if either of us was by ourselves. We [each] strengthened the other person."

Zane found out he had AIDS in 1985 and started a dance called "The Gift / No God Logic." He recalled: "There were 30,000 people dead from this disease. I did not want to make a dance about AIDS. I would not know how to *begin* to make a dance about AIDS." On the other hand, he was angry. "I thought it was going to be the last dance I was making, and went into the studio and I was very angry.... Because [before that I thought] I could make dances for another 40 years."

Near the end of his decline, Zane choreographed, like Gillis and Stierle, even from his sick-bed. He made a solo for company member Janet Miller called "Prejudice" and described the process: "I was not well, I was in bed here, and she was on the floor there, and I would get up and I would try to do some steps and she would instantly have to play them back to me, and I'd keep what I kept.... I was throwing out words like MALIGN, PREJUDICE, RAGE, and she'd have to do something physical with her body."

The anger that Zane felt facing AIDS was not new but was linked to the prejudice and superficiality that he had long struggled against in both dance and life: "I was angry well before I was sick. I'm only *angrier* [now].... I'm so put off by the dance world that I come from, the *passing*, the way people are constantly trying to pass in a heterosexualized way, the way we continue to act out the dreams of a lifestyle which we ourselves don't live, and I'm saying that as a gay man. This has always left a bad taste in my mouth.... I'm not into accepting tradition, or the lies of tradition. Heterosexuals are just as limited by the portrayal of the Prince and Princess *as* the Prince and Princess as homosexuals are by the non-portrayal of a lifestyle that exists."

He speaks about writing a letter to critic Deborah Jowitt after he felt she had misstated the cause of death of two dancers who had died of AIDS: "Pretending that these were not AIDS-related [deaths] was in no way helping people with the disease, or helping to point out to the public at large that *we have a problem* and it is *your problem.*" When Jowitt wrote back that she was respecting the wishes of one dancer's parents, Zane was in no way placated: "I was very taken aback. Because this is not the time to be protecting people's parents, the feelings of people's parents. We have too many lives at stake."

Earlier Joanna Simon, in the PBS "MacNeil-Lehrer Report" segment on AIDS and the arts, had asked Zane how he felt on hearing he was ill: "I was incredibly frightened," he said. "I was in a panic. It was great desperation, great desperation. When someone at age 38 discovers that they have a life-threatening disease and one that is degenerating the body, making you smaller, one which you are losing control over, one that you may not be victorious over, there's no room for that in the marketplace of the dance world as such."[17]

When Simon asked Zane's partner Bill T. Jones how Arnie's diagnosis had affected the company, he replied that he was "more than aware of the stigma attached to this illness" but that, regarding funding, it would do little good to deny Arnie's condition because "the irony is that the news travels anyway."

Without missing a beat, Zane added with a mixture of anger and spunk: "The news should travel.

In Demian Acquavella's taped interview at the library, he discusses the various transformations (physical, emotional, and spiritual) that he went through after being diagnosed. He stresses the importance of being open about the disease and also of letting it go: "Try to make it as comfortable as possible when you tell someone and then tell them not to treat you like an invalid.... You know, it's not the kind of thing we talk about it all day. We just live with it. You have a problem and you have to deal with it.... I feel like I am normal, I just have AIDS, and that's no big deal."[18]

On another of the tapes, former Joffrey dancer Burton Taylor speaks of a similar self-acceptance that an unspecified 12-step program brought him to: "I'm complete. I'm absolutely complete. I had the most fabulous life.... So a day at a time.... All I have is real gratitude. And I know that my final lesson is to make sure to forgive myself and to forgive everybody else. And to be very patient with people and very loving. And very patient and loving with myself. I've usually been very hard on myself. That is really where I am and what is going on with my life. And we'll see how it unfolds."[19]

Ted Hershey, a dancer with the Hartford Ballet and co-founder of the Hartford-based Works Dance Company, speaks of the transforming experience of caring for his lover (and Works co-founder) Rob Kowalski when he was dying with AIDS: "I guess in the process of Rob dying, it was the most powerful experience in my life. We really were very fortunate in the process.... Rob decided that he didn't want to struggle on for months and gradually deteriorate with less and less ability to feel like he was living. And Rob was so in his body—he was such a physical being—that I really appreciate that decision.... He was a dancer, and not to have his body there, for him, was really tough. And so he made the decision to go.... It was my responsibility at that time, and my joy and my love to allow him to die with as much grace and comfort and love as possible."[20]

After Kowalksi's death, however, Hershey faced the dilemma of all caretakers: "What's my responsibility to him and his work now? All the pieces, you know? The physical things that we leave behind. His check stubs and the things he touched. It's just so hard to make a decision about what you're going to let go of."

Still, Hershey says he has learned stamina from Kowalski, and that stamina now supports him as he faces the disease himself: "The other thing about AIDS and living through this, I've learned, is that nothing is unlivable. It really kind of holds things up in your face more. It says, 'You better heal this.' I mean, it puts it right in front of you." Not that that makes things easy: "What's hard is that having AIDS is—for me, right now—it's like a part-time job. When you're sicker, it can be a full-time job. And there's not as much time and energy for all the things that you might want to do."

Clark Tippet, the dynamic young ABT dancer who beat drug addiction to make a comeback as both a performer and a choreographer of sensual, body-celebrating dances of his own before coming down with the disease, spoke of the difficulties—both physical and emotional—of continuing to work while ill, wondering how "that cute little guy from the Joffrey" managed to do it. But the glory that was dance haunts Tippet throughout the interview, right down to an anecdote about Balanchine on his deathbed insisting, "You know, I can still see it"— meaning dance, the same dance that Tippet describes as the "ballet moment," echoing Siegel's "at the vanishing point" metaphor: "It's breathtaking in its purity. That's what's so, sort of, breakable about it is that it's only for a really short time. It blooms for just a night, a minute, sort of a second.... This machine is over in a second and you only have a couple of years."[21]

11

Music: Of Rage & Remembrance

hen John Corigliano began working on his AIDS-inspired Symphony No. 1 (which premiered in Chicago in March 1990, with Daniel Barenboim conducting), he asked his friend and collaborator, playwright William M. Hoffman, to eulogize several friends who had died of the epidemic. Hoffman entitled the resulting poem "Of Rage and Remembrance." Corigliano wrote music for each of the verbal eulogies, then removed the words and kept the solo instrumental phrases for each one and incorporated them as musical motifs in the symphony. Since that time, he has also composed a choral setting of the original poem; the choral work was premiered by the Seattle Men's Chorus.

The phrase "of rage and remembrance" could summarize the dichotomy of most art about AIDS, especially the world of contemporary classical music. But most of this art (and music) aligns itself with one side or the other; few works juxtapose the two attitudes as expertly as Corigliano's symphony, where feelings of anger (dissonance, sudden bursts of volume) interweave with lyrical, gentle, fun-loving, and life-affirming recollections of the friends who have been killed by the epidemic. Corigliano clearly intended the musical tapestry to reflect the weaving of "rage and remembrance" in the NAMES Project AIDS Memorial Quilt:

A few years ago, I was extremely moved when I first saw "the Quilt," an ambitious interweaving of several thousand fabric panels, each memorializing a person who had died of AIDS, and, most importantly, each designed and constructed by his or her loved ones. This made me want to memorialize in music those I have lost, and reflect on those I am losing. I decided to relate the first three movements of the Symphony to three lifelong musician-friends. In the third movement, still other friends are recalled in a quilt-like interweaving of motivic melodies.[1]

In the first movement of the symphony, the rage comes first, beginning with an "angry-sounding...nasal open A" played by the strings, joined by the rest of the orchestra led by a thumping timpani and "antagonistic chattering of antiphonal brass."[2] The rage spends itself and the soft tinkle of an offstage piano is heard, playing a tango by Isaac Albéniz that had been a favorite of Sheldon Shkolnik, the friend to whom Corigliano dedicates the symphony. Inspired by the piano interlude, the whole tone of the work changes: becoming soft, delicate, understated. The strings come back, but lyrical and tender this time, touched increasingly by a kind of sad longing, enfolding the piano sound, then moving on without it. The volume grows, the anger and dissonance reemerges. Everything accelerates, then slows down again to a tender softness, then builds angrily again until it collapses into a final softness as the Albéniz piano line returns, juxtaposed gently with the same A note in the strings, which has become painfully sad.

The second movement is a tarantella, which Corigliano defines, quoting *Grove's Music Dictionary*, as a "South Italian dance played at continually increasing speed [and] by means of dancing it a strange kind of insanity [attributed to tarantula bite] could be cured." This movement is dedicated to a music industry executive who suffered from AIDS-related dementia at the end. Here, the frenetic tarantella is played against slower, sadder sounds: "I tried to picture some of the schizophrenic and hallucinatory images that would have accompanied that madness, as well as the moments of lucidity. This movement is formally less organized than the previous one, and intentionally so—but there is a slow and relentless progression toward an accelerated 'madness.' The ending can only be described as a brutal scream."

The third and longest movement is entitled "Chaconne: Giulio's Song," dedicated to a cellist friend and that cellist's teacher, both of whom had died of AIDS and who are represented in the movement by two solo cellos, which mingle with the other instrumental solos mentioned above, based on the eliminated short eulogies written by Hoffman and now represented by a single violin, or trombone, or clarinet, among others, each silently speaking the memory of a specific lost friend. At the end of the section, the cacophony from the first movement returns, chimes ring, and drums pound out a funeral march.

The short "Epilogue" brings back the Albéniz piano and the sad violins from the opening section, the tarantella, and the two cellos from the "Chaconne," all played against "a repeated pattern consisting of waves of brass chords" which Corigliano indicates represent for him a sense of timelessness. At the very end, the solo cello holds the A note that began the symphony, letting it fade to a soft whisper.

If Corigliano's symphony begins in dissonance and ends with a whisper, Diamanda Galas's *Plague Mass* begins—and ends—with a scream. First performed on two consecutive nights at the Cathedral of St. John the Divine in New York City in October 1990, Galas's angry diatribe against the gods (and God), the medical establishment, and the government for allowing AIDS to spread and kill, is a work of undeniable power. But like Tom Joslin's video death-diary, *Silverlake Life*, it is at times almost literally unbearable. I doubt that Galas herself would deny that, or wish it otherwise.

Taking the components of a traditional mass and transforming them into rage (which is in part, at least, a remembrance of her brother, Philip Dmitri Galas, who died of the epidemic), Galas has created something that is not quite a black mass (as some have accused it of being) but certainly a work of brazen challenge to most institutions (including churches and the Church) that she finds guilty of silence and collusion. During the Consecration, that part of the regular Catholic mass where the priest offers communion, Galas drenches her body (already naked to the waist) in what appears to be blood.

She opens her *Plague Mass* with an accusational wail that proclaims, chillingly, "There are no more tickets to the funeral. There are NO MORE TICKETS to the funeral! The funeral is CROWDED!"

"Were you a witness?" she demands of the audience, then segues into Roy Acuff's gospel song, "Were You There When They Crucified My Lord?," starting with the verse "Were you there when they dragged him to the grave?" Her delivery has uncanny overtones of the version

Marian Anderson used to sing—its phrasing, its chilling clarity, its spine-tingling challenge to personal responsibility. This similarity to Anderson's rendition can't be coincidental: at the end of the mass, Galas also does her own version of "Let My People Go," in which even the piano accompaniment is virtually identical to the arrangement Anderson used on her RCA *Spirituals* album. But the new lyrics are distinctly Galas's own:

> O Lord Jesus, do you think I've served my time?
> The eight legs of the Devil are now crawling up my spine.
>
> I go to sleep each evening now
> dreaming of the grave
> and see the friend I used to know
> calling out my name.
>
> O Lord Jesus, here's the news from those below:
> The eight legs of the Devil will not let my people go.[3]

In between these two revisionist spirituals, Galas vocalizes all sorts of texts, including scriptural passages from Leviticus, Psalms, and Revelations, as well as delivering a hair-raising "Blind Man's Cry," by a nineteenth century French writer named Tristan Corbiere's comparing his suffering with that of Christ during the Crucifixion.

Galas, a singer with an extraordinary vocal range who has performed premieres by composers including Iannis Xenakis and Yugoslavian avant-gardist Vinko Globokar, has been working on another AIDS-related work, her *Masque of the Red Death* trilogy since 1984. The work, which has also been recorded and has been performed in 25 locations around the world, is:

> dedicated to people who are HIV-positive, PWArcs and PWAs, who fight to stay alive in a hostile environment that offers disgusting pity and pacifying lies to persuade the diseased man to desist from fighting, and participate instead in his own burial; that offers the constant threat of mandatory testing, reporting and quarantine; and that offers slow torture and continuing design of death, or genocide, through a failure to act responsibly in a medical emergency.[4]

Galas is a performer who had dedicated herself almost completely to the struggle against AIDS. She has literally branded herself an activist: On the knuckles of her left hand are tatooed the words "We are all HIV +."

William Parker was an internationally known baritone who discovered that he had AIDS in 1988. He was best known for his moving renditions of works by American composers: John Jacob Niles' settings of some Thomas Merton poems, for instance, or works by Ned Rorem, Aaron Copland, Charles Ives and others. He sang in French and German as well, but it is his native repertory—often ignored by his peers—that he warmed up to most and for which he found a particularly appreciative audience. On discovering his condition, his reaction had an all-American pragmatism about it. He didn't take his diagnosis as a retirement notice—let alone a death sentence— but determined to keep singing, which he did until shortly before he died in March 1993. And he was determined not only to sing, but to sing about AIDS, asking his friends in the classical music world to join him in putting together what became *The AIDS Quilt Songbook*. It premiered at New York's Alice Tully Hall on June 4, 1992 and is available from Harmonia Mundi Records.

Parker described the genesis of the project to critic Will Crutchfield:

> In Santa Fe last summer, I was thinking about what we sing about all the time in opera and song—grief, separation, death, fear of death, traumatic events in life—and I had to ask, "Why are we not singing about AIDS?" For singers, we are being pretty unvocal about this. Something left me unsatisfied about AIDS benefits where the music is all Mozart and Puccini and the word AIDS never gets said.[5]

Indeed, the New York music establishment had responded quite emphatically to AIDS with concerts like *Best of the Best* (November 1985), *Music for Life* (November 1987), *Season of Concern* (August 1989), and a second and third *Music for Life* (in October 1990 and March 1993). All the big names turned out; lots of money was raised. But no one spoke (or sang) directly to the losses of AIDS, no matter how symbolic such gestures as Leonard Bernstein's conducting of Charles Ives's *The Unanswered Question* might have been.

Other than sponsoring such black-tie benefits, the classical music world has been as quick as any other profession to turn its back on people who actually contracted the syndrome. Parker's own management dropped him, in spite of his worldwide reputation as a recitalist, fearing he would not be able to fulfill commitments. When another top manager, John Gingrich, was approached through a third party about whether or not he would handle a singer with AIDS, he replied, "I'd take on a *good* singer with AIDS." When told that the singer was Will Parker, he quickly said yes.

"It's naive to believe that the music industry is generous or gracious about this," said Philip Caggiano of Gingrich's office, who worked closely with Parker on promoting the songbook. "This is not *Philadelphia*, where the whole family stands up for you. It's a lot more complex than that. Sometimes it seems like there's no art in this world, only commerce."[6]

At any rate, Parker had found a support in his new management—and a commitment to his new project: a cycle of songs about AIDS, to be sung by himself and other baritones. He put out the word to composers he knew, many of whom had composed original material for him previously, that he was looking for AIDS material, incorporating lyrics either by people with AIDS or directly focusing on the epidemic. By the time of the premiere performance, he had collected 18 songs. The cycle continues to be performed and new songs (not all for baritones) will be added over the years. Parker called the first performance *The AIDS Quilt Songbook—1992*, as he told several interviewers, because he wanted it to become an annual affair.

As Crutchfield wrote just prior to the first performance, Parker was driven by the project (much as Edward Stierle must have been to finish his last ballet): "Like all the others [who have AIDS], the 48-year-old Mr. Parker has been making his choices about what to fight and what to accept, what to do with his time, and what to do when his time comes."[7] Parker sang in the premiere performance, along with three other baritones, and continued to perform selections of the work up until two months before his death, in March 1993.

Of the 18 original selections (15 are included on the Harmonia Mundi release), the composers include Ned Rorem, Lee Hoiby, John Harbison, William Bolcom, Ricky Ian Gordon, Elizabeth Brown, and Chris DeBlasio (who himself later died of AIDS, in July 1993); the poets and librettists include James Merrill, Melvin Dixon (two works), Ethyl Eichelberger, and Perry Brass.

There are works of rage, led by Susan Snively's poem "Fury," set to music by Donald Wheelock, which opens the program:

I have a poisoned hand,
I have a bitter voice.
I look death in the face.

I have no choice.

And when death looks on me,
its hollow eye and frown
makes light leap in my eye
to stare him down.[8]

Others, like Eichelberger's "Vaslav's Song" from his theater piece
Dasvedanya, Mama, or Richard Pearson Thomas's trio, "AIDS Anxiety,"
have a spunky humor that undercuts the seriousness behind their irony.
Thomas has one of the three baritones wonder: "Can I get it / If I'm
licked by a kitten / That a friend is babysitting / For someone I don't
know, / And that loveable kitten / Likes to drink from the toilet bowl?"
Then comes the refrain: "AIDS anxiety is getting me down. / It's going
around, / And all my friends have got it too."[9]

Dixon, a black poet and novelist who died of AIDS in 1992, writes
with a tough pithiness that reduces both symptoms and mounting
despair, plus the thoughts of the ill and the caregiving, to two-word
phrases, which reverberate with the rhythm of a heartbeat:

Night sweats. Dry cough.
Loose stools. Weight loss.

Get mad. Fight back.
Call home. Rest well....

Black out. White rooms.
Head hot. Feet cold....

Six months? Three weeks?
Can't eat. No air....

Sweet heart. Don't stop.
Breathe in. Breathe out.[10]

Other selections also offer blunt details of the illness or deeply pained
responses of caregivers. Musically the selections often opt for forlorn
minor keys, often drifting off at the end without any resolution to their
pain. As Parker said in an interview in early 1992:

Some of the texts are very graphic. They're about taking medica-
tion, being sick, throwing up, having to take it over again, the
night sweats—the horror of the number of diseases that exist.
We're not sugar-coating it and saying, "Well, we're just having a

little difficulty." We must show some of the rough sides. After all, most songs are about crucial times in our lives—someone has died, someone has left you, you've inherited a lot of money, the boy's gotten the girl. So why can't we sing about AIDS?[11]

Some of the poems—especially Merrill's "Investiture at Cecconi's"—seem almost too convoluted to be set to song. But others, like Brass's "Walt Whitman in 1989," take gloriously to flight. In DeBlasio's lyric, full-throated setting, we meet the poet of the War Between the States, almost 130 years later, this time chronicling the casualties of another civil war and gently nursing them (as Whitman himself did young soldiers in that earlier battle):

He has written many lines
about these years: the disfigurement
of young men and the wars

of hard tongues and closed minds.
The body in pain will bear such nobility,
but words have the edge

of poison when spoken bitterly.
Now he takes a dying man
in his arms and tells him

How deeply flows the River....[12]

DeBlasio used the last words of the song, "All the Way Through Evening," as the title of a song cycle of his own (all to poems by Brass) that became part of his own memorial service on January 11, 1994, in the same Lincoln Center concert hall where Parker's *AIDS Quilt Songbook* was premiered. In the DeBlasio cycle, there is one piece called "An Elegy to Paul Jacobs," another of the friends remembered in the last movement of Symphony No. 1 by John Corigliano; Corigliano in turn was one of DeBlasio's teachers. The interconnections in the Quilt, the way the panels fit together in an unending round of rage and remembrance, are becoming heartbreakingly familiar.

Quilts

he NAMES Project AIDS Memorial Quilt has been ana-
lyzed as art, theater, politics, spirituality and even (in a
panel at the 1993 Modern Language Association convention) as "rhetoric." It has appeared on a daytime
television soap opera and has inspired a musical equivalent, a video, a book, and countless articles in both the popular
press and academic journals. But, curiously enough, it is seldom
described as being what it most basically is: a communal folk craft
known as quilting.

A quilt, or "comforter," as it is called in some rural communities,
is a warm double-layered blanket, usually with stuffing inside (to
make it even warmer) and decorated in some sort of pattern with
small geometric shapes of colored cloth "pieced" in various elaborate
designs onto one or both surfaces.

As a child growing up in a small town in southern Indiana, I have
many memories of quilts and quilting. The quilt on my bed was purple, blue, and white, with the pieces of cloth stitched into a kind of
repeating octagonal design that I used to contemplate in the moon-
light while trying to fall asleep or observe in the early morning sunlight on awakening. The quilt itself wasn't very thick or heavy, but it
provided a perfect cover under which to snuggle on winter nights in
the cold attic room of our farmhouse.

My grandmother, who raised me, did not quilt, but her sister
(whom I called Aunt Addie) did. I remember how the quilts-in-
progress would be on frames in her living room when we would visit
and I would stuff myself with her homemade rolls (my grandmother
made terrific cornbread, but she could never match her sister's
rolls). Aunt Addie held periodic quilting bees with other farm
women from the neighborhood. I was never invited, but I enjoyed
imagining what that communal craft must have been like, pep-

pered as I'm sure it was with laughter, gossip, and easy country-
lady-like camaraderie.

My grandmother's best friend Carrie had a step-daughter named
Ella who was large and plain and used to cut and sort pieces of cloth
for quilting on Carrie's front porch. I used to go over and help her
after school, and we each took a childlike pride in our cutting and
sorting of these building blocks.

After Ella went away (to "a home," my grandmother told me, for
the "simple-minded"), I moved on to visits with Aunt Lola Barfus,
who lived on the town square and who quilted with pieces of material
like those that Ella and I used to sort. Aunt Lola (we pronounced it
"Lo-lee" and she wasn't really anybody's aunt, as far as I can recall,
but the whole town called her that) loved quilting, requiring only the
assistance of a good listener. As she quilted, Aunt Lola also constructed stories, drawing from her own personal history and that of
the town. I sat spellbound, and stories now seem inseparable from
the designs for the quilts she was piecing.

After I went away to college and Aunt Lola died, I didn't think too
much about quilts for a number of years, depending on what my
grandmother would call "store-bought" blankets instead.

Then on the Sunday of Thanksgiving weekend in 1987, I made a
quick trip down to Washington, D.C. to see the Georgia O'Keeffe and
Lucian Freud exhibits, after ten non-stop months of caretaking
Peter through five bouts of PCP. "Get away for a few days," his doctor
had urged. "You need some rest." I begrudgingly allowed myself one
afternoon. After first walking numbly through Freud's harrowing
neorealistic portraits in the Hirschheim Gallery, then dreamily sur-
veying O'Keeffe's pink clouds and flowers and seashells at the
National Gallery, I had some extra time and took in the Shaker
quilts at the same location. In a flash, my memories of quilts came
back to me, gently comforting the stress and fear I'd been living
with, day in day out, for the past ten months. Leaving the quilt
exhibit, I called home. Peter was worse. I took a cab to the airport
and arrived at our apartment just three hours before he died, at
home, the way he wanted it.

The following May, I saw a portion of the NAMES project quilt for
the first time, at a book convention in Anaheim, California. The
power of the statements—so simple, so eloquent, so individual, yet so
powerful—overwhelmed me. The following month, the whole quilt
was on display in New York. I began to recognize the scope and size of
the whole, the way feelings and memories were being stitched

together out of an endless array of materials, like those Ella and I had sorted through on Carrie's porch. Some of the pieces were similar, almost matched, having been cut perhaps from the same cloth, but each was startlingly unique. And what a patchwork they made, stretched out together on the ground.

It took almost a year for Peter's twin sister Patti and I to begin working on our own quilt panel for Peter. We included one of his favorite shirts (bright yellow, with little green stripes), a green Tibetan prayer flag that our friend Kate had brought back from Ladakh, some felt flowers and a felt panda, his name (in a bold purple that almost matched the triangles from the quilt on my bed back in Indiana), and a little pouch that included a poem (from me), a dollar (from Patti), a St. Jude medal, and a few other memories.

We didn't "quilt" our panel with the proper stitching and backing and formally arranged pieces of cloth. If I'd ever learned how, from watching Aunt Lola Barfus, I'd forgotten. Our collaboration was more free-form, personal. But it was a quilt nonetheless. A comforter. It still is, each time I see it as a part of the whole.

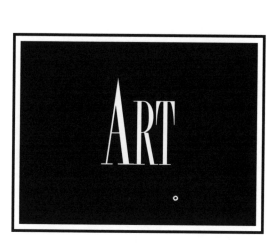

12

The NAMES Project AIDS Memorial Quilt

They brought me some of his clothes. The hospital gown,
those too-tight dungarees, his blue choir robe
with the gold sash. How that boy could sing!
His favorite color in a necktie. A Sunday shirt.
What I'm gonna do with all this stuff?
I can remember Junie without this business.
My niece Francine say they quilting all over the country.
So many good boys like her boy, gone.
                — Melvin Dixon, "Aunt Ida Pieces a Quilt"[1]

o response to AIDS has touched so many people in quite
the same way as the NAMES Project AIDS Memorial
Quilt. It's hard to analyze something so personal, so
heartfelt as the Quilt, but the responses have raised questions central to any discussion of the art of AIDS, so this
chapter finds itself, not coincidentally, near the center of this book.

The NAMES Project AIDS Memorial Quilt is a traveling exhibition
of memorial panels, each 3 feet by 6 feet (the size of a cemetery plot)
honoring the memory of a person who has died of AIDS. Most are made
by friends, lovers, and families of the person who has died; some are
made by total strangers. There are no rules, no requirements other than
the dimensions. Those making the panels can use any material they
choose, and they can decorate their panels as simply or as elaborately as
they wish.

The panels are sent to a regional office, where they are stitched

129

together to form 12-foot-by-12-foot blocks of 8 panels each. A number of permutations exist for combining the 8 panels in the block, and those who assemble them vary the combinations, so that the effect is that of a large crazy quilt, not uniform in either color or design.

When the Quilt is displayed, usually in some large outdoor space (such as the Ellipse next to the Washington Monument in the nation's capital), the 12 x 12s are combined further into groups of four, with white walkways in between them. An even larger grid, of square blocks 24 feet by 24 feet, now containing 32 panels each, is achieved.

Viewed from a slight distance, the Quilt presents a true patchwork of lives remembered: wild colors and soft pastels, somber blacks and browns, rainbows and clouds, and most of all names: formal names, familiar names, nicknames and drag names, first names only and "anonymous," for those afraid or unable to speak out, for whatever reason. One panel has a large hole where a family ripped out a man's last name that his lover had sewn on: the first name remains, proud and defiant, beside the gaping hole.

There are sometimes groupings of panels in the 12 x 12s: Lovers or brothers, remembered with matching panels; similarly constructed panels celebrating a whole group of friends or co-workers, like that remembering a group from San Francisco's Pacific Gas and Electric Co.

Walking closer, viewers can see how individual the panels are: what fabrics are used (everything from silk to gunny sack, from chintz to leather), what accessories (ribbons, buttons, flags, college pennants, napkins, jewelry, even a 4-H blue ribbon), what representations of persons remembered (photos, drawings, cut-outs, empty garments), what words (not only names and dates, but poems, phrases, favorite quotes, sometimes whole volumes on a single panel). The words and memories are sewn, glued, magic-markered or even penciled to the panels: some sturdily, intent on weathering the passage of time, some so fragilely that they're already beginning to fade and fall off.

The panels celebrate occupations, identities, relationships: the departed as brother, son, lover, father, mother, daughter, sister, teacher, poet, actor, singer, dancer, bird-watcher, opera lover, disco bunny, drag queen, leatherman. Charles Ludlam as Camille. Roy Cohn: "Bully. Coward. Victim." An Edward Gorey cartoon. A staff of music containing no notes, only a single rest. A name over 12 candles (12 friends), 9 of which are extinguished.

As the viewers walk down the white paths between the grouped panels, names are read aloud over a sound system, minute after minute, hour after hour. All these names, as if the list will never end.

Cleve Jones says he got the idea for the Quilt during a memorial parade in November 1985, honoring the late Harvey Milk, the San Francisco supervisor assassinated in 1978. As part of the march, those in the parade had been asked to bring cardboard placards with the names of people who had died of AIDS and place them on the wall of the old Federal Building. In *The Quilt: Stories from the NAMES Project,* Cindy Ruskin quotes Jones as recalling: "It was such a startling image. The wind and the rain tore some of the cardboard names loose, but people stood there for hours reading names. I knew then that we needed a monument, a memorial."[2]

It took Jones over a year to formulate and organize his project, working initially with a friend, Mike Smith. By the annual San Francisco Lesbian and Gay Freedom Day Parade, June 28, 1987, there were 40 panels, including the first, made by Jones for Marvin Feldman, a close friend who had died the previous October. The panels were hung from the mayor's balcony at City Hall.

Word spread quickly about the project. The NAMES Project opened an office on Castro Street, starting with seven volunteers, and quickly grew into an operation with ten sewing machines and scores of helpers. Pushing for a display in Washington in October, where there was to be a National March for Lesbian and Gay Rights, the Project had 400 panels by August. As Ruskin reports, "Ultimately, 1,920 quilt panels made it to the Capitol Mall in Washington, where they covered the size of two football fields. But nearly 3,000 panels had reached the San Francisco workshop by the time of the March and they haven't stopped coming."[3]

The Quilt had grown to such proportions by October 1992 that organizers of the project predicted that this showing would be the last time that all the panels could be shown together (there are many regional showings around the country, where panels specific to that geographic location are featured). At that time, according to one report,[4] the Quilt consisted of 22,000 panels, weighed 26 tons, filled 48 tractor trailers and, when unfolded, covered an area that was the equivalent of 12 football fields. (As of April 1, 1994, the NAMES Project reports it now has 26, 613 panels)

Like any phenomenon that has received so much attention, the Quilt has drawn its share of critical (and often contradictory) responses: that it is too personal (or too impersonal), that it is too political (or not political enough), that it favors elegy or emotionalism over action and resistance, that it is aesthetically flawed, that its real attention is on those who mourn or grieve (those who make the panels and come to see them) rather than on those persons with AIDS being remembered, that it is a work by the living presuming to speak for the dead.

Peter S. Hawkins, a professor of religion and literature at Yale Divinity School, has noted the basic human impulse for naming that the Quilt satisfies: "Human beings are alone in imagining their own deaths; they are also unique in their need to remember the dead and to keep on imagining them. Central to this act of memory is the name of the deceased, that familiar formula of identity by which a person seems to live on after life is over. To forget a name is in effect to allow death to have the last word." [5]

Hawkins compares the Quilt to the Vietnam Veterans Memorial, which unlike the towering edifices surrounding it in Washington, is instead "a minimalist sculpture, an earthwork in which the spectator moves down rather than up, to view names engraved not in the capital's customary white stone but in highly polished black granite."[6] As he continues to describe the Vietnam memorial, conceived by architectural student Maya Lin, the parallels with the Quilt experience are startling:

> In effect, the walls of the memorial were turned into mirrors in which the living would see themselves superimposed upon the names of the dead. Lin also decided against arranging the soldiers alphabetically, choosing instead to place them in the order of the day they died. The wall, she said, would read like a Greek epic. To locate specific names, with the aid of a directory, would be like entering a tour of duty, like finding bodies on a battlefield.[7]

There are distinct differences, of course: The Quilt has no permanent installation but travels around the country; it is made of cloth, not stone; its list of names continues to grow, while the Vietnam list is complete. But "the Quilt in any of its forms is most profoundly about the naming of names: the sight of them on the myriad panels, the sound of them read aloud. As with the Vietnam Veterans Memorial, the names themselves are the memorial. In both cases they are the destination of pilgrimage, the occasion for candlelight vigils and song."[8]

Hawkins goes on to relate the Quilt to the history of quilting, which he points out was traditionally a way that women memorialized their dead, in a softer, more intuitive way, while men chiseled names in stone. He is intrigued that the originators of the Quilt, being gay men, chose this method, which often recorded more than just birth dates and death dates about a particular name:

> Some of the panels are indeed "volumes of hieroglyphics," recon-
> structions of human narrative that rely as much on private associa-
> tions as on any public discourse—life stories that need to be decod-
> ed. Moreover, intimacies are everywhere confided to strangers. The
> panels betray a delight in the telling of tales, revealing in those who
> have died a taste for leather or for chintz, for motorbikes or drag
> shows. Secrets are shared with everybody. It is as if the survivors
> had decided that the greatest gift they could offer the dead would
> be telling everything, breaking the silence that has surrounded gay
> life long before the advent of AIDS.[9]

Still, it is the name itself that holds the real intimacies, the real secrets, and its repetition, like a litany, is the real empowerment. One panel in particular caught Hawkins attention—as it did many others (including John Corigliano, who chose it as one of three panels on the album cover of his *Symphony No. 1*). The panel was made by David Kemmeries for his lover Jac Wall: a simple white outlined figure stands against a patterned background of light blue. If you walk close enough, you can read the black printing which outlines this reverse shadow, this body turning to light:

> Jac Wall is my lover. Jac Wall had AIDS. Jac Wall died. I love
> Jac Wall. Jac Wall is a good guy. Jac Wall made me a better per-
> son. Jac Wall could beat me in wrestling. Jac Wall loves me. Jac
> Wall is thoughtful. Jac Wall is great in bed. Jac Wall is intelli-
> gent. I love Jac Wall. Jac Wall is with me. Jac Wall turns me on.
> I miss Jac Wall. Jac Wall is faithful. Jac Wall is a natural Indian.
> Jac Wall is young at heart. Jac Wall looks good naked. I love Jac
> Wall. Jac Wall improved my life. Jac Wall is my lover. Jac Wall
> loves me. I miss Jac Wall. I will be with you soon.[10]

Another writer, Robert Dawidoff, has given an achingly clear repre-sentation of what it is like to be "lost" in the Quilt, moving from panel to panel, hearing the names read over a loudspeaker, drifting from life to life, name to name, memory to memory: "The experience of the Quilt is overwhelming. It is not like visiting a place or viewing something, it is being in the Quilt, as if enfolded by it. You go to look and suddenly the

Quilt makes you present in your own life because of the surrounding atmosphere of lives, lives, lives."[11] He also points out, importantly, that the experience is not a solitary one: "The other thing in The NAMES Project is the other people there seeing it with you."[12] The audience of the Quilt, like its makers and those memorialized, is a kind of Rainbow Coalition:

> AIDS has taken every kind of life, male, female, young, old, child, adult; every kind of person has died of AIDS. The NAMES Project reminds us of that. A child's bed strewn with her stuffed animals remembers a little girl. But, as everyone knows, gay men have been especially hard hit by AIDS. The NAMES Project is, among other things, a remarkable, living record of the recent history of gay Americans. The panels unfold a story of love, friendship, creativity, and human worth that chokes the viewer with pride and sadness.... AIDS is not only happening to gays, let alone to gay men, but it is happening to them and The NAMES Project is an extraordinary tribute to and by and for a community under desperate, unlooked for, unmerited siege.[13]

Like a few others, gay theorist Richard Mohr has criticized the Quilt for omitting certain details (specifically the more sexual details) of the lives of those remembered—that those memorializing friends and family they have lost, in other words, paint their own distorted pictures of the deceased instead of letting the deceased represent themselves: "The proper focus of moral concern in mourning is he who is mourned, not he who does the mourning."[14] But surely mourning—and certainly the mourning associated with the Quilt—almost has to be at least partly about the survivors and caregivers, who make the panels, who view the panels, who live the other half of the stories being told and cannot be arbitrarily denied their part in those stories, or in the grieving that must be a kind of final chapter in those stories. "The NAMES Project Quilt is not only a memorial," Susan Grant Rosen of Union Theological Seminary has written. "If this were its sole aim, the job could have been commissioned, and a work of consistent artistic quality produced. But the Quilt exists to honor the survivors along with the dead."[15] Or, as Judy Elsley has written: "In part the panels provide a way for survivors to make a difference. Because caretakers feel particularly helpless in terms of healing those afflicted with the disease, the quilt is something concrete and lasting over which they do have control."[16]

Each panel is, in a sense, a bond between the maker and the person memorialized, and can in turn serve as a bridge to the viewer as well. It is in this respect that Elinor Fuchs's initially surprising analysis of the Quilt as a "performance" in *American Theatre* makes most sense: "the Quilt is more relaxed, more inclusive, more sensual, more human, more *theatrical* than anything previously imagined in the protocols of mourning."[17] Its spunky sense of humor helps alleviate the sadness and sobriety of the ritual performance:

> With all the suffering it represents, the Quilt playfully sends up the solemnity, the *rigidity*, of mourning, including "permanence." Imagine a cemetery putting all its attendants in white jeans and sneakers. Then imagine rows and rows of marble headstones etched with teddy bears, Hawaiian shirts and Mickey Mouse. Imagine jumbling Jews, Catholics, Muslims and New Age Buddhists in the same subdivision of the "everlasting abode." *Imagine* finding a sublime design of mountains, bordered with "Comfort, oh comfort my people" in Hebrew and English right next to a splash of sequins celebrating "Boogie," and directly below a grinning depiction of Bugs Bunny. The Quilt is cemetery as All Fools' Days, a carnival of the sacred, the homely, the joyous and the downright tacky, resisting, even *in extremis*, the solemnity of mourning.[18]

However, at the same time that the Quilt is performance or a kind of camp celebration, more like a wake than a visit to the funeral home, it also has a very serious, solemn, and perhaps sacred purpose: to honor in death persons who, more often than not were not accorded proper honor and respect in life, especially during their final disease. As Susan Grant Rosen notes, "The Quilt emerges from the profound need human beings feel to mark the passage from life to death in a way that is 'right and fitting.' In our culture, with its religious heritage, 'right and fitting' death ceremonial means honoring the sacred quality in human life."[19] It is that very sacred quality that is often denied to people who die of AIDS, Rosen states: "Many AIDS patients die without the support of family or faith community. Even when they are remembered in conventional funeral rites, one can question the degree to which the ceremony honors the dead or permits a full expression of grief, since the cause of death is often obscured to protect the family and the community from stigma."[20]

Rosen quotes a woman from Nebraska who made a panel for a colleague of her son, whom she had never met, because she was afraid his own family would not recognize him: "I felt bad about that. I feel bad about all the people who die of AIDS that nobody knows."[21] A similar touching anecdote is included by Ruskin in *The Quilt*: a woman who had never met a man who died of AIDS decided to make a panel for him after seeing an "In Memoriam" notice by his lover in the local paper. She sent it to the NAMES Project with this note:

> Dear David's Lover:
>
> Please know my intent, when making this panel, was not to invade your memories or life with David. I have no memories to share of him but I do share one thing with you. On October 23, 1986 [when I read the death notice in the paper], a pain went through my heart that was unbearable. A loneliness for the loss of a complete stranger—a potential friend. To this day I cry when I think of how you must miss each other. . . .
>
> Love, Cindy[22]

The letters, like the panels themselves, are strikingly democratic: They open the Quilt up to anyone who wants to participate. There are no aliens, no outsiders, no foreigners or outcasts. They include the writer or maker in a dialogue with the person remembered and are intended, as Timothy F. Murphy, has written, "to preserve the memory of a life that has touched them, that deserves something better than silence." [23] Like Aunt Ida in Melvin Dixon's poem, each quilter chips away at that silence. Aunt Ida is shocked at first when she hears her nephew Junie's quilt is going to be displayed: "A quilt ain't no showpiece," she insists. "It's to keep you warm. Francine say it can do both."[24] And perhaps even more:

> Francine say she gonna send this quilt to Washington
> like folks doing from all 'cross the country,
> so many good people gone. Babies, mothers, fathers
> and boys like our Junie. Francine say
> they gonna piece this quilt to another one,
> another name and another patch
> all in a larger quilt getting larger and larger.
>
> Maybe we all like that, patches waiting to be pieced....
> Now where did I put that needle?[25]

13

Confrontations & Critical Agendas

... [A]rt *does* have the power to save lives, and it is this power that must be recognized, fostered, and supported in every way possible. But if we are to do this, we will have to abandon the idealist conception of art. We don't need a cultural renaissance; we need cultural practices actively participating in the struggle against AIDS. We don't need to transcend the epidemic; we need to end it.

—Douglas Crimp, *AIDS: Cultural Analysis/Cultural Activism*[1]

ow to represent AIDS in the visual arts—painting, sculpture, and photography—is a particularly perplexing question, one that has generated more answers (usually quite forceful and didactic manifestos) than reasonable dialogue on the subject. Should the art under discussion represent people with AIDS directly, or should it turn its focus outward, portraying the world surrounding—and often oppressing—PWAs? If PWAs are to be represented, how graphic should the representations be? If outer-directed, what should the work then address? Government inaction? The world of medical research? The virus itself? How can more abstract notions like homophobia, fear, anger, or dementia be shown? How can survival, resistance, or being HIV positive be depicted?

The art of AIDS reflects almost all these approaches at one time or another. Each of the artists who treats AIDS in his or her work usually succeeds or fails not because of the subject matter, but because of his or her inherent talent. But does AIDS art, by the very fragility of its nature, demand different or less stringent standards than other art? Perhaps yes, in an immediate sense, for artists (and others) fighting for their lives, as critic Douglas Crimp insists. But will such an art have a lasting relevance (something Crimp appears to consider a moot point)?

There's no real answer to such a dilemma. Much of the work of AIDS artists has been presented in group shows, the nature of which allows an egalitarianism and broad spectrum of styles and approaches. One of the first of these, *Witnesses: Against Our Vanishing*, got considerable attention in the mainstream press for reasons that had little to do with its shared but varied aesthetic; indeed, the most virulent criticism centered not on the artworks exhibited but on a controversial and angry catalogue essay by one of the artists in the show, David Wojnarowicz.

The exhibit, curated by Nan Goldin at Artists Space in the Soho district of New York City, *Witnesses* opened on November 16, 1989. The space quickly lost its grant from the National Endowment of the Arts, whose chairman, John Frohnmayer, denounced the exhibit (though he later reversed himself and restored the grant). The story made front-page headlines across the country, as did two other government funding "gay pornography" scandals at about the same time: the brouhaha surrounding a Robert Mapplethorpe photography exhibit (first in Washington, then in Cincinnati), and the cancellation of NEA grants to four artists deemed obscene by the Endowment.

But the Artists Space scandal had less to do with art and more to do with words, namely Wojnarowicz's description of New York Cardinal John J. O'Connor as a "fat cannibal" and a "creep in black skirts," calling rather explicitly for his extinction: "I believe in the death penalty for people in positions of power who commit crimes against humanity, i.e., fascism."[2] The Cardinal's death warrant, however, paled beside Wojnarowicz's comments against two elected members of the U. S. Government, Senator Jesse Helms and Rep. William Dannemayer, whose outspoken opposition to gay rights and AIDS legislation has been legendary: "At least in my ungoverned imagination I can fuck somebody without a rubber or I can, in the privacy of my own skull, douse Helms with a bucket of gasoline and set his putrid ass on fire or throw rep. William Dannemayer off the empire state building. These fantasies give me distance from my outrage for a few seconds." [3]

Certainly Wojnarowicz and Goldin knew what they were doing: pushing good taste to the extreme, skirting on ice as thin as the First

Amendment would allow. This tactic has been standard in much visual art about AIDS, as in AIDS activism in general. The gallery lost its $1,000 grant (temporarily) but got probably 100 times that in free publicity. And New Yorkers flocked to see the show.

The exhibit, like the controversy that surrounded it, relied more on words and media manipulation than conventional artistic displays. There were photos or paintings of people with AIDS, hospital rooms, an empty chair. Almost all of these reached their fullest impact when the viewer referred to the catalogue or to typed notices on the wall beside the works, as with Dorit Cyprus's four rows of snapshots of a woman's body on little shelves under a large blue nude: "AIDS is symptomatic of a culture which has lost its 'body,'" the commentary states, even adding its own quotation marks for emphasis to make sure the viewer gets the message. *YIELD (the body)* is moreover "a step towards celebrating many bodies; a step toward recovery."[4]

Darrel Ellis's painting, a self-portrait, has a particularly thought-provoking statement by the artist appended: "I struggle to resist the frozen images of myself taken by Robert Mapplethorpe and Peter Hujar. They haunt me." Shillburne Thurber offers snapshots of empty bedrooms and motel rooms, stating: "AIDS has left empty spaces in many lives including my own. Hopefully these images help to convey some sense of the implacable finality associated with this loss." Greer Lankton's *Freddy and Ellen* is a seven-foot-tall sculpture of two emaciated, doll-like creatures holding on to each other while sitting on a couch; the two could be lovers, mother and son, or just friends. Lankton has written: "Having watched so many friends die from AIDS has been like surgery without anesthesia. I have found it very difficult to relate my emotional responses to my art work. It seems like nothing I could make would adequately describe the grief I feel. The skins I have made are just mementos, like the skin we wear when we are alive becomes just a memento after we die." Wojnarowicz's *America* is one of his photo-negative collages, juxtaposing words and images (some of them distinctly homoerotic) to shock his audience awake.

Philip Lorca di Corcia's *Vittorio* shows a haunted young man staring at the camera; he is in a hospital bed, surrounded by balloons, an IV pole, get-well cards, hospital gifts. Just down the wall in the exhibit, the viewer comes to some pencil drawings, self-portraits by the same Vittorio Scarpati in his hospital bed. Curator Goldin describes them as "a visual diary of his days living in suspension.... He has left behind an indelible record of his fight for life and given us a gift of wit and wisdom."

It becomes apparent that the participants in the show are for the most part friends of each other, members of a kind of loose community of artists and activists, many of them fighting for their lives. Stephen Tashjian's *Tabboo!* is a "portrait of Mark Morrisroe," but Morrisroe has made his own horrifying statement as well, a Polaroid self-portrait entitled "Mark Morrisroe (1959-1989)," with this accompanying text:

> They have stopped listening to me, so I wrote everything down in a note; who was trying to murder me and how, and then smashed the vase of flowers Pat Hearn sent me so I would have something to mutilate myself with by carving in my leg, "evening nurses murdered me"; and I took the phone receiver and pummeled my face over and over and sprayed blood all over the walls and on this book; and then I took the butter pat from my dinner tray and greased up the note and stuffed it up my asshole so they would find it during my autopsy.

This is no exhibit—no crisis—for the faint-hearted or squeamish.

Goldin herself chronicles the sense of both desperation and community she feels the exhibit represents, writing in the catalogue: "I feel my own recent recovery from addiction, and that of many of my friends, is directly related to AIDS. With the advent of a fatal illness in our midst, the glorification of self-destruction wore thin.... We have been forced to make survival, recovery and healing our priorities as individuals and as a community. We realize that we can live the same lifestyle, but in the light. That we can still live fully in the moment but with an awareness of consequences."[5]

The exhibit has its own manifesto: "to prove that a gay aesthetic continues to flourish. To prove that sex = death is a false equation.... That the sexual liberation movement need not become extinct but requires a new responsibility."[6] Goldin speaks of her own rage "in the face of this plague" and her wish to "empower others with a forum to voice their grief and anger in the hope that this public ritual of mourning can be cathartic in the process of recovery, both for those among us who are now ill and those survivors who are left behind."[7] Then she throws down the gauntlet, insisting "AIDS has not and will not eliminate our community, or succeed in wiping out our sensibility or silencing our voice," then concludes with an upfront challenge to those who would dismiss the exhibit: "We are all clumsy in dealing with grief. I do not believe we need to develop a correct etiquette. Every one of our responses is valid. Passivity and silence are the gravest dangers. It is not the time to distract ourselves with divisiveness." [8]

Many of the earliest examples of art about AIDS made extensive use of text and graphic design, much like propaganda art or "agitprop" of earlier decades— "agitprop" being a term used primarily by the right wing artistic establishment to dismiss any attempt at political consciousness in the arts. In the AIDS community, such graphic art is closely linked to political action groups like ACT UP which identifies itself as "a diverse, nonpartisan group united in anger and committed to direct action to end the AIDS crisis."

From the beginning, as Douglas Crimp and Adam Rolston have chronicled in their study *AIDS DemoGraphics*, all of ACT UP's actions were accompanied by posters signs, buttons, and stickers—the graphics of open, acknowledged propaganda: "We have no patent on the politics or the designs. There are AIDS activist graphics wherever there are AIDS activists.... We want others to keep using our graphics and making their own. Part of our point is that nobody owns these images They belong to a movement that is constantly growing—in numbers, in militancy, in political awareness." [9]

As Crimp and Rolston point out, such activism was not welcomed by the New York gallery and museum establishment. When an exhibit was mounted at the Museum of Modern Art in early 1988 entitled "Committed to Print: Social and Political Themes in Recent American Printed Art," there was no work included detailing either gay rights or the AIDS crisis, and "When asked by a critic at the *Village Voice* why there was nothing about AIDS, the curator [Deborah Wye] blithely replied that she knew of no graphic work of artistic merit dealing with the epidemic." [10]

Yet the most famous graphic to arise out of the AIDS crisis had been created over a year before, and the streets of New York had been plastered with posters and stickers containing it. The design was simple: a poster (and later a button) proclaiming "SILENCE = DEATH" on a pink triangle against a black background. The emblem was originally created by the Silence = Death Project, six gay men who later joined the original ACT UP organization and offered the symbol to ACT UP for its second demonstration in April 1987. It has since become the sort of unofficial symbol of the group.

The symbolic significance goes back to use of the pink triangle by the Nazis to single out homosexuals, to which the collective added the phrase SILENCE = DEATH, stating:

> SILENCE = DEATH declares that silence about the oppression and annihilation of gay people, *then and now*, must be broken as a matter of our survival.... But it is not merely what SILENCE = DEATH says, but also how it looks, that gives it its particular force. The power of this equation under a triangle is the compression of its connotation into a logo, a logo so striking that you ultimately *have* to ask, if you don't already know, "What does that mean?" And it is the answers we are constantly called upon to give to others—small, everyday direct actions that make SILENCE = DEATH signify beyond a community of lesbian and gay cognoscenti.[11]

The next major artistic statement by the graphics arm of ACT UP was *Let the Record Show*, a window exhibit at the New Museum of Contemporary Art on lower Broadway in New York. Produced by a collaborative group of artists within the larger ACT UP organization, it featured a neon version of the SILENCE = DEATH symbol, a photomural of the Nuremberg Trials, an electronic information display, and "six life-size, silhouetted photographs of 'AIDS criminals' in separate, boxed-in spaces, and below each one the words by which he or she may be judged by history, cast—literally—in concrete."[12] The "rogues gallery" of the window display included then President Ronald Reagan: Senator Jesse Helms; evangelist Jerry Falwell; Cory Servaas, a particularly controversial member of the Presidential AIDS Commission; William F. Buckley, who had advocated the tattooing of "everyone detected with AIDS"; and an anonymous surgeon who declares "We used to hate faggots on an emotional basis. Now we have a good reason."

AIDS activist artists formed a number of other collectives in the next few years, including New York-based (and ACT UP-associated) Gran Fury, Little Elvis, and Group Material, as well as General Idea in Toronto, which took the "general idea" of Robert Indiana's "LOVE" painting, substituting another four-letter word, "AIDS," in paintings, billboards, flyers, and sculptures—not to parody or rip-off Indiana's quintessential statement of the sixties, but to try to "domesticate" the acronym for the late eighties.

As Lois Nesbitt has written:

> The activist groups seize the incidental as well as paid advertising
> spaces and surfaces that comprise the urban fabric. In New York,
> where such activity has been especially visible . . . AIDS-related
> posters and stickers have appeared on buildings, automatic teller
> machines, subway cars, phone booths, mailboxes and elsewhere, tes-
> tifying to the ingenuity and determination of guerrilla artists.

> AIDS street graphics have coopted the techniques of Madison
> Avenue advertising, blurring the distinction between their offerings
> and those of the marketplace and thus deliberately catching viewers
> off-guard. In keeping with the visual language of urban ads, quick
> impact is the goal, effected through simple, striking visuals and
> brief, provocative slogans, often underscored by fine print elaborat-
> ing a point or supplying further information.[13]

It is important, also, to keep in mind the collective nature of this art.
Though many of the artists involved were also painters or performance
artists of some note, they insistently submerged their own identities as
artists into making a concise and significant group statement. Anyone
who has tried to write—or create anything—with other people can grasp
the extreme difficulty of such a project—and can also understand the
striking rewards when ego is finally overcome and the process really
begins to work.

The New York based groups started to produce an array of posters
and other art that captured the attention not only of the AIDS activist
and gay community, but the general public as well. Among the messages
were an AIDSGATE poster, with Ronald Reagan's photo (by the Silence
= Death Collective); a yellow bumper sticker reading "THE AIDS CRI-
SIS IS NOT OVER" by Little Elvis; Gran Fury's "WALL STREET
MONEY" series, with photocopies of ten, fifty, and one hundred dollar
bills, with AIDS messages on the back; and Gran Fury's "READ MY
LIPS" posters (and later T-shirts) with same sex couples kissing and the
message "FIGHT HOMOPHOBIA: FIGHT AIDS"; Gran Fury's staggering powerful bumper sticker challenge, black type on a bold yellow
background, insisting "MEN: USE CONDOMS OR BEAT IT"; Gran
Fury's "THE GOVERNMENT HAS BLOOD ON ITS HANDS:
ONE AIDS DEATH EVERY HALF HOUR," illustrated by a bloody
handprint; and the same group's 4-page replica of the *New York Times* calling itself the *New York Crimes* and containing AIDS stories which the actu-

al newspaper had up until then never deemed part of its "All the News That's Fit to Print."

In January 1992, a traveling exhibit entitled *From Media to Metaphor: Art About AIDS* opened at Hamilton College in Clinton, New York. After touring to a varied assortment of rural and urban outposts—Seattle, Washington; Kutztown, Pennsylvania; Montreal, Canada; Miami Beach, Florida; Columbia, South Carolina; Bloomington, Indiana; and Santa Barbara, California—the exhibit came home to the Grey Gallery in the Greenwich Village section of New York City, where its co-curators (Thomas Sokolowski, director of the Grey Gallery, and Robert Atkins, an art critic for the *Village Voice*) had planned it for almost two years prior to its original opening in the small upstate college town.

From the beginning, the show was meant to offer education about AIDS as well as a wide range of artistic representations about the epidemic. In each venue, AIDS information was made available at the exhibit, videos were shown in addition to the paintings, photos, and sculptures on display, and the local hosts would update the exhibit with works by local artists.

The show's selections indicate how diverse representations of AIDS have become in the four years since the *Witnesses* exhibit. Many of the works are larger and more elaborate and incorporate a broader range of styles, from photographic portraits to architectural models and figurative painting. At the Grey Gallery, sculptor Dui Seid contributed the updating: *Artist's Estate*, a green dumpster filled with the remains of the days and lives of artist friends who had recently died of AIDS—a chilling reminder of what happens to many of the works of PWAs, especially in a large city like New York. Included in the debris were objects signifying both personal and artistic loss: empty picture frames, rolled prints and canvases, paint containers, and brushes, plus bottles of Retrovir (an AIDS treatment drug), personal snapshots and slides, issues of *Playguy*, *AIDS Treatment News*, and the *New York Times*, cut-out obituaries, letters to arts organizations and government agencies, Depends (diapers for adults), rubber gloves, a telephone, a tennis shoe, a wheelchair. One of the letters was from the Tony Shafrazi Gallery protesting an AIDS treatment center in its neighborhood (Shafrazi's most famous client was Keith Haring, who died of AIDS in 1990).

If Seid's dumpster may not look like "art" to some of viewers, they shouldn't have any such problem with other pieces in the show, such as

Paul Marcus's *Maze of AIDS*, with its slice-of-life scenes from the life of a young Hispanic woman with AIDS in the Bronx; Haring's version of the SILENCE = DEATH as "see no evil, hear no evil, speak no evil"; Thomas Woodruff's portrait of himself as a crying clown; or Masami Teraoka's Japanese Ukiyo-e print of a traditional geisha clutching a condom. The black and white or color portraits by Rosalind Solomon, Jane Rosett, Nicholas Nixon, Robert Mapplethorpe, and Gypsy Ray—all of PWAs—should also speak to these audiences. But some of the less traditional statements are also very accessible, like Jo Shane's shrink-wrapped bundle of 972 rolls of President's Choice toilet paper, incorporating photos of similarly "disposable" people who died of AIDS; the (ART)^n collective's illuminated cross featuring colorized CAT scans, with two hands of hope (a Wisconsin folk art image) and two pairs of rolling dice superimposed; Kathe Burkhart's pop art rendition of Liz Taylor absurdly forced to declare, tabloid-style, "I DON'T HAVE AIDS!"; Ross Bleckner's muted abstractions of med school magnifications of human cells, the very home of the virus; or Nancy Burson's blown-up photos of an HIV-infected and a healthy T-cell with the printed admonition "VISUALIZE THIS" —a piece that was particularly controversial, according to the catalogue description: "Detractors felt that it placed the responsibility for the AIDS crisis on PWAs rather than on the government. This position may be a polarizing example of either/or thinking not necessarily in the best interests of PWAs. Some PWAs employ Eastern and Western medicine, visualize and meditate, and participate in demonstrations as well." [14]

In early January 1994, just before the *From Media to Metaphor* exhibit opened in New York City, Thomas Sokolowski reflected on how the art of AIDS has changed since he and Atkins originally curated the exhibit two-and-a-half years earlier. "I think we reached a kind of benchmark with President Clinton's election," he said. "Things have changed. People's energies are not focused on Clinton the way they were on Bush and Reagan. The enemy has been kicked out. Clinton may not be a good guy, but he's not a monster." [15]

As a result, the work he is looking at today is different from the work three years ago, when he was choosing pieces to include in the original exhibit. "There wasn't as much brand new work being made. We went to those artists who were still alive to see their new work, with the idea that maybe we would freshen up the show, or to just see what they were

doing. Most of them were not making works about AIDS any more."
Sokolowski felt there were several explanations for this, ranging from
burn-out to the fact that "people just can't scream all the time." Perhaps
"AIDS isn't the fear that it was before. It's more distant now—not right
up at our doorstep. People have to step back and get some perspective.
We're still at a crisis—I don't mean to imply that we're not. But how do
we speak in a new way, to different communities? Especially since we
don't speak in the same language."

For one thing, Sokolowski feels, the message needs to be more global.
"In Britain and France, for example, there's very little work being done.
In India, where the epidemic is reaching really alarming proportions, you
can't even show two people kissing. How can you talk about sex and
condoms?" He mentions Cheri Samba, a poster artist from Zaire, whose
work addresses such issues. But elsewhere the status of information-pro-
viding art is bleak.

One of the messages of the exhibit is that there is no single "message"
to such art. "Everyone has tried to find one logo, one symbol, and to
make it THE one." says Sokolowski. "But one symbol or one strategy
does not suffice. Artistic responses are always individual."

There is also no single audience. Such an exhibit thus offers both aesthetics and politics, allowing both Douglas Crimp's manifesto (which
opened this chapter) and a less didactic interpretation of how to represent
so complex an issue.

AIDS art criticism has, rightly or wrongly, reflected some of the deep
divisions in the gay and art communities on how AIDS and homosexuality should be "represented" in the arts. On one hand, there are critics
like Crimp writing essays like "How to Have Promiscuity in an
Epidemic"[16] as if compulsive, multi-partner sex were some sort of god-
given right and the defining characteristic of the gay lifestyle; on the
other there are people like Larry Kramer or Jim Fouratt questioning the
emotional and physical toll of "transgressive sexual acts" as a path to
real gay identity, especially in the age of AIDS. Somewhere in the middle, there's what British activist and critic Simon Watney has worried
about as "the re-homosexualisation of gay culture"[17]—where the straight
media, in particularly, uses the threat of AIDS to try to drive gays back
into the closet and to abandon the modicum of liberation they have
wrested from society.

A number of activists also have tried to proscribe (or at least dismiss) a whole canon of works by certain painters, sculptors, and photographers of the epidemic, as suggested by the much-quoted ACT UP flyer that greeted the exhibit of AIDS photographs by Nicholas Nixon at the Museum of Modern Art in New York. Under the headline "NO MORE PICTURES WITHOUT CONTEXT," the flyer proclaimed:

> We believe that the representation of people with AIDS (PWAs) affects not only how viewers will perceive PWAs outside the museum, but, ultimately, crucial issues of AIDS funding, legislation, and education.
>
> The artist's choice to produce representational work always affects more than a single artist's career, going beyond issues of curatorship, beyond the walls on which an artist's work is displayed.
>
> Ultimately, representations affect those portrayed.
>
> In portraying PWAs as people to be pitied or feared, as people alone and lonely, we believe that this show perpetuates general misconceptions about AIDS without addressing the realities of those of us living every day with this crisis as PWAs and people who love PWAs.[18]

The flyer then ends with another proclamation: "We demand the visibility of PWAs who are vibrant, angry, loving, sexy, beautiful, acting up and fighting back. STOP LOOKING AT US; START LISTENING TO US."

Though few would deny the validity of ACT UP's basic plea (to represent the other side of the AIDS picture fairly), the tone of the manifesto comes dangerously close to insisting that *only* positive images of PWAs be presented, which in itself would be tantamount to censorship and misrepresentation. Many observers worry that this is an attempt to not only whitewash AIDS, but to control art.

But at the same time, the reverse approach is even more scary: the attempt by critics and curators, both inside and outside the world of AIDS, to dismiss AIDS art as mere propaganda or amateurism. Many AIDS artists, who are painting as fast as they can in face of their own mortality, don't always make neat aesthetic statements which fit under any existing critical agendas. The works, indeed, both out of necessity and intentionally, are often crude, angry, even "unfinished." To dismiss them, or to subject them to standards completely removed from their own context or immediacy, is to miss the point completely.

INTERLUDE

Critics & Spectators

I've spent most of my life trying to work as a critic, first of pop music, then, variously, of theater, dance, film, and video. But being a critic is a conceit I've never felt comfortable with, implying, as it does, judgment, condescension, special privilege, and (often) dismissal of the art being criticized. At its best, criticism is description, analysis, classification, but even those acts are almost always presumptuous. I've always thought there must, somehow, be a better way.

When I first met Peter, one of the first things that struck me was that when we went to a play or cabaret performance, he didn't turn to me at the intermission and say, "Well, what did you think of that?"—something previous boyfriends, and even casual acquaintances, had done, without fail. I hated being put on the spot, having to make snap judgments, even if I was not writing about what we were watching or listening to. I desperately wanted to be just another member of the audience.

Peter allowed me that: never challenged me, never argued with me. Writing was my space—something I did as an occupation. It happened to coincide with what we usually did socially, but it didn't (as far as he was concerned) have to interfere. I felt at times he'd just as soon be at home watching "Family Feud," but he never complained, even when I took him to opera, where he usually quietly slept.

What about writing in general: how can it be more honest, more direct? I've had several clues over the years. One goes all the way back to my freshman year in high school. A friend and teacher named Wilma Dyck read over two short stories I had just written: one about a mad scientist running a mental institution on the heaths of England, the other about a young sailor on the high seas, separated from his true love. Wilma said that it was very nice that I was reading things like *The Island of Doctor Moreau, Wuthering Heights,* and *Moby-Dick,* but maybe it would be helpful if I tried writing about people or situations that I actually knew.

Concerning "criticism" itself, my first boss in the field, Thomas Willis from the *Chicago Tribune,* once sent me, as a green young rock 'n' roll columnist to review my first dance concert and my first art exhibit (he was dance, music, and art critic at the *Trib*). "But I don't know a thing about dance!" I protested. "You like theater, right? And pop music? Well, just write down what you see." He hesitated a moment, then added the zinger: "And don't make anything up. Don't ever pretend to know something you don't, because the reader will see through you every time."

The second lesson also came from Tom. I came back very excited from a dance concert—I think it was Erick Hawkins— and started babbling to Tom, who was trying to write his review of the Chicago Symphony, about how great it had been. "Write a four-head," he said, not even looking up from his typewriter. That meant three short paragraphs, less than a hundred words. I was crushed. But I probably learned more about writing concise descriptive criticism that night than at any trip to the keyboard before or since.

This lesson was pounded into my head again in the summer of 1972 at a conference for dance critics at Connecticut College. It was conducted by Marcia B. Siegel and Deborah Jowitt, two critics for whom I've always had considerable respect. Both Siegel and Jowitt were adamant about one thing: criticism starts with description, not judgment. One's first duty is to explain what is going on up on stage as accurately as possible, not to condemn or praise it.

Each morning the seminar started with Siegel leading the writers in movement exercises—getting us to experience everyday movement (though not any particular style of "dance") in our own bodies. How else would we ever be able to describe a moving art, without a direct experience of such basics?

At the end of one session, someone asked Siegel whom she wrote for: Was her responsibility to the artist (and Art with a capital A) or to the audience? I've never forgotten her reply. "I write for myself," she said. "It's the only honest thing I can do." The questioner was stunned, as we all were initially. How egotistical, I thought at first, how presumptuous. But the more I thought about it, the more sense it made. A critic cannot be a flack for the artist, but the presumption that anyone can be totally objective (writing just for "the audience") is equally absurd. The most any of us can do is to write as honestly as possible about our response to what we see.

Another interesting question was directed at Jowitt: "How can I review a concert by a friend?" one young woman asked. Without hesitating, Jowitt, a former dancer with lots of friends among the dancers whose concerts she covers regularly for the *Village Voice*, replied, "I review everyone as if they could possibly be a friend."

I think Peter would have approved of that. I think he would define a critic as some guy (or gal) who gets a free seat and therefore has a responsibility to do his/her job—but no special privileges. Other than the free seat, the critic is just one of the crowd.

It goes deeper than that. Why are we, as groups and individuals, in life even more than art, so quick to criticize each other? Why do we react so violently and quickly to the criticism of others: presuming we can compare (but should not be compared), that we can judge (but should not be judged), that we can classify (but should not be classified)?

The critic's seat is not a royal box, and those in the profession who admit that are more likely to succeed in offering something (of t*heir own*, as Siegel would say) to the public at large.

14

What the Camera Saw: Mapplethorpe &
Other Photographic Responses

n spite of what we're told as children about the camera never lying, the truth is that cameras lie all the time. By freezing a moment out of time and by framing that moment, no matter how casually, the camera lies about the big picture and about the flow of time and about the myriad, constant changes in life itself.

Taking pictures of people with AIDS thus becomes a very sticky proposition. Pictures of people with AIDS always stack the deck in one way or another: being too arty or too artless, too negative or too positive—editing out (or in) certain details or symbols to elicit a particular response in the viewer. All of this is simply part of the nature of the craft of photography, how it's practiced, how it operates. Given and acknowledging its limitations, however, the camera can be a tool. It does record information, and that record can be both aesthetically and honestly done.

Look, for example, at Robert Mapplethorpe's final self-portrait of himself as a man dying of AIDS, which was showcased in the premiere exhibit of the new Mapplethorpe photo gallery of the Guggenheim Museum, along with lots of other examples of Mapplethorpe looking longingly at himself. Made the year before his death, *Self-Portrait, 1988* (a print of which also traveled with the *From Media to Metaphor* show) shows the face of the subject, haggard and somewhat careworn (there's just the hint of a frown, but the eyes are fixed with a kind of determined acceptance), staring straight ahead. Other than the face, only the right hand is visible (no arm, no body, no neck) clutching a walking stick with a carved skull on the end of it.

This is hardly a snapshot of a person with AIDS. It is a premeditated statement, clearly calculated to elicit certain responses (as are all Mapplethorpe's self-portraits) including shock (as are most of Mapplethorpe's best known works). Here is this once handsome, sexy man, grown "old" and pale and emaciated (though rather artily so), walking with Death. His body, his limbs—other than the hand clutching the stick—have already disappeared. His head floats in space in the upper right-hand corner of the all-black space, without even a walking stick to ground it.

Next to this at the Guggenheim (where the photos are arranged chronologically around the walls of the room but where, at least on the day I was there, almost all of the viewers chose to walk backwards, viewing them in reverse time sequence) is a 1987 portrait that shows Mapplethorpe also gaunt and obviously ill. Here he allows the viewer to see his whole frame, in a loose gray sweater and baggy trousers. It is less theatricalized, more "ordinary" than the skull portrait, which seems to suggest its subject is some medieval monk on a pilgrimage. Yet both are self-portraits, equally valid, of a man confronting disease and death, which are now a part of him, just like the nudity and drag and S&M regalia were in other, earlier, stations of the cross around the room.[1]

Since Mapplethorpe was an artist who particularly relished the beauty of the human body—particularly the male, homoerotic body—his works raise a deep question of concern in exploring AIDS: What happens when beauty itself—form, fitness, sensuality—begins to dissolve, uncontrollably?

John Preston, a writer and editor, has dealt with this powerful and affecting metaphor in his introduction to *Personal Dispatches: Writers Confront AIDS*. Preston also does erotic photography, and one day he got a call at his home in rural Maine from a young man he'd never met who wanted him to photograph him:

> He'd just been diagnosed and he was concerned that his attractiveness, the one thing he'd always been able to count on, was going to go soon. There were warnings about KS lesions and almost a certainty of weight loss. He no longer had the energy for his strenuous workouts and his muscle tone would soon fade. His body had been

his one great work of art and now he was going to lose it along with everything else. He wanted a totem of who he had become before the disease took over, and his photographs in a national magazine were the best answer he could come up with.[2]

Preston then continues: "It was then, that evening when I was alone, that my heart broke, and I wasn't sure I could ever put it back together again. It wasn't just him; it was what was happening to all of us.... This one episode became the focal point for my utter exhaustion and the erosion of my spirit."

In 1990, Marvin Heiferman curated a photography exhibit entitled *The Indomitable Spirit* which opened at New York's International Center of Photography Midtown, then moved to the Los Angeles Municipal Art Gallery—then to Sotheby's, where the photos (and some paintings which were also submitted) were sold to raise money for AIDS organizations. In the introduction to the accompanying catalogue, Heiferman explains that "leading members of the photography and art communities were asked to contribute an image that affirmed the human will to live, one that celebrated human endurance and resiliency in the face of overwhelming obstacles."[3] The exhibit was "consciously . . . not an exhibition of photographs of people with AIDS," he wrote, questioning such an approach as "voyeuristic, exploitative and morally wrong."[4] In his preface, Andy Grundberg echoes the same hands-off attitude towards photographing people with AIDS: "To many of us in the art world, no photographic images of AIDS itself are really necessary: we see the toll of AIDS in human form, among our friends and families."[5]

Heiferman's and Grundberg's comments echo the public outcry from groups like ACT UP/NY to two exhibits of photos of PWAs which appeared in 1988: Rosalind Solomon's *Portraits in the Time of AIDS* at the Grey Gallery and Nicholas Nixon's *Portraits of People* at the Museum of Modern Art. (The latter drew the manifesto from ACT UP cited in Chapter 13.)

When Nixon published his photos in 1991, featuring interviews and texts by Bebe Nixon along with his photo series of 15 people with AIDS, the introduction clarified the Nixons' position in light of such criticism, stating that the collection reflected not one point of view, but many often contradictory ones:

> It is about bravery and cowardice and style and weakness, about
> honesty and self-deception, humor and bitterness. . . . It is about
> what happens to the body and spirit as a person, a young person,
> faces the certainty and unfamiliar hugeness of death. It is about dis-
> covering that your family is with you, or that it is not. It is about
> how different we human beings are from one another, how inconsis-
> tent, how contradictory and how unlike characters in literature,
> whose lives and deaths so often have a harmony about them. Those
> lives and deaths are imaginary. These are real.[6]

The Nixons furthermore readily admit this is not a complete picture,
even of the 15 persons photographed: "We never knew them when they
were well. We only knew them when they were sick, terribly sick, and
we knew them only *because* they were sick." (They thus acknowledge one
of the chief criticisms leveled at the book and photos, namely, that they
are outsiders, not part of the gay or AIDS community, but people who
just saw "it" as a good photo opportunity.[7])

It must also be acknowledged that some of Nixon's photos are
depressingly graphic. In one series in the book, Nixon presents a young
man lying in bed, surrounded by his IV, his walker, his wheelchair. His
spine and facial bones seem ready to push through the skin. His lips are
parched, he's unshaven, his hair thin, his eyes vacant over an oxygen
mask. Another series shows a man named George, who initially looks
healthy, with no KS lesions showing, cradling his white cat, but then he
too wastes away and disappears.

Solomon's photos also alternate between the disturbing and the comforting. One young man in particular stands out, confronting the camera
with neither sadness nor defiance, wearing a straw hat and an array of
buttons: SILENCE = DEATH, CURE AIDS NOW, and one celebrating
the NAMES Project Memorial Quilt. But another man lies emaciated
and shirtless in the middle of a rumpled bed in what appears to be an
SRO flophouse, surrounding by the clutter of his life: empty cigarette
packs, soda cans, newspapers, dirty clothes, a jar of Skippy peanut butter.

"We live in a culture where youth should be perpetual," Solomon
writes in her artist's statement. "Illness and death are taboo. Some of the
isolation of people with AIDS comes from that general taboo."[8] But this
depiction of the isolation of PWAs is one thing critics have contended is
negative about Solomon's photos, even when she tries to undercut the
loneliness by photographing the PWAs outdoors or in gardens.

Tom Sokolowski, who curated Solomon's show for the Grey Gallery and who writes the introduction to the catalogue, points out that unlike hospital deathwatch media images of PWAs as part of a basically "faceless epidemic," Solomon's photos are *posed*, voluntary portraits and thus constitute "a unique portrait gallery of the faces of AIDS."[9] He acknowledges that the images may not always be easy to look at: "A sense of body is at the heart of the dilemma: body as the physical reminder of presentness, of material reality, and hence, of aliveness. Since these portraits reflect people who are ill, they must reflect a proper balance between the tact and immediacy in their rendering." [10] Sokolowski uses the photo of the man in straw hat mentioned above to elucidate his point:

> Solomon forces the viewer to contemplate the formal differences between the haphazard pattern of facial [KS] lesions and the thoughtful placement of buttons on the man's pullover. Each in its own way, lesion or badge, is a symbol, a mark of distinction, one more indelible than the other. The lettering and slogans respond to the external awareness of AIDS, the lesions, an externalization of its reality to the PLWA [person living with AIDS]. The fixed gaze hovers somewhere between confrontational and meditative.[11]

The question remains: Are these images true, positive, honest? Do they invade a world of pain and suffering that should remain private? And ultimately whose comfort and privacy do they really invade: that of the PWAs and their loved ones, or that of the viewer?

One is reminded of Nan Goldin's statement in the *Witnesses: Against Our Vanishing* catalogue: "We are all clumsy in dealing with grief. I do not believe we need to develop a correct etiquette. Every one of our responses is valid." Among those responses, one of which stands out powerfully is Goldin's own shimmering portrait of art critic and performance artist Cookie Mueller laughing, included in the *Nan Goldin/David Armstrong: A Double Life* show in early 1994 at Matthew Mark Gallery in New York. In the color print, Mueller's broad smile and haystack blonde presence occupy the lower-left-hand corner of the frame, charging the rest of the rectangle with whiteness and light. In contrast to Mapplethorpe's self-proclaimed floating head in a sea of black, which occupies the opposite corner of its rectangle, Goldin allows Mueller her body and her laughter. Equally valid, opposing views of AIDS. Like Mapplethorpe's, Mueller's life went on for another year after the photo, but Goldin chooses to remember her with a smile and wave of light—a nice way to manipulate a frozen moment in time, for subject and viewer alike.

Frank Moore: Canvases from an Epidemic

rank Moore pretty much epitomizes what the art of AIDS represents: He is an activist as well as a painter. He weighs his time between collective art projects and individual ones. His work is personal as well as political, balancing anger and elegy. His approach is interdisciplinary—having encompassed contributions in dance, theater, and performance art as well as painting—and his style is eclectic. Without denying the devastating force of AIDS as a theme, he nonetheless sees it as part of a larger picture, a larger disease of the human condition and the ecology of the planet.

He also happens to be one of the finest painters working today, and his canvases would hold their own in any museum anywhere. He fills those canvases with the entire iconography of the AIDS epidemic: hospitals, nurses, hypodermic needles, demonstrators, healing circles, blood plasma, books, toilets, erotica—all sorts of signs and symbols, including representations of the virus itself, of PWAs as well as of their tormentors and their caregivers. The canvases are bold and bright and alive with detail, but they are never crammed or crowded, just brimming with life. The stories they contain draw the viewer back again and again to read and reread their messages. I'm reminded a bit of how I used to pore over each issue of *Mad Magazine* when I was a kid in the fifties, always finding something new on each perusal, tucked away in a corner of a frame or squeezed into a margin. I relished each of those jokes and messages, the way I find myself nourished and stimulated by reviewing the many details—often contradictory and astonishing—in Moore's complex canvases of the epidemic.

Critic David Hirsh, reviewing Moore's January 1993 show at Sperone Westwater Gallery in New York, described his work as being situated "at a shifting intersection of American Realism, European surrealism, and South American Magical Realism (by way of the East Village)."[1] To that stew one might add Hieronymus Bosch and Pieter Brueghel, whose medieval canvases similarly swarmed with life, peopled by tiny, doll-like figures toiling through everyday life or struggling with the nightmare of death. Or, in literary terms, imagine Upton Sinclair meeting Kafka in Dante's Inferno, as described by Gabriel Garcia-Marquez: deep social, political, and ecological concerns interpreted through three or four layers of symbolism, without losing touch with the art of storytelling as the fount of interpretation.

Moore was born in New York City in 1953, grew up on Long Island, spent summers upstate in the Adirondacks, where he acquired a love of nature and a concern for ecology. From his parents he gained a love of American folk art and the painting style of the WPA era ("There was a certain political quality to that work that I came back to later," he recalls). He studied painting at Yale, then for two years in Paris, coming back to New York and started to work figuratively. "What I do is often called 'representational,'" Moore says, "but the term bothers me a little. I'm not really re-presenting something that exists in the world. It's more presentational—presenting something that only exists in the paintings and couldn't really exist outside of a painting." He spent most of the eighties "dealing with technical problems, how to make a painting work. I can understand painters who say it takes them forty years just to get the basics down."[2]

At the same time, he started designing for theater, dance, and film, working with Jim Self, Charles Moulton, Lar Lubovitch, and others, while continuing to hone his painting skills and explore his social conscience: "I was moving gradually toward work that dealt with social, sexual, and political issues. At first these were coded, especially the gay references. I was also trying to deal with environmental issues, which dated back to my childhood, sort of from my grandfather on down, kind of a conservation aesthetic. And then at a certain point, AIDS reared its head. I was mounting a piece at Cornell when my lover died in 1990. By that time I was already doing work that combined environmental issues, health care issues, and gender issues and treated them essentially as a single problem."

Even before AIDS really hit home in his life, Moore's paintings began to foreshadow its impact. One canvas depicted a broken window, with shards of glass flying into a room and over the furniture and objects inside, with nothing but a deep blackness outside the window. "It was like a brick had been thrown through the window, but you couldn't see the brick." Another was about sharks and swimmers sharing the same waters. "It's amazing now to look back. There was almost a sense of dread or foreboding in those paintings."

There were also several paintings with plants whose flowers were eyeballs. "I had done this picture called *Farewell*, and it was a kind of fantasy about my lover and me. What we were faced with. And it's kind of curious because it was before either one of us knew we were positive, but it was already sort of anticipated. In the painting there's a rain cloud bursting in the distance. I was dealing with deforestation as a metaphor for what was happening because of AIDS—and about our attitude towards the natural environment. In a sense both AIDS and the ecological crisis are the product of a certain lack of compassion or sensitivity or concern. But at that time in my work, I was still coding things, because dealing with gay issues in the arts is a very difficult thing to do, without having your work be ultimately relegated to a mere curiosity."

Then came the epidemic: "AIDS in a sense freed me of all that. It wasn't something I was dreading anymore. It was right in front of me. The suspense of waiting for something to happen was gone." Over the next two years, Moore began painting more directly and openly about AIDS, though still within a framework of general ecological and health care concerns. One painting depicts a beach strewn with hospital waste. Another a desert with a billboard promising "PANACEA." Another has a hospital bed on a polar ice flow, with an Exxon Valdez-type leaking oil tanker in the background, a confluence of ecological and personal nightmares ("I've always found hospitals to be among the most surreal places in the world," says Moore, "and not just because of the bizarre nature of their sterile architecture and rather fascist environment. Also because when you're in a hospital, you're also mentally in kind of an altered state.")

In *Debutantes*, two interracial adolescent same-sex couples ride a tricycle and walk a Scotty through a garden where all the flowers hold medical diagrams and the marble sculptures are, on closer examination, depictions of gay men being tortured. On a sundial there is an innocent looking Rectal Pear, a torture device used on homosexual sodomites in the Middle Ages. The garden itself is surrounded by a high prison fence, which holds two pink triangles. The painting is framed in barbed wire.

In *Arena* (a detail of which forms the jacket of this book), Moore has depicted an operating theater, such as those used in medical teaching schools (but actually based on a seventeenth-century Dutch dissecting theater), placing it inside a labyrinth of nine circles, the same number as those in Dante's *Inferno*. In the center, a doctor is placing a Hickman catheter into a person with AIDS, from whom a cloud of gray gas is escaping. Various onlookers watch the proceedings, and many other scenes of the AIDS epidemic take place around or inside the labyrinth: body-builders pose, demonstrators march, Buddhists meditate, a mother carries her son, whose body has suddenly deflated like a painted balloon. Someone is even selling hot-dogs. But in spite of this nine-ring circus of conflicting responses, *Arena* holds up a sense of hope, as Hirsh points out: "Buried in the structure of this tangled scene of death is the hope for gentle care which includes respect for an ill person's ability to, in some sense, transcend his illness. *Arena* suggests that learning how to care for the AIDS patient could, proceeding back up through the nine circles, change humankind's knowledge of and functioning within the world for the better." [3]

Moore himself might describe this transformative or hopeful quality in slightly different (more political, perhaps, and less spiritual) terms: "One of the transformative effects I've seen of AIDS is an awareness of interrelatedness—how many people who previously defined their focus and their interests rather narrowly have opened up to realize that in fact racism does affect everyone, and homelessness, and environmental degradation. All these are tied together and it's impossible to deal with one problem without invoking all the others somehow. One has to be aware of the entire context of a situation, or a solution won't work."

At the time of the 1993 show, Moore told Hirsh: "It might seem that this is obsessional work about a medical condition. In a sense it is, but the struggle, from my point of view, has been to integrate AIDS into my life without it seizing control. The only way for me to successfully do this was to plunge into learning as much as I could about it, think about it exhaustively and move to a point of acceptance. AIDS, for some people, can be a dark core of dread that stops their minds from working. I got sick of that." [4]

In another painting from the show, this image of information overkill achieves a special impact. In it, a large stack of books about AIDS are in the foreground; in the background there is a fire and a Trinidadian fishing boat. Moore relates the genesis of the canvas: "I had a friend who was Trinidadian. He lived in an apartment with huge mounds of books everywhere. It was an amazing accumulation of literature, information, and art history, that had become completely unmanageable—he didn't even know what was there anymore. And then there was this fire and it all burned." In the painting, there is also the sense that the stack of books has become unmanageable—too much, perhaps, of a good thing: "It's all there. Susan Sontag on the top of the pile. A complete AIDS library. Even Louise Hay. And it's a portrait of a certain kind of individual. The kind I became for a while myself, but am moving away from now. Where everything was filtered through AIDS."[5]

Like the character at the end of the film *Savage Nights*, Moore no longer allows his life (or art) to be completely dominated by AIDS. His next show will feature another large, extremely complex canvas like *Arena*, but this time the subject is ecology and the landscape is the Grand Canyon. Moore relates AIDS to a larger context now, in both his work and his thinking: "I connect AIDS, this immune dysfunction that we call AIDS, to the larger phenomenon of Chronic Fatigue Syndrome and the epidemic in breast cancer. To look at AIDS itself is ultimately too limited an approach. Because all of the underlying factors that led to making AIDS the nightmare that it is will still be there after there's a cure for AIDS. We could come out with this magic bullet that would cure all these people with AIDS, but the racism, the homophobia, the lack of access to health care, the environmental degradation—all these factors will continue. And if we're not calling it AIDS, and we're not calling it Chronic Fatigue Syndrome, and we're not calling it breast cancer, we'll call it something else. But there will continue to be this imbalance and this destructive impact."

Unlike many contemporary artists, Moore frames all of his paintings, and he frames them personally and in rather unconventional and imaginative ways. He explains it as a natural progression of the particular kind of message his works contain: "I began to embrace more and more this idea of literary painting, where there's a suspension of disbelief, the creation of a fantasy that the viewer is invited into—that a painting can be an arena where you can allow your thoughts to enter and be transformed. A place of change. There's a kind of tension set up between all the elements in the picture that creates a mentally charged field, and you need a way to approach that. Usually in any given picture, there are a lot of ways to get into it and a lot of ways to get out of it. There's not a single point of view that is correct. But the frame can be like a threshold of that experience, something you have to cross to get into the experience."

So Moore began contructing frames that were signifiers in their own right, ways to lead the viewer into the larger dialogue. Plastic icicles hang from the top of the frame of the the hospital bed on the polar ice flow. Barbed wire entraps the gay concentration camp. Three bluebirds herald the "Panacea" desert scene; one of them is lying dead on its back, feet up in the air. "I was making a play on both the symbol of the Bluebird of Happiness and the tradition of the canary in the coal mine," says Moore—that canary that miners use to test the air in the mine: if it's bad enough to kill the canary, it's probably time for the "general population" to get out as fast as they can.

Other painters, including Hugh Steers, Robert Farber, Sue Coe, and Billy Quinn, are working, like Moore, in a somewhat representational mode about AIDS. Sculptors Robert Gober and Felix Gonzales-Torres also address the subject, but in less traditional, more "conceptual" ways. All of them seem to view representing AIDS as almost a contradiction in terms: their art is about vanishing, shrinking, disappearing.

Hugh Steers often paints people with paper bags over their heads. He has a 1990 painting called *Flag* in which a couple sit ramrod straight in wooden chairs, like the pair in Grant Wood's *American Gothic*, but with paper bags over their heads and a black cat slinking behind them. In *Blue Towel, Red Tank* (from 1988), a man gives mouth-to-mouth resuscitation to another man who has collapsed naked on the bathroom floor. In *Mask and Mirror* (from 1990) an emaciated actor in high heels is caught between a skull mask and a mirror in his dressing room. Steers' paintings have a brutal, agonizing edge to their realism, like the portraits by Lucian Freud.

In Robert Farber's "I thought I had time" exhibit at Artists Space

in the fall of 1992, the artist juxtaposed texts from diaries of the
Black Death in Europe in 1348-49 with contemporary AIDS chronicles, placing the texts over washes of stark grey, brown, and black,
next to medieval gargoyles or church cornices. In *Western Blot No. 15*
(1992), he superimposes a text of his own, about his own treatment
for AIDS, over a washed out, disappearing portrait of himself.

Irish painter Billy Quinn offers lush canvases of nude PWAs,
angels, and religious iconography. His celebration of the male body—
even the ill male body—stands in stark contrast to the disturbing (one
might even say horrific) representations of the sick and dying by illus-
trator Sue Coe or Steers. But both points of view are absolutely essential and necessary to fully picture AIDS.

Many artists who have been touched by AIDS have chosen to represent it by a kind of blankness or absence. Ross Bleckner went
through a period of painting funeral urns and other symbolic object-
icons of grief. Now he is painting soft-focus abstract studies of
human cells: a close-up of the very stage in which the drama is being
enacted, deep inside.

Robert Gober's sculptures are often described as "haunted by
death" in spite of their spunky humor. There are sinks and urinals,
detached from utilitarian use, as well as wax castings human limbs,
also detached from everyday life. There are no whole figures, no
whole people, no functional commodities left any more, he seems to
suggest, even in our own bathrooms.

Felix Gonzales-Torres makes art that is not so much disposable as
dispensable: people can take a sheet of paper or a piece of candy home
with them. The art is the stack of papers, the candy constructions:
when the components are gone, the art is finished, complete, memory.

Charles LeDray makes clothes for small dolls, celebrating a real
world that is similarly becoming more and more fragile and reduced
in size. As William Harris has described his work, LeDray

> sews clothes by hand, miniature versions of everyday garments that
> seem to have once been worn and that allude to a world that is
> shrinking. "There is life after death in the things we leave behind,"
> says LeDray, who recently had his first one-person show at Tom
> Cugliani Gallery in New York. "I like to think these objects are
> about that memory."[6]

Art thus becomes, as Nan Goldin proclaimed in her 1989 exhibit at Artists Space, not only a "witness against our vanishing" (as artists, as individuals, and as a community threatened by extinction), but also, ironically a testimonial to that disappearance: a steady depletion that is shrinking, short-circuiting, fast-forwarding the world of the visual arts—not only in New York City but around the world—with tragic consequences not just for those making and viewing art today, but for all of posterity.

16

Days Without Art

O n December 1, 1989, to coincide with World AIDS Day, a
group of art galleries and museums, primarily in the New
York City area, decided to close their doors or drape certain
works of art in memory of those who had died of AIDS. By
December 1, 1993, the memorial had spread around the
world and involved over 5,000 cultural institutions, artist organizations,
and AIDS service providers. A parallel project, entitled Night Without
Light, had been added to the observance in 1990; in 1993 the blackout of
city skylines—skyscrapers, bridges, and monuments—occurred between
7:45 and 8 p.m. in Montreal, Vienna, London, Seoul, Seattle, and San
Francisco as well as New York City, where it had begun as a gesture on
the part of Broadway theaters to acknowledge their industry's loss to the
epidemic. In 1993, the White House also joined in observing Night
Without Light, dimming the floodlights which illuminate the presidential residence for the 15 minutes of darkness.

Day Without Art began as the brainchild of a group called Visual
AIDS, founded in 1988 as "a diverse group of artists and arts profession-
als concerned about AIDS." In 1991, it added the Ribbon Project to its
list of activities. The idea came originally from Frank Moore, a member

of Visual AIDS, who conceived of it as a symbol of compassion for PWAs and their lovers or families, just as the yellow ribbon was for the those imprisoned and their loved ones during the Iran hostage crisis. Red ribbons became particularly popular at awards ceremonies—like the Oscars, the Emmys, the Tonys, and the Grammys—as a show of solidarity with PWAs; perhaps because of their popularity at such events, now there has been a certain amount of backlash against them in the AIDS community, though the resistance is in no way universal. For the 1993 Day Without Art and World AIDS Day celebration, the U.S. Postal Department issued a stamp featuring the ribbon.

For the 1993 Day Without Art, National Endowment of the Arts Chairman Jane Alexander stated:

> DAY WITHOUT ART is a powerful symbol of the devastating effect of AIDS on the arts community. This day reinforces the vitality and power art brings to our daily lives by showing how the absence of art leaves a void of spirit. We miss the young men and women who will never again grace the stage, paint the canvases, write the poems, or release from their imagination the ability to make the world a better place. We must work together to remember their legacy, to tender compassion to those now suffering, and to find a cure.[1]

Participants in New York's 1993 observance included The American Museum of Natural History, which draped various exhibit cases ("the shrouding of art from cultures around the world reflects the global impact of AIDS"); the Museum of Modern Art, where visitors were asked to bring index cards with the name of someone who had died of AIDS and place them on a wall of the museum (similar to the placards that inspired Cleve Jones to create the NAMES Project); the Metropolitan Museum of Art, which draped Pablo Picasso's portrait of Gertrude Stein in black, as it had in previous years; the Pierpont Morgan Library, which featured a display of manuscripts left unfinished when a writer or composer died before they were finished (like Thackery's *Denis Duval* and Puccini's *Turandot*); El Museo del Barrio, which closed its doors and draped "statistics about the impact of AIDS on the Latino/a community" across its courtyard; the Museum of African Art, which darkened all of the displays in its then-current exhibit, *Faces of the Gods: Art and Altars of Africa and the African Americas*, except the altar created by Brazilian artist Pai Balbino de Paula to Omolu, the *candomblé* god of healing, with all of its offering pots turned upside down in memory of those dead of AIDS; and the Studio Museum of Harlem, which likewise darkened all exhibits other than Joe Lewis's "HIV—What You Don't Know Can Kill You."

Cable channel CUNY in New York presented 24 hours of uninterrupted programming about AIDS, most of it made by groups like AIDS Community TV, a production company allied with ACT UP. Various cable stations around the country observed a "Moment Without Television," a 60-second blackout with an AIDS message, and several aired "We Interrupt This Program," a half-hour AIDS performance art program featuring memorial tributes, readings, and short skits about AIDS. Various museums, galleries, and performance spaces around the country likewise gave live readings or performances to mark the occasion—and to provide material for future incarnations of "We Interrupt This Program."

At the United Nations, Liza Minnelli unveiled her anthem, "The Day After That," from Broadway's *Kiss of the Spider Woman*, introduced by U.N. Secretary General Boutros Boutros-Ghali, who called on all governments to take action to combat AIDS and declare it a "common enemy" of humanity. Across the country and around the world, spokespersons from Texas Governor Ann Richards to Polish president Lech Walesa, spoke out against AIDS. Nepal and Uruguay also issued AIDS stamps on the occasion of World AIDS Day. Princess Diana attended a sold-out British benefit concert entitled "Symphony of Hope" at Wembley Stadium in London. The event starred George Michael and Simply Red's Mick Hucknall and was co-hosted by David Bowie, who told the crowd: "Like myself I am sure that many of you this evening have friends who are either affected by HIV or have AIDS, or have died from AIDS. Until a cure is found for this most terrible of diseases, it is our duty to make life more bearable for them."[2]

In Paris, ACT UP positioned a giant pink condom on the obelisk on the Place de la Concorde, and President François Mitterrand, in an unrelated show of concern, toured the AIDS ward of a local hospital and announced that his nephew had died of the disease. Bars in Paris and elsewhere in France were reported to be serving customers a condom instead of a croissant with their morning coffee.[3]

AIDS activists in Germany placed paving stones engraved with the names of dozens of people who have died from AIDS across the entrance to Bonn's Art and Exhibition Hall in a project called "Names and

Stones," a sort of German hard-core version of the Quilt. "Everyone who wants to visit the gallery will be forced to step on the names, and hopefully, to think about them and why they died," said the gallery's managing director, Wenzel Jacob.[4]

In Rabat, Morocco, 500 young Moroccans handed out condoms and literature in schools to mark the day. "We should not talk here specifically about Moslem fundamentalists. We are all in this together," said Abdelkader Lamhader, vice-president of the Moroccan Young Peoples' Anti-AIDS Association.[5] Many of the group were expected to join a march from Rabat to Marrakesh the following week to attend the 8th African AIDS conference there. (As an Associated Press story reported the following day, The African Development Bank, with headquarters in Abidjan, estimates more than 7.5 million Africans are infected with the AIDS virus and that 1.2 million Africans have already died of AIDS. In seven years time, the bank estimated, 14 million sub-Saharan Africans will be infected.)[6]

But back in New York, playwright Larry Kramer declared "World AIDS Day is a joke. It allows everyone one day a year to say the word and feel better about themselves without doing anything. What are we celebrating? A plague that's going to kill a billion people."[7] And members of ACT UP demonstrated at the post office where the U.S. stamp was introduced. "We need a cure, not a stamp," shouted David Robinson, one of the organizers of the demonstration. "The issuance of the red-ribbon stamp is nothing more than a public-relations campaign to gloss over the government's inaction. Making speeches and selling stamps will not alleviate the AIDS pandemic. It is an insult to the 13 million people living with HIV worldwide."[8]

The original concept behind all this needs restating: What would a day, a week, a year, a world without art really be like? How much art has been lost already, and will continue to be lost, because of AIDS? How many paintings, or manuscripts, or unfinished films or plays have ended up already in green dumpsters, like Dui Seid's *Artist's Estate* in *From Media to Metaphor?* And who can save such art from vanishing? Even if families and friends care enough to preserve the work of PWAs, they often have no knowledge or means at their disposal for caretaking such works. And if they call a museum, like the Grey Gallery, the results are often equally sad. As Tom Sokolowski says: "Usually the most we can do is interest one or two museums in a couple of pieces, and then they're usually only interested if they don't have to pay crating and shipping costs. And with unknown artists, whose work was never given a whole exhibition on its own, the problems are even more severe. We ourselves can't possibly take everything that's offered to us. You would need a building the size of the Pentagon, just for storage."

Furthermore, though it's nice for the art world to take one day off to remember those lost to AIDS, is this really enough? No major museum in the country has mounted a show about AIDS. Activists have legitimately pointed out that gay curators in those institutions have consistently refused to confront the epidemic, like the closeted Hollywood executives and the powerbrokers in pop and classical music. And, they ask, why have older, established gay artists done nothing to address the issue? Contributing to fundraisers, sporting a red ribbon, or draping a painting or sculpture seem feeble gestures indeed an epidemic of such proportions, these voices insist.

Cereal Box Marionettes & Adventure Games

s a child, I never for a minute doubted that I preferred make-believe to reality, whether it was reading for hours in my room; walking the woods near my grandfather's farm with my pack of mongrel dogs, pretending I was a famous African explorer; or dressing up in a wild old blond braided wig and multicolored striped dress that my grandmother once wore in a Farm Bureau play. Fantasy was a lot more fun than making my bed or doing my chores around the farm, or having to play silly sports, like the other kids always wanted to do, or games (indoors or out) where I always seemed to lose.

When I played with other kids at all, I usually tried to drag them into my fantasy worlds: dress-up plays, improvised make-believe, scenarios picked up mostly from books or TV. I also was friendly with two brothers who used to build elaborate treehouses on the ground out of cardboard and wooden crating from their father's business. Each of the three of us would have our own room, and we would invite the other two to come visit. I must have orchestrated my part in this a bit too elaborately, for one day I overheard my friends' mother tell them—loudly enough, I've always been convinced, for me to hear—"I don't want you playing with him anymore. He's such a sissy."

Out in the woods with my dogs, I didn't have to bother with attitudes like that. Or when I went stomping down pathways and through elaborate mazes I had created in a fresh green ryefield. With no one but the dogs for company, I wasn't so much lonely as in complete control of my own fantasy: director, stage manager, designer, and sole actor in my own productions.

About this time, I got my first puppets. They were both marionettes. One was Howdy Doody; the other a little boy puppet, dressed in black and white, and blond just like me. Howdy Doody was fun for awhile, but I never believed that he was the *real* Howdy Doody, who lived on television with Mister Bluster and Buffalo Bob and Princess Summer-Fall-Winter-Spring. And the other puppet was not only mine alone: it really *was* me. I could make him do anything or say anything I wanted, just by pulling the strings and speaking for him. He never got embarrassed or hurt or called a sissy; he never had to play stupid games where he was awkward and lost all the time; he didn't have a mother and father who were divorced and both lived somewhere else while he stayed behind with his grandparents.

When I went to visit my mother, stepfather, and two stepsisters in the summertime, I didn't take my puppets along. So I tried to get my sisters to help me make hand-puppets, out of putty and papier-mâché. But the hand-puppets were dumb looking, and wriggling a glove around on your hand is nowhere near as fun as manipulating a marionette by its strings. That was art; the other was just kids playing around.

Then it was General Mills to the rescue. That very summer was the time they brought out all sorts of cut-out marionettes on the back of cereal boxes. You would take the scissors and carefully trim them out, then string their various joints (neck, arms, legs, feet, hands) together with thread, then tie strings on them so that you could make them move and dance. They weren't terribly elaborate: two-dimensional cut-outs which were basically cartoon characters (mostly animals: I remember a family of skunks in particular). But none of that really mattered: I had marionettes again.

For the first time, I began to think big. I built stages, painted sets, wrote whole plays. I drafted my sisters as fellow puppeteers. We put on shows for the whole neighborhood. I was of course still chief manipulator, the creator of a world where I was in charge and appreciated. I had little patience with people who didn't want to play my way, calling them names I'd heard others around me use when they wanted to assert their superiority, like "freak" or "queer," until my mother overheard me one day and explained—with a nonjudgmental clarity that I still recall—exactly what such terms meant. It didn't seem like such good theater after that to exclude people for no good reason. After all, the really good parts were always the outsiders, the loners, the outcasts—like the Ugly Duckling or Dumbo—though onstage they always got to have a happy ending and the villains got their comeuppance.

Grade school, high school, college all brought more theater, more role-playing, more manipulation. I started acting lessons in nearby Louisville, Kentucky, convinced I was headed for Broadway. I formed a local acting troupe in my hometown, mounting productions of *Wizard of Oz* and *The Glass Menagerie*. I got married—"to a real woman," as Peter used to say—whom I'd met in my acting class in Louisville. The marriage, like the courtship, was conducted mostly through improvisations and conversations employing imaginary animals. The illusion didn't last when it was put to the test, any more than the illusion that I could really act. After taking a stab at directing (where I was convinced my real talent as a manipulator lay) and discovering that it was harder to control live human beings than imaginary characters, I decided to be a writer, a journalist, a critic instead. Then I could really tell people how to act, or at least what they had done wrong.

There were two years in Chicago—biding my time, treading water, coming out as a gay man—before I took the plunge and headed to New York, where I'd been convinced since grade school that I would finally belong. It worked, in a way, like the woods of Indiana or (much later) the mountains of Montana: I could play all by myself, without interference and with no real responsibility to anyone except myself.

My first years in New York were when Off-Off-Broadway was in its heyday: I practically lived at LaMama (and actually lived next door once, for six months or so, in an apartment with no bathroom—but what did minor details like that matter in an improvised world?) and at the other wild, zany playhouses-of-the-ridiculous of that era. I saw as many as ten or twelve shows a week sometimes, including, often, a triple-header at LaMama on a Saturday night. Nothing else seemed to matter.

If a boyfriend wanted to join in this improvisation for a month or so, fine, as long as the play didn't get too serious. Once some friends and I improvised a whole house in Brooklyn, running it like an Off-Off-Broadway play for two years. We were our own *Glass Menagerie*: Sallie as Amanda, the long-suffering mother-of-us-all; Tone, the quiet one, dreaming and curating her glass animals; my cousin Gary and I playing our old roles from back in Indiana a decade before: the perky, happy-go-lucky Gentleman Caller and long-suffering Tom, presuming he could narrate the whole play. How we paid the rent or managed to eat could often be a camp cliff-hanger all its own. (Sallie recently recalled the time I threw some frozen fish into a dish in the oven with a can of peaches and a can of pears, declaring it *poisson pas sans pêches*—"fish not without peaches," in my fumbling high school French. As I recall, it wasn't bad.)

In the next twenty years, all of our lives would be devastated by AIDS, as we all lost friends and lovers (and one of our number) to the epidemic, but that scenario wasn't even dreamed of yet in 1973. We all went our separate ways. Sallie writes cookbooks. Tone lives in Florida and occasionally returns to New York to perform (out of all of us, she was the only one who could really act). I left the house to fumble around for another five years before finding Peter and beginning to learn to live with realities I couldn't manipulate. Gary ended up doing PR for the Bureau of Consumer Affairs of the City of New York—which he always did with considerable theatrical flair—until he, too, was diagnosed with AIDS and went off to live with that reality (and a loving, supportive family) in Oregon until his death in June 1993.

I traveled to Off-Off-Broadway less and less after leaving the house in Brooklyn, and even less when the actors, the playwrights, the directors, the set and lighting designers, and even the publicists all began to die. I had my own reality to deal with by then, and I retreated again into that private world, but this time no amount of improvising or fantasizing could change what was happening. Still, on those long nights after Peter would finally fall asleep during the last two years of his decline, I would turn on my computer and boot up the Dungeons and Dragons-like adventure game, *Wizardry*, descending deeper and deeper into the maze of fantasy role-playing. It was almost like being in the labyrinth of passages in my grandfather's ryefield or being able, for a few hours at least, to pull the strings of the marionettes rather than being jerked around, myself, by a brutal manipulator over which I had no control whatsoever.

17

Early Stages: Larry Kramer, William M. Hoffman, & Robert Chesley

n my first day of research for this study, I was browsing through the books in the open stacks at the Library of the Performing Arts in New York's Lincoln Center, checking out what dramatic titles the library had available on the subject of AIDS. I picked up one of several circulating copies of Larry Kramer's *The Normal Heart* and discovered that at several spots in the text, someone had scribbled comments in blunt pencil, furiously challenging some of Kramer's own angry statements. Having been raised as a kid who was taught not to deface public property—most particularly library books—I had a strong negative reaction to this crude attempt by someone to make his or her own addendum to a work of literature—this presumptive, unofficial revisionism.

On page 22, in response to Kramer's suggestion that the silence of the general populace about AIDS is reminiscent of silence of the German public when Hitler began killing Jews, someone had written in the margin: "In Gods name how DARE you pretend that AIDS is equivalent to the Holocaust!! HOW DARE YOU!! FOOLS!! HOW DARE YOU use the slaughter [underlined twice] of innocent people to further your selfish sexual gratification!!!"

Kramer, himself Jewish, clearly had no intent to belittle the Holocaust, but rather to point out some obvious parallels to another holocaust that was then just beginning: the AIDS crisis. But the phantom scrawler curiously refused to let anyone share the drama of his or

her remembered pain, to allow anyone else into that arena of discrimination and rage. And the anger didn't stop there: the scribbler also reacts
almost as violently to Kramer's questioning of why the media paid so
much more attention to an outbreak of Legionnaires Disease in a
Philadelphia hotel than it did to the continuing casualties of the AIDS
epidemic: "That's because <u>everyone</u> stays in hotels. Very few people
have homosexual sex or use injected drugs." Unlike "innocent"
Legionnaires or European Jews, in other words, people with AIDS presumably deserved their fate.

On the following page, the scribbler becomes almost magnanimous
without losing his (or her) condescension: "I'm sorry for you, but I
never forced you to be <u>promiscuous</u>."

Theater has traditionally been an art form that directly challenges its
audience. Especially in the more intimate settings (Off-Broadway or Off-
Off-Broadway in New York, or the smaller regional stages around the
country), actors often deliver their lines mere feet from the audience,
confronting the viewer directly not only with the playwright's ideas, but
the very presences and actions of the actors. Such theater is by nature a
confrontational, often upsetting experience, a long way from the pabu-
lum dished out in most Broadway matinees, where the form is more like
a TV sitcom or "Movie of the Week": occasionally "meaningful" or
"significant," but hardly something that's really going to make its audience squirm or think very deeply.

It is thus not surprising that some of the first strong statements about
AIDS were those written by playwrights, and that onstage depictions of
the epidemic have continued to be among the most outspoken and most
successful examples of AIDS art. Three radical voices in particular pioneered this challenge to the status quo early in the epidemic, in 1984 and
1985: Larry Kramer, whose *Normal Heart* elicited the above angry
response; William M. Hoffman, author of the other best-known "early
AIDS play," *As Is*, and a veteran Off-Off-Broadway playwright already
skilled at theatricalizing the offbeat and the outspoken; and Robert
Chesley, whose dramas *Night Sweat* and *Jerker* shocked audiences by examining not only AIDS and homosexuality, but the further underground
taboo of sadomasochism as well.

Larry Kramer's notoriety as the shrill Cassandra of AIDS activism precedes his reputation as a playwright, and he has hardly toned down the

shrillness of his attacks in the years since *The Normal Heart* opened to almost unanimous rave reviews at the New York Shakespeare Festival Public Theater on April 21, 1985.[1] Kramer had already made his mark in the arts fifteen years earlier, writing the screenplay and producing Ken Russell's movie version of the D. H. Lawrence novel *Women in Love*. But it was his role as a pioneer AIDS activist—even before the epidemic had a name—that made him well known in the gay community long before the play opened. Kramer co-founded the Gay Men's Health Crisis, the first important AIDS activist organization in early 1982. After becoming disillusioned with GMHC for being too bureaucratic and centered on fundaising—a family feud he doesn't hesitate to air in *The Normal Heart*—he quit that group and went on to found the more populist ACT UP in 1987.

Even before he turned to organizing, Kramer's voice was one of the first raised about the new, mysterious disease in the gay community, in a series of articles in the *New York Native*, a gay newspaper in 1981. When his initial warnings—that the immune disorder might be sexually transmitted—were first carried by the paper, it was fellow future playwright Robert Chesley who wrote a letter to the editor in response, calling him a dangerous alarmist and accusing him of "gay homophobia and anti-eroticism."[2] Kramer responded:

> Something we are doing is ticking off the timebomb that is causing the breakdown of immunity in certain bodies, and while it is true that we don't know what it is specifically, isn't it better to be cautious until various suspected causes have been discounted rather than be reckless? An individual can choose to continue or cease smoking...but isn't it stupid to rail against the very presentation of these warnings?
>
> I am not glorying in death. I am overwhelmed by it. The death of my friends. The death of whatever community there is here in New York. The death of any visible love.[3]

Kramer's main target from the beginning was not other homosexuals or their behavior, but the lack of response to the new disease on the part of the medical establishment and the government, but he never hesitated to ruffle the feathers of gays—especially promiscuous gays—as well. The stage was set by all this for the play that became *The Normal Heart*, which dramatizes the crisis—and the conflicting attitudes toward it, both inside and outside the gay community—with a force and conviction that still manage to overwhelm readers and viewers almost a decade later. Columnist Michael Musto, describing a June 1993 benefit reading of the play chaired by Barbra Streisand (who's optioned the play for a film), states the play had proven "every bit as effective as in '85." He continued:

> Back then, the play was an eloquent call to arms demanding an immediate and drastic reply to a relatively new crisis. It tapped powerfully into our terror and frustrations, and as the reply never really came, we became increasingly in tune with Kramer's outrage. But in the last few years, a lot of the anger fizzled as we either lapsed back into denial or just dropped out of the fight in total defeat. Nearly insane from so much caring, we'd coddled ourselves right back into the old complacence. In just two hours, the reading made us feel responsible again.[4]

The Normal Heart personalizes the story of AIDS and the founding of GMHC in bold strokes. The character Ned (originally played by Brad Davis, who himself later died of the epidemic) is clearly based on Kramer himself, insisting on "a new definition of what it means to be gay" since the old one was virtually suicidal: "Being defined by our cocks is literally killing us."[5] At the same time, Ned is imminently human: his relationships to others (and to himself) form the bedrock of the drama, as he interacts with old friends, a new lover (who coincidentally works as a writer for the newspaper Ned rages against the most vehemently, the *New York Times*), his straight brother, and even his doctors and various squirmy politicians.

Ned's lover Felix dies near the end of *The Normal Heart*, but the real conclusion is the reunion of Ned with his brother Ben, from whom he has been estranged for years. Critics over the years have pointed out the political resonance of this ("Kramer's work makes the point that everyone, regardless of sexual identity, must cooperate in facing this crisis, for all of us belong to the same tribe."[6]), but what makes the scene really work is that it rescues itself from political rhetoric, offering a profoundly personal statement instead.

Kramer went on to explore such moments of personal truth seven-and-a-half years later in the sequel to *The Normal Heart*, entitled *The Destiny of Me*. Again the protagonist is Ned Weeks; again the parallels seem to be with Kramer's own persona. Ned is now sick himself and is being treated by a Washington, D. C., doctor who seems clearly patterned after the National Institute of Health's Dr. Anthony Fauci. The dialogue between Ned and the doctor (and between Ned and the nurse who is the doctor's wife) again have a force that is both documentary and deeply personal. But what is really being explored in the 1992 play is Kramer/Ned's relationship to his own childhood memories (represented by a younger actor who plays Ned as a child, then called Alexander), and his family: his mother Rena, his violent and homophobic father Richard, and (again) his brother Ben.

Two crises are thus examined in tandem, in scenes that juxtapose two time-frames: Alexander with his family, and Ned with his doctor and nurse. No oversimplified connections are made between the two: when the anger in one time zone gets too great, shifting the dramatic focus momentarily to the other manages to defuse the explosiveness of the situation. In one scene Ned confronts his dying father Richard, who offers a painful deathbed explanation of his lifelong discomfort with his son's homosexuality, linking it to his hatred of his own father, a *mohel* ("the man who does the circumcision") who had abandoned Richard and his mother after mutilating a rich man's son in a circumcision. The grandfather had brainwashed the father with religion—then abandoned him:

> I helped my father. I was his assistant. All the time, the blood. Bawling babies terrified out of their wits. Tiny little cocks with pieces peeled off them. I had to dispose of the pieces. I buried them. He made me memorize all the Orthodox laws. If I made a mistake, he beat me. "You are forbidden to touch your membrum in self-gratification. You are forbidden to bring on an erection. It is forbidden to discharge semen in vain. Two bachelors must not sleep together.... It is forbidden." He made me learn all that and then he ran away. I never stopped hating him. It's hard living with your gut filled with hate. Good luck to you, my boy. Anything you want to say to me?[7]

Ned is speechless, and when he finally manages to speak his mind ("I'm sorry your life was a disappointment, Poppa. Poppa, you were cruel to me, Poppa."[8]), the old man has already died. But, significantly, Kramer the playwright is not silent on the subject; he gives a dying man—a homophobe and hater and discriminator—his due, his say, his attempt (however feeble) to explain his side. It's a noble moment, rare indeed in the art of AIDS, and that it comes from as cranky and seemingly unforgiving a voice as Kramer is rather startling and wonderful.

But such magnanimity isn't the final note of the play. At the end, when the doctor's latest experiment on Ned seems to have failed, the patient reacts violently, throwing off his IVs and splattering blood plasma against the walls of the hospital room. Then, after that shocker, to calm things down a bit for the final curtain, Alexander and Ned (who have been singing Broadway musical ditties to each other throughout the play) end up in an ironic duet to "Make Believe" from *Show Boat*, and Ned admits to his younger self that the only thing he's really learned from all this is: "I want to stay a little longer."[9]

However, writing in the introduction to the published version of *The Destiny of Me*, Kramer makes it clear that this ending is not a curtain call to his rage or commitment: "I discovered long ago that writing doesn't bring catharsis   getting things off your chest doesn't get them off for very long."[10]

William M. Hoffman's *As Is* opened at the Circle Repertory Company in New York about six weeks before Kramer's *Normal Heart* premiered at the Public Theatre. Both productions later moved to Broadway, and the two plays are often mentioned in tandem (in reviews and elsewhere) because of this synchronicity. That their combined presence helped to clarify the AIDS crisis for New York theatergoers is undeniable. But they are also very different plays.

Hoffman's play centers on two lovers who have just split up because one of them, Rich, has found a new boyfriend, leaving Saul, his ex, with nothing but his considerable Jewish humor for armor. In the course of their conversation, it is revealed that many of their friends are sick and dying from AIDS—and then Rich, too, announces, with quiet simplicity, "I have it." In short order, Rich's new boyfriend, Chet, leaves him, and Saul becomes Rich's caregiver. By exploring their relationship to each other and to various friends and family members (again, there is a straight brother who's a key figure in Rich's story), Hoffman draws a vivid portrait of the impact AIDS had, even at this early date, on everyday gay life in an urban center like New York. And as with Kramer's *Normal Heart*, Hoffman's play (and the TV movie version of it adapted by the playwright for the Showtime cable channel) holds up remarkably well in the mid-nineties as a work of character, drama, and ideas—peppered throughout with humor, information, and humanity.

As a kind of prelude to the main drama, Hoffman offers an extraordinary soliloquy by a "dowdy middle-aged" hospice worker, an ex-nun (wonderfully played by Colleen Dewhurst in the TV version). Her monologue mixes irony and pathos, setting the tone for the whole play:

> My job is to ease the way for those who are dying. I've done this for the last couple of years.... During the day I have a boring secretarial job, which is how I support my career as a saint. I was much more idealistic when I started.... I thought I'd be able to impart my great wisdom to those in need of improvement. I wanted to bear witness to dramatic deathbed conversations, see shafts of light emanating from heaven, multicolored auras hovering above the heads of those in the process of expiring.[11]

It doesn't turn out that way—for the hospice worker, or for Saul and Rich. AIDS is realistically presented: a fact of life, as is. The main section of the play balances scenes between Saul and Rich with others that allow the audience to see the broadening impact of AIDS on the world outside the personal drama of Rich and Saul, both on other people with AIDS and on the larger gay and straight communities. There are short scenes of Rich in a gay leather bar, full of clones; of a group of outsiders discussing "the first time I heard about AIDS"; of two workers on an AIDS hotline answering calls; of Rich at an AIDS support group. At the end Rich and Saul have reconciled, and the hospice worker is back, talking about her new patient named Richard who's "a fighter." Sometimes, she adds, the people she's caring for tell her "the most amazing things":

> The other night Jean-Jacques—he's this real queen, there's no other word for it—he told me what he misses most in the hospital is his corset and high heels. I mean he weighs all of ninety pounds and he's half dead. But I admire his spirit. The way they treat him. Sometimes they won't even bring the food to his bed. And I'm afraid to complain for fear they take it out on him! Damn them! . . . I've lost some of my idealism, as I said. Last night I painted his nails for him. Flaming red. He loved it.[12]

Hoffman spent a number of years writing for the wild and often wicked world of Off-Off-Broadway before *As Is*. He is also librettist to the opera *The Ghosts of Versailles*, with music by John Corigliano, which was a considerable success in its premiere at the Metropolitan Opera in 1992. In early 1994, he presented a laboratory production of *Riga*, a work-in-progress dealing with both AIDS and the Holocaust. The play is scheduled to be produced by Circle Repertory Company, with Marshall W. Mason directing, but in its raw workshop form in early February 1994, *Riga* harked back to the style of Hoffman's earlier, free-wheeling downtown productions. One scene in particular recalls the confrontational experimental theater of the late sixties: the actors in the cast spread out along the aisles of the theater, so that they surround the audience completely and their voices seem to be coming from everywhere, spewing out anti-Semitic remarks along with right-wing religious homophobia. Near the beginning, there's a similar effect, with the sound system blasting out gunfire and the recorded voices of Adolf Hitler and Louis Farrakhan and Jesse Helms, all oozing hot hatred against Jews and gays. In both instances, the audience members are trapped in the crossfire of words and attitudes: there's no escape, no dramatic distance to protect or shield them from the force of the ideas being catapulted into the space.

In the main drama onstage, Wolf and Z, who are Jewish and black, respectively, are in the process of breaking up (somewhat like Rich and Saul in *As Is*, although Wolf and Z have been together only a short time). But here the primary problem is not so much AIDS (neither seems to be infected) as its after-effect: Z's ex-lover Dennis has recently died, and Z can't turn loose of his memories of that earlier relationship in order to attempt a new one. But Wolf is equally locked into memory-obsession, agonizing over the deaths of his mother's relatives at the hands of the Nazis in Latvia during the Second World War. (Some 80,000 Jews were killed in Latvia during the war, including most of Hoffman's mother's family. The slaughters on the beach of Liepaja and in the forests of Rumbula and Bikierniki, near Riga, specifically haunt Hoffman's play.)

As Wolf and Z discuss AIDS and activism and the question of their relationship in the fragile present, often with a certain amount of humor ("Why don't you join Queer Nation then?" "I don't like their haircuts."), scenes unfold relating to the brutal Holocaust in Riga and its impact on Wolf's family. In one especially harrowing scene, the secondary actors all play members of the Riga League for the Advancement of Scientific Racialism, and the parallels between anti-Semitism, racism, and homophobia are chilling.

As Wolf grows more and more impatient with Z's avoidance of commitment, Z resents what he considers Wolf's obsession with his family's past. Eventually each manages to open the other to an acknowledgment of the two pains being faced, without comparing the traumas. Something seems possible.

"The two men are haunted by the past, and they have to come to terms with the past to have a present," said Hoffman in an interview shortly before the workshop production opened. "How do we deal with this grief? How do we go on? How do we live with this kind of over-whelming rage? How do we go past this? I think all the newer AIDS works deal with that. *Normal Heart* and *As Is* deal with the recognition that there was a phenomenon called AIDS. We had to deal with just that. That was plenty for that time. But now we're dealing with *living* with AIDS, in the present."[13]

Hoffman, who anticipates that disgruntled critics may object to the discussion of AIDS and the Holocaust in the same play, shrugs: "I don't want to get into a discussion about comparing the Holocaust and AIDS because there is no comparison, except in terms of lives being lost and people's reactions to that." He defines himself as a rebel who has "never been politically correct"—intentionally: "I've seen a lot of politically correct plays. I taught at two politically correct schools: the New School and the University of Michigan. And these were two places that were very frightened of saying anything from the gut. So there were two topics you couldn't say anything about, namely race and sex, in any honest fashion. You couldn't admit to preferences or any negative feel-ings. You were always looking at the thought police behind your shoul-der. I think there's a special place in hell for people that do that."

In the same independent mood, Hoffman goes on to challenge the automatic equation that is often made between homophobia and fear of AIDS: "It is very normal to be terrified of a plague and to behave irra-tionally. It may not be good, but in the history of plagues, this kind of behavior is normal, this kind of despicable behavior. This fear cuts across everything, and you'll find it among gay people too. You'll find gay people comparing themselves: 'I wasn't as promiscuous as that one. It's those promiscuous ones that are to blame.' It's always the OTHER. It's those cats that caused the plague, it's those Jews, it's those gays, those OTHER people. I'm sure in Africa it's the same: it's that other tribe, or those women, or those bad people, those Christians, or Muslims, or whatever. I think it's normal not to want to deal with this.

I think we have to realize how frightening and how repulsive this disease is, to make progress."

AIDS should be treated realistically onstage, Hoffman feels, not as a metaphor or an abstraction. (Critic Joel Shatzky has pointed out that it is because neither Kramer nor Hoffman has "tried to treat AIDS in symbolic terms or to compromise his portrayal of gay men that these dramas have had such an electrifying effect on their audiences."[14]) AIDS simply exists, Hoffman feels: it has no secret or symbolic meanings: "What does AIDS 'mean'? Not a damn thing, as far as I can tell. I don't even see it as extraordinary. I don't see what is extraordinary about AIDS. There have been lots of plagues before, including plagues that were much worse than AIDS in terms of the number of people killed. What has been extraordinary is the blindness we've had toward disease in general."[15]

He is not particularly upset by the tendency of some critics to refer to his play and *The Normal Heart* as "first generation AIDS plays." Theater does have a history, a lineage, after all, like any other art form. But what does bother him, however, about the question of generations of AIDS plays is: "How many generations are we going to have? That's frightening. We shouldn't have to have any more AIDS plays."

Robert Chesley's *Night Sweat* opened in New York almost a year before either *As Is* or *The Normal Heart*, but it opened at a small, predominantly gay showcase without the clout and reputation of Circle Repertory Theater or New York Public Theater. Though it later went on to have productions in Los Angeles and San Francisco, its subject matter also kept it from getting the mainstream media attention that the other two plays enjoyed. *Night Sweat* was also considerably more shocking in its sexual content than either Hoffman's or Kramer's plays, including several scenes of simulated gay sex. Though Tony Kushner was later to insert similar material in both parts of *Angels in America*, when Chesley wrote *Night Sweat* in 1984, onstage sex scenes (certainly onstage *gay* sex scenes) were still unthinkable outside the realm of out-and-out pornography.

As Chesley writes in the introduction to the published edition of the play, reactions to the piece were varied:

> *Night Sweat, A Romantic Comedy* has the dubious distinction of being the first produced, full-length play dealing with the AIDS crisis. Reaction to its original production, in New York, was very divid-

ed. Some people loved it, but even closest friends behaved as if I had placed something at their feet which it was best to step over and politely ignore. My best buddy told me he wished I had never written it.[16]

Chesley goes on to acknowledge that his approach to the subject may be a bit skewed, and that the Hoffman and Kramer plays are probably "better introductions to the subject of AIDS" than his "comic nightmare about a fantasy suicide club."

Night Sweat, which never explains its own title (though night sweats are among the earliest indicators of a compromised immune system), is exactly what Chesley says: an eerie vision of a disco/sex club where gay men (presumably suffering from AIDS, though the word is never spoken) can pay $10,000 each to arrange the death of their choice, from the stabbing scene of *Lucia di Lammermoor* to a Disco Bunny's Dance of Death. As the Director of the establishment puts it to a new customer: "The Experience is the ultimate moment of life, a joyous celebration of the gift of self-awareness, self-realization. We are here to help you plan that wonderful, transcendent moment."

Chesley has taken what some have imagined as the ultimate S&M experience (death during sex) and used it to both shock and arouse his audience. Even on paper, the play is intensely sexy and erotic. Adding AIDS to this is extremely unsettling, as the playwright continues to parody various self-help and accept-your-disease attitudes by having the Director say things like: "You cannot save him. All you can do is interfere with his right to avoid pointless suffering, and his right to choose a death that is dignified and, if I may so, beautiful and truly romantic."

When a blond bombshell dressed as a nun enters to save the day and rescue the guy who has paid his fee but then decides he wants to live, there's something very phony and *deus ex machina* about it all. Like his character, Chesley seems to be still gazing longingly at the humpy leather-clad executioners who were seducing the hero towards a final climax. The message for the despairing persons with AIDS ("But meanwhile you're going to live. Live until the very *moment* you die! And make love! Make love in every possible, safe and sensible way! Enjoy it all, from the most delicate cruising to the heaviest S&M trips!") rings curiously hollow, giving way to the discorama finale, as the dancing Bunny also changes his mind, echoing Susan Hayward ("I want to live!") as the thumping music stops abruptly and the blackout comes.

Chesley's next play, *Jerker, or The Helping Hand*, caused almost as much consternation. It is a two-character play about two gay men having phone sex. When it was aired on Pacifica radio station KPFK in September 1986 (after a staging that premiered in Los Angeles six weeks earlier), the station almost lost its broadcast license from the FCC. As Chesley describes it, though the FCC eventually chose not to prosecute, the harm had been done: "The broadcast media responded with a show of chickenshit gutlessness, reminiscent of the betrayals of the '50s, and a 'chilling effect' on the broadcast of sexual material took hold across the nation. This was of course, just when simple, honest information about sex was most vitally and undeniably necessary."

One might challenge Chesley's implication that the dialogue here is "simple, honest information about sex," especially during the first half of the play, when the verbal (and visual) material has far more to do with graphic eroticism than with information or instruction. The telephone fantasies are vivid and compelling, though as in *Night Sweat*, they rely heavily on role-playing and S&M fantasizing rather than (as the blond in *Night Sweat* puts it at one point) more ordinary "vanilla" sex.

About half-way through the play based on these conversations between two strangers, a certain uncanny intimacy begins to develop between them. One guy begs off on the fantasy trip one night, not wanting to indulge because he's just heard a friend is sick with "it." Then the same man develops a cough, and suddenly there's nothing but his answering machine (an old Judy Garland song) when his phone-sex partner calls, and, at the end, the telephone company clincher in the age of AIDS: "The number you have dialed has been disconnected."

With *Dog Plays*, the third play in the collection, written in 1989, Chesley himself had been diagnosed (there's a photo of him at the end of the book, shirtless, revealing his KS lesions):

> These odd little plays, which can, of course, be performed separately, are all that I have written for theater in the past two years, since getting the Diagnosis. In a sense, they are my first AIDS plays. The previous plays deal with the impact of AIDS on gay-identified lives and communities. But getting the diagnosis yourself thrusts you instantly out of the Golden Land of the (seemingly) Healthy, and into a different territory. These plays are from that territory.

They are sad little plays indeed, peopled by the sick, the sicker, and the dead: each of the three has a ghost. One character in particular echoes Chesley's warning that everything changes with *actual* diagnosis:

> Time was . . . before *I* got the Diagnosis, time was if a guy told me he'd been diagnosed, there was something I used to say. Words I had ready, I guess. Words I *meant*, though. I'd tell him, "Well, you know, we're all in this together." And I *did* mean it. And it *is* true. But funny thing: when I got the Diagnosis myself, I stopped saying that. I sure as hell didn't say it to anyone who *didn't* have the Diagnosis, even though I still believe it. But it seemed—it seems—discourteous.

In the third short play, the character Fido (all the characters in this trilogy have dog names) talks about Rover, who died after a bout of disorientation and dementia, but kept playing with fire until the end:

> I loved your beauty. And I'll admit that if I'd had your beauty, I might have gone off to play, too. But I loved your beauty because—because it lit up the world, so brightly, lit up *my* life, *too*, and because I *knew*. I *knew* you had that *same yearning I had*, that same *gaping, aching hole*, right *here*.... A guy can light himself up and go off like a Roman candle, and be very beautiful, and give off a *brilliant*, blinding light. And maybe it's hellfire for him, and maybe it isn't. Maybe there isn't any right or wrong about it. Maybe there's just joy and sorrow. I don't know.

Even Edna St. Vincent Millay, burning her candle at both ends, couldn't say it better: that poignant blaze of glory, then nothing but shadows and memories.

According to Chesley's introduction, Stephen Foster songs are to be sung before, after, and between the three plays: simple, unadorned, in the original arrangements. After the last play (the one about Fido and Rover and beauty's blinding light), the selection is "My Old Kentucky Home, Good Night" and, Chesley indicates, "The houselights were brought up, and the audience joined in: 'Weep no more my lady...' It helped."

Chesley himself died in early December, 1990, having left some Roman candles of his own: these disturbing firecrackers of poignant, explosive power.

18

Further Confrontations
Across the Proscenium Arch

The theatre is there to explore these issues, not to decide them for us, just as it can't, being fiction, assuage our grief at the many real losses we've suffered. What it can do best, perhaps, in the long term, is teach us the processes we are likely to go through: not make us cry, but show us the how and why of crying. Not make us grieve, but display the changing nature of grief. Not preach anger or love or despair, but dramatize—*dramatize*—the way we experience those feelings. And when the theatre does this—as the many tentative stances in these plays do, each in its own measure—then something else happens: because of art, our experience of ourselves awakens. We unfreeze. Our sense of shared feelings, shared events, overcomes the numbness. Humanity, and not the syndrome, becomes the protagonist. If we can do that in art, then it can be done in life. Sharing our losses creatively, we can begin to share our hope.[1]

—Michael Feingold, *The Way We Live Now*

n his introduction to *The Way We Live Now: American Plays and the AIDS Crisis*, Michael Feingold, longtime theater critic of the *Village Voice*, chronicles the numbness of a contemporary theater community in which AIDS itself has taken center stage as the main actor. As a critic in New York City, Feingold himself has known the pain of becoming "uncomfortably proficient in the writing of obituaries" and attending "the informal memorial services that have become a prevailing theatrical form of our time."[2] His conclusion, that the real gift of art about AIDS is that it brings us back to life and hope, seems a valid one and a good way to describe the extremely varied plays which have come out of the epidemic. Whether their approach is one of anger and confrontation or elegy and personal loss, they reach beyond the proscenium arch and across the footlights to touch and change the viewer, making a difference in "the way we live now" (as the title of the collection indicates).

Joe Pintauro's *Raft of the Medusa* is structured as an AIDS support group session: a psychiatrist sits stage center, flanked on either side by patients who are a cross-section of the AIDS community: straight and gay, black and white, male and female, angry and accepting. One of the first to speak is Cora, an attractive blonde Yuppie who's one of the angriest ("I don't deserve this shit") and blames the gay men in the room—blames all gay men, in fact—because she was infected by a bisexual she picked up at a singles bar.

One former member of the group, Donald, has just died, though he keeps appearing onstage and the characters (including one who was his lover) have to talk though how they feel about his death. They talk about a lot of other things as well, including how they feel about each other and how they feel about their various conditions and options (including suicide, which is referred to as "the Amsterdam solution").

Described on paper, the concept sounds static: a semi-circle of group therapy monologues, with occasional interplay. The actual effect is much more wrenching because of the clarity of the characterizations and the careful arrangement of their speeches; with good cross-cutting, the play would work even better as a film or teleplay. It reaches its dramatic peak when one of the members is revealed to be a plant: a reporter researching a magazine article. A black bag lady named Nairobi, who is mute and has sat immobile throughout the proceedings thus far, jumps up and stabs the spy with what appears to be an infected needle. She signs to the psychiatrist, who interprets: "This is my weapon against everyone who makes fun of my pain. They watched my babies die." The spy collapses, convinced he's been infected, then Nairobi admits it was a clean needle. The relief in the room is chilling. One of the others sums up the irony they all feel: "At least one of us got to feel it. The miracle we've all been waiting for."

Other plays are beginning to try to balance the picture of the actual demographics of AIDS by presenting the impact of the epidemic on straights as well as gays, on women as well as men, and on Blacks and Latinos as well as whites.

A Better Life by Louis Delgado Jr., which had a brief run at the Theater Row Theater in New York in August 1993, is set in a hospital room shared by two AIDS patients, one gay and the other an IV drug user. Both have been abandoned by their significant others when they became sick, and the drama explores their coming to terms not only with having AIDS, but also with their feelings about each other (AIDS patients are not free from discrimination themselves, especially against others not in their own particular "risk group," as both *A Better Life* and *Raft of the Medusa* indicate). The playwright is himself a recovering drug addict and received financial assistance for the production from the state office of Alcoholism and Substance Abuse Services.

Cheryl L. West's *Before It Hits Home* opened at Arena Stage in Washington, then at the New York Shakespeare Festival Public Theater. Its primary focus is on a black bisexual jazz musician who is diagnosed with AIDS and returns to his small home town, where he at first tries to keep his condition a secret from his family. In the New York production, the musician was played by James McDaniel, who had originated the key role of the young man who tries to pass himself off as Sidney Poitier's son in John Guare's *Six Degrees of Separation*. As Michael Kuchwara, the Associated Press drama critic, pointed out in his review: "In *Six Degrees*, McDaniel played a con man who charmed a collection of wealthy white New Yorkers. In *Before It Hits Home*, he's a con man of another sort, duping his family about his sexuality and his illness, until he can lie no more."[3]

The San Francisco three-man performance group Pomo Afro Homos, whose name declares their aesthetic (postmodern), racial (African American), and sexual identities, have dealt openly with various questions of discrimination since their formation in 1990. Like West did with *Before It Hits Home*, the group has consistently challenged the black community's silence on the AIDS crisis and homosexuality. The group has been pointedly excluded from the National Black Theatre Festival for three consecutive years (1991 to 1993), perhaps because, as Brian Freeman of the group has been quoted as saying: "We are gay. We are black. We are not one or the other. We are often asked to choose between one or the other and we cannot. We need to find the strength to be both."[4] In their performance at the Serious Fun! festival at Lincoln Center in New York in the summer of 1993, the trio closed with a segment called "Dark Fruit":

> The three Pomos began their finale, reading letters of rage and loss. To Magic Johnson. To AIDS organizations. To Afro-centrics. To all black churches. To the media. To America. The lines were sharp: "Dear . . . First Baptist, Second Baptist, Third, Last Baptist, and all black churches. How many organists will you go through before you do more than light a candle?"[5]

The most controversial play to deal with AIDS among heterosexuals to date is Alan Bowne's *Beirut*, which caused a minor furor even in the anything-goes atmosphere of the New York experimental theater scene when it debuted at the Nat Horne Theatre in March 1987. The short play is set in a dystopia, where the futuristic hell is the Lower East Side of New York City, when that part of Manhattan has been transformed into a kind of war zone (thus the title) where people who test positive to an unnamed disease (clearly AIDS, with Kaposi's sarcoma being a kind of mark of Cain) are kept prisoners in their own apartments in a neighborhood patrolled by storm troopers and riddled with surveillance camera "sex detectors." People in the quarantine zone are all tattooed with the letter P (for positive) on their buttocks; outsiders ("blood-negatives") are forbidden to enter the quarantine zone and (on pain of execution) to have sex (gay or straight) with a P.

Bowne, who himself died of AIDS in 1988, raised the ire of the activist community by presenting what many considered misinformation about the condition in his dystopia (the disease in *Beirut* can be spread by saliva, for example, and "even a Trojan [condom] won't protect you"), but what gives the play its eerie resonance is the grungy realism of its language (Bowne is best known for his play *Forty Deuce*, about male hustlers in a seedy SRO hotel in New York's Times Square area, which exhibited the playwright's brilliant ear for New York street talk) and the uneasy proposition that lies at its center: a kind of Romeo and Juliet love affair between an HIV-negative woman and a positive man. Blue (originally played by Marisa Tomei) has sneaked into the quarantine zone because she's obsessed with a hot number named Torch (Michael

David Morrison), who's just been diagnosed and branded. As in Robert Chesley's similarly disturbing *Night Sweat* or Cyril Collard's film *Savage Nights*, Bowne's drama is charged with an erotic power that is staggering: the audience, almost in spite of itself, feels pulled into the growing onstage lust. The real focus becomes not AIDS or quarantine, but a game of Russian roulette between someone infected and someone who's not—and seems not to care that she might become so.

The question of quarantine was also raised by a Hot Peaches show called *Concentrated Camp* in 1989. The free-wheeling drag troupe, who have been performing in New York and Europe since the earlys seventies, took a very different approach to the subject than Bowne did, but their credo has always been rather different than that of most of their peers Off-Off-Broadway: The Peaches epitomize what one might call the politics of trash. There are no sacred cows, either sexual or political. The troupe is always street-wise and self-critical, able to laugh at and cry about themselves at the same time. There's a line in one of their earlier plays, called *Gay?*, which pretty much sums up the Peaches philosophy by quoting one of Off-Off-Broadway's legendary transvestite actresses, Candy Darling: "Come down off that trapeze, honey, into the sawdust with the rest of the circus!"

In *Concentrated Camp*, the company satirized a situation expertly described by Robert Massa as follows:

> To protect the public health, the government decides to round up gay men and put them in camps. At the risk of chipping their nail polish, some drag queens dig a tunnel and escape. They meet grave diggers and persuade them to come out of the closet, then all hide out at a Homosexuals Anonymous meeting in the suburbs. The authorities track them down and bang at the door. Remembering Stonewall, the queens pull out guns and prepare to fight back. Then they decide—gee whiz, let's put on a show—to do a Copacabana finale instead.[6]

In spite of this zippy description, Massa didn't much like the show, finding the idea of quarantine outdated and not really relevant to AIDS activism of the present moment. It's also possible that some subjects— like quarantines and tattooing—are touchier to handle, even with satire and camp, than others. (This was again evidenced by the outrage of some AIDS activists in response to the Benetton HIV tattoo ads in the fall of 1993. Instead of seeing the ad as an act of political defiance, like a Gran Fury poster, the groups attacked the youth-market-oriented clothing company, long famous for its controversial ads, for poor taste in giving a serious subject a kind of Calvin Klein sex-sell. The ads of the tattooed male buttocks and muscular male biceps were indeed homoerotic and appeared to be clearly geared toward a gay audience. But were they, as the protesters maintained, "exploiting the illness and suffering of others for commercial gain"[7]? Or might the company simply be coopting the symbolism of the oppressor and making it their own, as the Danish population did in World War II when the general public all donned yellow Star of David armbands in defiance of the Nazi's singling out the Jews in that country?)

Scott McPherson's *Marvin's Room* did not directly deal with AIDS, although almost everyone in the play is sick or helping care for someone who is sick: an exact depiction of the life crisis of the playwright, who, as he wrote the play, was not only ill himself, but was caring for a lover dying with AIDS. In the published edition of the play, he writes:

> Now I am 31 and my lover has AIDS. Our friends have AIDS. And we all take care of each other, the less sick caring for the more sick. At times, an unbelievably harsh fate is transcended by a simple act of love, by caring for another.
>
> By most, we are thought of as "dying." But as dying becomes a way of life, the meaning of the world blurs.[8]

Marvin's Room, however, is the story of Bessie, a middle-aged spinster who has spent the past two decades of her life caring for a bedridden father and a disabled aunt. As the play opens, she discovers that she, too, is ill, with leukemia: her caring, her being a caregiver, has not exempted her from disease, and she must now turn to others. As Larry Kramer writes in the introduction to the published version of the play: "*Marvin's Room* is not a play about AIDS. And *Marvin's Room* is not a gay play. Yet *Marvin's Room* is a magnificent gay play about AIDS."[9]

Terrence McNally has never written a play exclusively about AIDS (except the brief "Andre's Mother," which he later expanded as a TV drama), but the subject has haunted most of his works in the past

decade. In his most outspokenly gay play, *The Lisbon Traviata*, one character is a doctor with a patient who has just died of the epidemic and
another offstage friend is assumed to be sick. In *Lips Together, Teeth Apart*,
two straight couples spend a weekend in a Fire Island summer house
which had belonged to one woman's gay brother, who has just died of
AIDS. In *Frankie and Johnny in the Clair de Lune*, the central characters (a
waitress and her ex-con boyfriend) agonize at length over safe sex techniques, and in the film version their relationship is paralleled by one
between two gay supporting characters in the film. Even in McNally's
book for the Broadway musical, *Kiss of the Spider Woman*, the specter of
AIDS hovers over the proceedings in a way, both in the fantasized
Death figure of the Spider Woman and in the gay character's compulsive attraction to that symbol of erotic danger.

In *A Perfect Ganesh*, a 1993 work at the Manhattan Theatre Club,
McNally addresses AIDS in a similarly oblique way. David Richards of
The New York Times has pointed out that McNally's works are not so
much about AIDS as "about loneliness and wants, reaching out when
you can and pulling back in spite of yourself...about the need to connect."[10] In *Ganesh*, two women in late middle age, friends and neighbors
in suburban Connecticut, take a trip to India seeking some sort of spiritual release. The son of one was killed by gay-bashers in an attack
shortly after his lover died of AIDS; the other woman years before had
seen her only son, as a baby, killed in a traffic accident. The second
woman now has a lump in her breast—a second secret that she keeps
locked up inside until almost the end of the play. Though they are never
able to share their similar losses with each other, the women help each
other through the trip. And along their journey through India, they
meet others who are suffering: a gay couple with AIDS and assorted
lepers and loners, angry locals and disillusioned travellers.

Commenting on everything is a character with an elephant head, the
Hindu god Ganesh, speaking sometimes as the god himself, sometimes as
minor characters in the play, but always reflecting the wisdom that is
India: "Be careful of India. You may find yourself here," he says, under
disguise of a Japanese businessman. And regarding the gay couple dying
of AIDS, he is particularly enigmatic: "Why must they die? Why not?"
Death in Hinduism is followed by rebirth; suffering paves the way for
more happiness, less pain in the life ahead.

In *Falsettos*, a musical by William Finn and James Lapine, Marvin, a gay Jewish man leaves his wife Trina and son Jason for another man, Whizzer. Things go relatively well until one day Whizzer collapses while he and Marvin are playing racquetball, and things disintegrate to the point that Jason's bar mitzvah has to be catered in Whizzer's hospital room. Throughout the lyrics are honest and direct. The published edition of the script contains an afterword by Frank Rich, then chief drama critic at the *New York Times*, about taking his two young sons to see the play, where they end up teaching him a lesson about family values and the open-mindedness of the youth, having no problem at all with the fact that two of the main characters were gay: "Surely not everyone they knew was so tolerant and free of the old sexual stereotypes, I insisted, but my children would have none of my adult pessimism. 'Kids are stereotyped,' said Nat, with an exasperated adolescent roll of the eyes meant to terminate the conversation." [11]

Finn's musical itself, which was nominated for a Tony as best play of the year in 1992, unfolds with a similar childlike grace and straightforwardness, allowing complex ideas and emotions the conciseness of song rather than the expansiveness of overblown rhetoric. At one point, Jason tries to make a deal with God for his father's lover's life: "Are you just a big psychiatrist? / Or can you make things not happen? / Do this for me / And I'll get bar mitzvahed / In exchange for: / Can you please make my friend stop dying?"[12] When the end comes, it too is simple and understated, with no deathbed melodrama: "There are no answers," Marvin and Whizzer sing to each other, "But what would I do / If you hadn't been my friend?"[13] Marvin's ex-psychiatrist, who has married Trina, sums everything up, with a Ganesh-like acceptance of life and death: "Lovers come and go. / Lovers live and die fortissimo. / This is where we take a stand. / Welcome to Falsettoland."[14]

In *Ancient Boys* by Jean-Claude van Itallie, a group of friends reminisce after the death of their friend Reuben, a painter, to AIDS. As they look at slides that relate to various aspects of their relationship to him, the ghost of Reuben himself wanders through the set, participating in flashbacks with the rest of the cast as they remember moments in his life. Intercut with this, Reuben also seems to be building a pyramid-shaped structure out of brooms and sticks. At one point, in a flashback just before Reuben's own diagnosis, he has a calmly detached discussion about the new epidemic with his friend Luke, trying to understand it in terms of metaphors of health and healing (which they're both interested in). "In autopsies of people who've died of AIDS, they've discovered the thymus gland is all shriveled," Reuben says, going on to explain that the thymus is "the sex clock which regulates when you reach puberty. It's right near the heart. Edgar Cayce says the thymus gland is the heart chakra. We're misusing heart energy.... Not just gay men—the whole society."[15]

Van Itallie, an established playwright who has worked over the years in both the United States and Europe and who is particularly known for his collaborations with director Joseph Chaikin, thus makes a brave foray into AIDS territory that few of his fellow playwrights have dared to try: questioning the meaning of AIDS beyond the medical. After Reuben himself is diagnosed, he continues to look for alternative explanations and alternative cures, rejecting chemotherapy for a macrobiotic diet, herbal medicine, psychic counseling, meditation, even a crystal—and that pyramid, which he's constructing onstage as the play unfolds.

In the final scene, the audience witnesses Reuben's ironic ode to pyramid power. In an earlier scene, he had told one of his friends, "On Atlantis and in Egypt a pyramid was used as an initiation vehicle, like a spaceship."[16] But Reuben's own initiation trip would appear to some more like a self-chosen foreshortening of his own journey: he swallows a bottleful of pills, steps into the pyramid, and folds his arms to await the end. Again, van Itallie has raised some deeply disturbing questions about AIDS that others have left unvoiced.

Copi, the Argentine-born French fashion designer and playwright, wrote *Grand Finale*, just before he died of AIDS in December 1987. Like the fourteen other plays he left behind, his swan song is a madcap farce. But this farce takes place in a hospital room, and the main character is dying of AIDS. Not that that inevitability causes any change of demeanor in the character or his friends. Witness the following exchange:

> HUBERT: Paris isn't the great city it used to be. Since they closed the baths, there's no place to hang out after the show. Of course, there are no more shows either. And even if there were, these days they're hardly a meeting place for people like us, of ambiguous sex and indeterminate age. There's always the park, but I'm afraid of

getting mugged. You're so lucky having AIDS; here you don't run any risks.

CYRIL: Ah, Hubert, you always know the right thing to say.

HUBERT: It's true, I'm jealous of you. Now that I no longer know how to spend my days, I'm terrified I'll live to be a hundred.

CYRIL: So go live in the third world: With all your money, you could be king of a court of little boys, waving banana leaves over you to brush away the flies.

HUBERT: I've had fantasies about that. But I'd be afraid of getting cut off from my friends.

CYRIL: All your friends are dead.

HUBERT: You're still alive, dear genius.

CYRIL: Well, not for long.[17]

The wild antics then begin in earnest, involving a cub reporter (or so he claims) who comes to interview the dying man but never asks him a question; an Italian diva who wants to marry Cyril ("What a sublime disease! . . . What a magnificent end for a true artist! And what a glorious fate for a widow!"[18]), a nurse (named Mary Jo Bongo) who smokes opium, and a doctor who eats all of Cyril's food and whose "hobby is lobotomy." Cyril is so busy rehearsing the death scene from *Hamlet* to impress the young reporter (who may or may not be his long-lost son by Hubert's sister) that whether or not he really dies—at precisely five in the afternoon, as he has decided—is never clear.

Harvey Fierstein's *Safe Sex* relies on more conventional humor, though it lacks both the bite and bawdiness of Fierstein's earlier works, including his best-known play, *Torch Song Trilogy*. And like Copi's *Grand Finale*, which was virtually ignored in its U. S. debut (having been a massive hit in Paris), Fierstein's *Safe Sex* got a relatively cool reception from New York audiences, most of whom seemed to agree with Edmund White's proclamation that AIDS was not a proper subject for comedy.

Safe Sex consists of three one-act plays, two of which deal with the changing sexual conventions of cruising and relationships in the age of AIDS, and one dealing with a confrontation between a dead man's two widows: his ex-wife and his male lover. All three are steeped in nostalgia for the days when sex was free and easy. As Manny says in "Manny and Jake," the first of the three plays:

> Two grown men stand in a bar. Watching. Each other. They stare at each other. Each wanting the other. Two grown men stare in a bar, feet apart, eyes together, they stare. They sip. They puff. They want. Two grown men stare in a bar and then travel on in opposite directions. Never touching. Never holding. Never having. And why? Why? They can't kiss. They want to. They used to. They can't anymore.... A moment of silence for what we used to do and how it felt.[19]

In the second play, "Safe Sex," two ex-lovers talk to each other from opposite ends of a seesaw, a clever metaphor for the uneasy balance of trying to relate in the new era, which again is woefully unlike the former fun times: "We had no lists of Do's and Don'ts. There was no death count. The worst you could get from loving was a broken heart.... Remember herpes? Remember crabs? Remember worrying about the clap?"[20] With liberation and the end of invisibility had come the virus and a fear of commitment, the danger of relationships teetering back and forth and never finding a balance.

In the third play, the ex-wife and lover battle for the spoils, and the playwright's sympathies clearly lie with the lover (the role Fierstein played both on stage and in the cable TV adaptation of "On Tidy Endings"—see Chapter 6). He points out that the ex-wife simply wasn't there in the five years since the divorce, and that it was he and he alone who fed his lover, pushed his wheelchair, cleaned up after him, took him to doctors and faith healers and to Mexico for non-FDA-approved drugs. "When you lived the way we did for three years, the battle becomes your life."[21] His anger at being "edited out of obituaries" and having condolence cards come through the ex-wife are hard to fault, though the piece never quite takes off and sings they way Feirstein's earlier, Off-Off-Broadway romps did, safe as they were (admittedly) in the very atmosphere of pre-AIDS camp iconoclasm that *Safe Sex* looks back upon with such perceptive nostalgia.

Harry Kondoleon (who died of AIDS in March 1994) wrote plays and novels from a decidedly skewed perspective, peopling these works with eccentric outsiders, dysfunctional families, and topsy-turvy relationships that wobble like a tall stack of magazines, ready to topple at any second. Even before he began to write more and more frequently about AIDS as his own health deteriorated, Kondoleon constructed plays whose titles place them in strange emotional territories: *Christmas on Mars*, for example, or *The Fairy Garden*, or a world of *Self Torture and Strenuous Exercise*. In *Slacks and Tops* a woman sits in an airport motel room planning a trip to Africa and cutting out pictures of clothing from *Vogue*. She then packs them carefully in her suitcase, clearly planning to wear the trim paper outfits on her trip. In *Christmas on Mars*, a character describes himself flatly: "I listen to records at the wrong speed and don't know it. I put quarters in other people's machines at the laundromat and watch the clothes spin and dry while mine sit in a wet unattended lump."[22] In *Anteroom*, a woman recalls eerily: "I read a short story once where a woman goes to the ladies room and while she's fixing her makeup in the mirror she doesn't know which woman in the reflection is herself and which are the others. She begins to wish to be one more than the others but soon one by one they all leave and the one she least wanted to be is the one she is."[23]

When AIDS enters this oddball *mise en scene* in Kondoleon's *Zero Positive*, the character already seems familiar. The action takes place in a "deathly apartment" on the Upper West Side of Manhattan. "Toy trains have the run of the place; tracks run into other rooms. trains are atop tables; they have shelves to themselves; they run."[24] It is "always lunchtime." The air-conditioner hums. A young man named Himmer prepares lunch for his mostly senile, mostly silent father, Jacob Blank. Two friends, Samantha and Prentice, arrive. Himmer asks Samantha about the results of tests that he and she had just had for the HIV virus. Both of them tested positive.

Discussion of the disease—its meaning or meaninglessness, who's sick, who's dead—permeates the dialogue, as the onstage action becomes more and more surreal. Himmer remembers a play, a kind of pseudo Greek tragedy, that his late mother, an alcoholic, had written in college. That was before she married his father the poet and before she left him (and Himmer) to go live with "two gay guys in the country" who got depressed and drowned themselves in a pond. Himmer invites an actor he knows, named Patrick, to look over the play. Patrick gets drunk and tries to slit his wrist with a pen-knife just as he remembers the name of a rich young woman who might want to produce Himmer's mother's play. The woman, Deborah Fine, arrives when Himmer is out and is

seduced by his father's trains (and by Jacob Blank himself, finally talking again) into stripping to the waist and portraying the old man's
favorite sex fantasy, the topless nurse.

Plans proceed for producing one of the mother's long-lost pseudo-
Greek plays, which, needless to say is about a plague, a pestilence, and
includes an elixir that turns out to be hemlock. Samantha, Himmer, and
Prentice all consider onstage exits, arguing over whose life is more
meaningless and miserable.

The play-within-a-play begins. "I arrive at dawn with heavy news of
a world crashing down," announces Patrick, as the messenger. "Woe to
me, sad herald, witness to the pestilence of the city."[25] Samantha plays
the Goddess of Battles All Lost. Deborah Fine wanders on as a Foolish
Servant Girl collecting the bones of the dead. Himmer and Prentice
arm-wrestle for the elixir/poison. Jacob grabs it instead, while they are
fighting, and downs it. Patrick rushes out for a doctor. Jacob and
Himmer share the same exit line: "I woke up early this morning and
what did I see? The end of me, the end of me."[26]

Paula Vogel's *The Baltimore Waltz* is, like many AIDS plays, a deeply
personal response to the playwright's experience with AIDS: the death
of her brother. In the play, a young schoolteacher named Anna goes on a
whirlwind tour of Europe with her gay brother Carl, even though just
before their departure, she is diagnosed with a new rare and invariably
fatal disease, ATD (Acquired Toilet Disease), which mysteriously
afflicts young single female schoolteachers. The brother and sister make
their way through Europe, with Carl carrying a stuffed rabbit which
seems to have something to do with smuggling illegal drugs to treat
ATD. Anna picks up waiters and bellboys right and left, leaving Carl
mostly in the hotel room, occasionally confronting her about her promiscuity and leaving him behind. At last they reach Zurich, where Anna is
to undergo a radical urine-drinking treatment from a Dr. Todesrocheln.
After this extremely oddball scene, the doctor says (in German) "WO
IST DEIN BRUDER?" Taking off his wig and glasses, he becomes the
doctor from the first scene who had informed Anna and Carl of Anna's
ATD, except of course, it was Carl who was sick, and the mysterious
disease was AIDS, not ATD, and they've been in Baltimore, at Johns
Hopkins all along. The stuffed rabbit in Anna's hands is nothing but
Carl's childhood toy. All the rest has been a feverish fantasy in Anna's

imagination. "You fool!" says the doctor (still part fantasy: no real doctor would say such a thing). "You left your brother in the room alone." Even that fantasy dissolves and Carl lies dead, under a white sheet, to the tune of Beethoven's "Emperor Waltz."

In the issue of *American Theatre* in which *The Baltimore Waltz* was published, Vogel writes: "In 1986, my brother Carl invited me to join him in a joint excursion to Europe. Due to pressures of time and money, I declined, never dreaming that he was HIV positive."[27] He was diagnosed with pneumonia at Johns Hopkins the following spring and died the next January. Vogel chronicled her response at a writers' workshop at the MacDowell Colony during the summer of 1989 and the production premiered at Circle Repertory Company in New York in January 1992.

Novelist and critic Susan Sontag is indirectly responsible for one of the more powerful theatrical statements about AIDS, *The Way We Live Now*, written originally as a short story in *The New Yorker* in November 1986 and then adapted for the stage by Edward Parone. In it, a group of people discuss the illness of a gay man with AIDS (though the word is never spoken). Parone staged it as "a reading for five voices," leaving in the "stage directions" from the original story: "At first he was just losing weight, he felt only a little ill, Max said to Ellen," begins Voice 1, and then Voice 2 continues, "and he didn't call for an appointment with his doctor, according to Greg, because he was managing to keep on working at more or less the same rhythm," (on to Voice 3) "but he did stop smoking, Tanya pointed out..." And so on.[28]

A few minutes later comes the title phrase: "Well, everybody is worried about everybody now, said Betsy, that seems to be the way we live, the way we live now."[29] The life of the man whose name we never learn is examined from an infinite number of viewpoints, voices, tones of caring and curiosity. In the original story, there are 26 friends, one for each letter of the alphabet. But there are an infinite number of responses. The truth is everywhere—and nowhere—in those responses, for words and voices both can and cannot contain this disease, these feelings. "I was thinking, Ursula said to Quentin, that the difference between a story and a painting or photograph is that in a story you can write, He's still alive. But in a painting or a photo you can't show 'still.' You can just show him being alive."[30]

Having offended a number of people with her dismissive, head-driven theorizing in *AIDS and Its Metaphors*, with this story/play and its panoply of voices, Sontag the artist outlasts Sontag the polemicist after all. "We unfreeze," as Michael Feingold says, and some of the numbness lifts.

Ron Vawter is a longtime member of The Wooster Group, one of the foremost experimental theater troupes in New York City (other leading members include actor and playwright Spalding Gray, actor Willem Dafoe, and director Elizabeth LeCompte). He played a pivotal minor role in Jonathan Demme's *Philadelphia* and has starred in an extraordinary theater piece of his own about AIDS, entitled *Roy Cohn/Jack Smith*. In his onstage introduction to that piece, both live in the theater and in the filmed version (produced by Demme and directed by Jill Godmillow), Vawter identifies himself as "a person living with AIDS." The show is also about two real-life people who had AIDS: lawyer Roy Cohn, who died of the epidemic in 1986, and underground theater director and film-maker Jack Smith, who died in 1989.

"This is not a documentary, but a subjective reaction," says Vawter to the audience, "a response to the lives of two very different white male homosexuals who had two very strong things in common: a virus and a society which sought to repress their homosexuality."[31] The Roy Cohn half of the program is a tour de force, written by Gary Indiana for Vawter, who portrays Cohn dressed in a purple velvet coat and black bow tie, giving an imaginary speech attacking the New York City gay rights bill to a right-wing family values group. The second half of the program features Vawter as Smith in a performance piece from the early eighties, involving lots of sequins and harem drag, camp old movie references, strange slide projections of a stuffed penguin, and a spaced-out, druggy ambiance.

Greg Mehrten, who is Vawter's companion and directed the piece, described the genesis of the piece, which Vawter started working on in Amsterdam in 1990: "He decided to make an homage to Jack Smith, who had just died that year of AIDS. Ron himself was HIV positive at the time, but that wasn't the only reason he wanted to do something about Jack. He had always admired his work a lot."[32] Vawter found an old audio tape of Smith doing a performance at the Theater for the New City in the early eighties. The performance was called *What's Underground About Marshmallows?* and like most of Smith's work, it was unscripted and changed nightly. He reconstructed the piece with the help of performance artist Penny Arcade, who had worked with Smith on the original.

After that piece was mounted in Amsterdam, Vawter wanted to bring *Jack Smith* back to New York but felt it needed something. At about the same time, he was negotiating with movie director Mark Rappaport about a Roy Cohn project, but the film never materialized, so Vawter decided to try a Roy Cohn theater piece on his own. He started researching Cohn's life and speeches, and brought Mehrten and novelist Gary Indiana in to work on the project. "The quotes are 80 percent made up," Mehrten admits. There was lots more to start with, including "a lot of Kennedy and J. Edgar Hoover stuff" that got cut from the work-in-progress, which was tried out in workshops in New York and elsewhere.

Discussing the riveting pauses where Vawter as Cohn stares out at the audience, Mehrten says, "As the piece evolved, those pauses got longer, going from being very prosaic little sips of water to more profound silences where the audience really begins to squirm and wonder, 'What's going on with him?' In a way, Ron needed those moments, physically and emotionally, but he was also confronting the audience. It became a very important moment in the play—time for the audience to absorb and reflect what was going on."

Mehrten says that Vawter never regretted "outing" himself as a person with AIDS in *Roy Cohn/Jack Smith*: "Before we did it, we had a long discussion. Ron thought he had to admit he has AIDS. It would be stupid and cowardly not to. That's what *informs* the work. After he did it, an incredible burden was lifted. And coincidentally, it did not make him a pariah in terms of finding work. It completely changed his relationship with Hollywood, for example. It changes your life."

Even though his health was increasingly fragile, Vawter continued to work in film and on stage. After helping promote *Philadelphia* and filming *Roy Cohn/Jack Smith*, plus directing Mehrten in Jim Strah's *Queer and Alone*, he took off for Amsterdam to appear as the title character in a Dutch production of Sophocles's *Philoctetes*, adapted by New York writer/director John Jesurun. In the play Philoctotes is an archer who is bitten by a scorpion and thus acquires an incurable condition and is exiled to a barrier island. After ten years, Ulysses hears of his plight and summons him to help fight the Trojan War, where the arrows of this pariah, this outcast, are the only ones that can slay the hero Paris and help win the war.

On his return to New York in Spring 1994, Vawter had planned to join Mehrten in a new project directed by Susan Sontag. It was to have involved brief scenes about dying and caretaking, drawn from literature and old movies. When Mehrten and I spoke in late January, he discussed how excited he and Vawter were about the project. "We're really enjoying the idea of switching off playing all those old Bette Davis and Deborah Kerr parts. But we haven't really dealt with the emotional part of the subject matter yet. Like me carrying a body up a staircase. Or Ron having to say, over and over, all those speeches about 'I'm dying,' or 'Help me.'"

In early April, Vawter became ill again and was hospitalized briefly in Italy. Merhrten went there to bring him home to New York. During the flight back, Vawter died quietly in his sleep, with his lover beside him. For his wake, Vawter wore his velvet smoking jacket from *Roy Cohn/Jack Smith*.

19

Allowing Humor: Jeffrey & Pterodactyls

n January 1987, when Edmund White wrote his classic manifesto, "Esthetics and Loss," giving his thoughts about the art of AIDS in the magazine *Artforum*. In it he states, "If art is to confront AIDS more honestly than the media has done, it must begin in tact, avoid humor, and end in anger."[1] The statement rang true for many of us facing the loss of friends and lovers, as did his proclamation that the epidemic was shifting the focus away from popular art to "high" art and that sex per se and emphasis on the body ("pumped up, pierced, ornamented") had ceased to be of prime importance to the gay community ("Fat is in; it means you're not dying, at least not yet"[2]).

White went even further in insisting that humor wasn't a proper response to AIDS:

> Avoid humor, because humor seems grotesquely inappropriate to the occasion. Humor puts the public (indifferent when not uneasy) on cozy terms with what is an unspeakable scandal: death. Humor domesticates terror, lays to rest misgivings that should be intensified. Humor suggests that AIDS is just another calamity to befall Mother Camp, whereas in truth AIDS is not one more item in a sequence, but a rupture in meaning itself. Humor, like melodrama,

205

is an assertion of bourgeois values; it falsely suggests that AIDS is all in the family.[3]

Times have changed in seven years, and White himself might be less dogmatic if he were to write his manifesto in the mid-nineties. Certainly there would be many people (including a number of the artists and critics discussed in these pages) who would now challenge his easy dismissal not only of humor, but also of camp, melodrama, and even bourgeois family values. One of them would be Paul Rudnick, author of the deliriously funny Off-Broadway hit, *Jeffrey*.

"I think that White later recanted that statement," says Rudnick. "But he did also say that humor lets you off the hook, which I don't think is true. At that time he was writing, though, there was so much ignorance and so much lack of any information about what was going on that you certainly wouldn't want to see it trivialized in any way or undermined by humor."[4]

Rudnick's *Jeffrey* definitely undermines standard thinking about AIDS as high art doom and gloom: it opens like a bedroom farce, with seven gay men piling out of a bed stage center, as if they were clowns crammed into a tiny car at a circus. ("People always wait forever for the first kiss in a gay play," Rudnick quips. "So I figured I'd get this sex thing out of the way in the first five seconds and *start* with an orgy.") It then quickly moves to a workout gym where the hero, who (in spite of the curtain-raiser fantasy) has sworn off all sex because of the epidemic—even safe, safer, or safest sex— meets the pumped-up man of his dreams, who turns out to be HIV positive. By examining their growing relationship in tandem with wry commentary on the world of AIDS all around them (benefits, memorial services, 12-step programs), Rudnick offers one of the most complete pictures of the epidemic thus far, insisting laughter must be a part of it.

The playwright readily acknowledges the delicacy of what he was trying to do. "I think up until now, maybe using humor and satire in the way that *Jeffrey* does would have seemed wildly inappropriate. But now ten years along, it began to be necessary actually." As a wickedly funny writer himself (he's also done two comic novels and the screenplays for two of the funniest Hollywood movies of recent years, *Sister Act* and *Addams Family Values*, plus serving as script doctor for the original *Addams Family* as well), he resents the elitist attitude that humor is not a serious art form: "I think Woody Allen once said, when you write comedy you're sitting at the children's table. What a sad and narrow-minded and simply wrong notion! What did he mean by that? Are you sitting at the children's table with Molière?"

Rudnick obviously sees things quite differently: "Humor can be such salvation and such a powerful weapon. Comedy explodes things. Plus, I think comedy is one of those things which separates us from the animals, along with, say, doing our hair. Somehow humor as celebration, or as defense, seems such a terrific and positive aspect of humanity. That we can take life and find it funny or make it funny. To neglect that or see it as lesser is such a mistake."

Frank Rich has celebrated the risks Rudnick took in writing a play that challenges "galloping defeatism" among gays rather as much as it confronts straight bigotry: "Far from being escapist, the laughter along the way is a battle cry, a defiant expression of who these idiosyncratic characters were before AIDS arrived and who they will still be after it has gone. While sex must be safe in the meantime, Mr. Rudnick's sharp, uninhibited wit must, as a matter of life-and-death mission, remain anything but."[5] Rich quotes one of the characters in the play as stating defiantly: "Think of AIDS as the guest who won't leave, the one we all hate. But it's still our party." (Rudnick's gay pride parade is so inclusive that there's even a mother marching with her "preoperative transsexual lesbian son."

Jeffrey's character was originally a supporting character in a different play on which Rudnick was working. "And that suddenly just leapt out as such a rich and comic idea," Rudnick recalls. "It demanded its own play." Like most New Yorkers in the arts, Rudnick had observed the AIDS crisis growing all around him and was impressed by the mobilization, especially among gay activist groups, that came in response to it. "It seemed that it was time to get off my butt. And it just seemed personally necessary. I felt it was the kind of play where I was working out how I felt about all this. I think that's why there has been such an outpouring of AIDS plays: it's one of the only ways we have of coping with it, of talking about the crisis, after being surrounded by so much illness and death. You can't just sit home and talk on the phone. There has to be some larger forum."

At times, the edge to the humor seems to skirt dangerously close to the margins of propriety, but Rudnick brings off scenes involving cruising at memorial services and rich society matrons staging a "Hoe-down for AIDS at the Waldorf" with real aplomb. Nothing is sacred, be it Barneys (the upscale men's clothing store in New York), Mother Teresa, 12-step recovery programs, or Catholic priests with a penchant for boys and old Broadway musicals. "There are so many questions of taste or appropriateness," says Rudnick, describing how he handled that uneasiness. "I found that if there was a moment that made me at all uncomfortable, instead of avoiding it, I would write right toward it. And in rehearsal, if anything felt borderline, we thought, no, that's where it will be exciting. Once in a while we found out there was a line that you did not cross, but that was very rare." For the first few minutes of the play, he recalls, audiences would look around to see if it was OK to laugh. "But by the end of the play, they were so involved with the characters that they forgot to worry."

The play has attracted a wide range of appreciative audiences. It was first presented in New York at a small theater called WPA, where the regular subscription crowd included "a lot of straight people in their sixties and seventies," Rudnick recalls. They were among his best audiences: "Older people, because they have been through the experience of losing friends, and endless experiences with health care, first of all understand that way of life. And they're also not so paranoid about illness, about death, about seeing an end to life. So laughter comes much more easily to them, as does understanding."

Rudnick very much wants the play to reach that wider audience, but at the same time, he has no qualms about admitting how important the core gay audience is to theater in general: "I want to get over that idea of treating the gay audience as if it's marginal and it's only a place to begin. It's so integral to the theater and so supportive of the arts in general that that's *plenty*." AIDS as a subject ups the ante, however: "AIDS is in many ways a litmus test for people's compassion, for people's ability to act either as individuals or as a political entity. It's really brought out the very best and the very worst in people."

Some viewers, for example, have objected to two of the main characters, Sterling and Darius, as "gay stereotypes," since they are an interior decorator and chorus boy, respectively. But Rudnick springs to his characters' defense: "There were outraged essays and editorials and letters, saying, 'This is a awful image for gay people.' I find *that* so horribly bigoted—the idea that these characters should not be allowed onstage. They're not being used for cheap incidental humor. In this play, they're heroes, and they're by far the smartest and sanest people onstage. To reject that kind of gay wit and gay style seems so offensive, among other things."

There are plans to bring *Jeffrey* to the screen, in an independent, low-budget production. "I'd like to have a gay film without that liberal earnestness that most of them always have. I always feel sorry for people involved in gay films, or any attempt at making a mainstream gay film, because every movie has this enormous burden on it of representing every possible gay voice. No movie should have to do that; no movie can do that. It's ridiculous. Every time you make *Philadelphia* or *Longtime Companion*, you go in knowing you are going to be attacked from every side. You can't win. You have to work in this incredible straight-jacket all the time."

To the inevitable question, Rudnick replies: "People ask me if I'm going to write another play about AIDS, and I say, hey, wait a minute, it's not a specialty act, it's not a tap moment. I wish I didn't have to write about it any more, wouldn't that be nice? How do you live with this, how do you acknowledge that this is going to be a part of everyone's life for at least the near future?" As the title character in *Jeffrey* laments, "Sex was never meant to be safe, or negotiated, or fatal." Drama—and comedy—is a way to explore that contradiction, to challenge its too-easy assumptions.

Nicky Silver's *Pterodactyls* offers another comic vision of the AIDS nightmare. In it, a young gay man named Todd returns home to his Philadelphia Main Line family after five years of sexual abandon in New York City. He has AIDS, he announces, though he has no symptoms whatsoever (one has to allow Silver this dramatic license, I suppose: it's an intriguing concept, though perhaps somewhat wanting in terms of medical correctness). All of the other members of the family are far sicker than Todd, in fact: His sister Emma is a neurasthenic hypochondriac who "forgets things" ("Facts run through me like Chinese food."); his mother is an alcoholic and compulsive shopper; and his father is a macho philanderer with sexual feelings for his daughter (parallelling those the mother has for Todd). Emma's fiancé, a wimpy waiter who dreams of being a movie director and agrees to be the family maid (short skirt and all), rounds out the household.

The play begins with Todd delivering a wacky monologue about the history of the earth and civilization. Since he has forgotten his notes, the lecture runs a bit awry, especially after the dinosaurs and pterodactyls die off and human history begins in earnest:

> During the Renaissance, people got very fat. Picasso sculpted *David*, Marco Polo invented pizza. Columbus discovered the New World and Gaetan Dugas discovered the Fountain of Youth. Europeans imported tea, to drink, and Africans, to do their work. Edison invented the telephone. Martha Graham invented modern dance. Hitler invented fascism and Rose Kennedy invented nepotism.[6]

The metaphor of the dinosaurs dying out haunts the play, especially after Todd begins to find strange bones in the back yard which turn out to be those of a Tyrannosaurus rex. Silver clarified the image in an interview that accompanies the publication of the script in *American Theatre*:

> In *Pterodactyls*, the characters—like all of us—have learned to survive in this grotesque world of disfigurement and dysfunction through denial. Well that fine's except now we have a situation, because of AIDS, where our denial could end up eliminating the species. As a culture, America condemned itself to be in this precarious state because we didn't care about the people who were dying to begin with—these were homosexuals, minorities, people of color, drug abusers, and we said, "Well, good, let them die. Who cares, we'll weed out the race. It's Darwinism." Because we didn't care, this disease expanded exponentially.[7]

In a wicked turn of fate, Todd survives all of the other characters and is left alone, still asymptomatic, with the T-rex skeleton at the end of the play. Or maybe he was a ghost all along, and simply came back to witness his revenge being played out. "Structurally, it's really a revenge play," says Silver. "Someone coming back and taking revenge on a family (ergo a society) that he could not please no matter what he did anyway. He comes home and seduces his sister's fiancé, and provides her with a gun to kill herself, and sends dad out into the tundra to die, and pours ma drinks until she's history."[8]

The fact that Todd is a survivor hardly makes him a hero, however, as Silver is quick to stress, both in conversation and the playwright's notes in the published edition of the play. "None of these people are heroes or villains, they're just sort of people muddling along, hurting each other willy-nilly. Todd is a survivor because he has some work to do." Todd's amoral stance throughout is one of the more disturbing aspects of this unsettling comic spin on sex and responsibility in the age of AIDS.

In his Sunday review in the *Times*, David Richards is struck by the "strange and compelling sadness" underlying the zany absurdism of the play.[9] A daily critic at the same paper, Ben Brantley, zeroed in on the "poignantly grotesque symbols of a species on the verge of extinction."[10] As a playwright, Silver is clearly playing with this delicate balance between high camp and deadly earnestness. "I would say that if there's a characteristic to my writing, stylistically, it is a desire as a playwright to go as far as I can for a laugh, and then to go as far as I can seriously, in a given piece of theater."[11]

Silver lost a close friend to AIDS in 1981 but had postponed dealing directly with the subject until *Pterodactyls*: "I had been wanting to write something on the subject of AIDS for a very long time. My closest friend in the whole world died very early in the history of the epidemic, in 1981, when he was diagnosed with GRID, or Gay Related Immune Deficiency, which is what they called it then. It had seeped into my work in minor ways, and I figure I needed to allow enough time to pass to have some kind of perspective on it. It took really about ten years until I got to the point where I no longer felt bad about it, until what sadness I had was equaled by the anger I was ready to vent."

In addition, Silver says, "There was a glut, well not a glut, but a number of plays that people now refer to as the first generation of AIDS plays. Or TV movies like *An Early Frost*, where sad, sweet homosexuals were slowly, sympathetically succumbing. It just was not my nature to write something like that, nor did I want to write something like that." In general, he felt, "The issue seemed too mammoth for me to present on stage. We were in a real global crisis, and I didn't see how to write about that for the stage, which is an intimate medium, where there's a small group of people standing in front of a slightly larger group of people telling a personal story. There have been some attempts at an epic approach to AIDS in the theater. But it's not the nature of theater to tell anything other than small stories. The most epic plays of all time, are still just really telling a small story that's symbolic of something bigger. Even *Angels in America* is telling three small stories at once."

"People who go to the theater go for the reasons that theater is known for: language, and the immediacy of being in the room, what's going on in front of you. All of my plays have that direct address thing, of some kind or another."

But that address is always in Silver's own idiosyncratic voice. "My natural inclination is to find humor in everything," he admits. That humor has tended to be madcap and relatively absurd in earlier works with titles like *My Marriage to Ernest Borgnine* and *Fat Men in Skirts*, and themes have run the gamut from incest to cannibalism ("There aren't many taboos left after that."). But in *Pterodactyls*, the loopy humor is mixed with a good deal of anger: "I think of it as a really angry play— the anger phase of mourning. I don't know whether that's supposed to come before or after grief. But I think it's more appropriate at this point in time to be angry than sad. We've been sad for a long time and it hasn't gotten us very far."

As he notes in his introduction to the play, that mixture of anger and ironic wit should be incorporated into the actual acting style of the play: "We were very blessed in the original production with actors who instinctively understood that broad comedy and utter despair are juxtaposed here, but not blended. The distinction between these two conflicting spirits must remain sharp. Humor should not be softened nor rage diluted in the hopes of achieving an even texture: the texture is not intended to be even." [12]

AIDS will continue to haunt his anger, he feels, if not his writing: "At first it was rather daunting to think of writing about anything else after this. There are other issues, but when you're dead, they're moot."

20

Alchemy & Angels in America

In fact alchemy may be called the art of the transmutation
of the soul. In saying this I am not seeking to deny that
alchemists also knew and practised metallurgical procedures such as the purification and alloying of metals; their
real work, however, for which all these procedures were
the outward supports or "operational" symbols, was the
transmutation of the soul.

—Titus Burckhardt, *Alchemy*[1]

t the end of the first part of *Angels in America*, Tony
Kushner's Pulitzer Prize-winning play about AIDS, an
angel does indeed appear in America, flying down from
the theatrical heavens and greeting the play's main character, a sassy young PWA named Prior, with the following enigmatic curtain line:

Greetings, Prophet;
The Great Work begins:
The Messenger has arrived.[2]

Critics have commented at length on the theatricality of the ending,
and—as the world awaited the premiere of Part Two of the play—spec-

ulation ran rampant about what "great work" Prior was going to undertake in Part Two.

Even after the second part (*Perestroika*) joined the first (*Millennium Approaches*) in regular rotation in New York and London, most commentators tended to take the angelic announcement as kind of a vague metaphor for Prior's struggle with AIDS. Virtually no mention has been made, in the press or elsewhere, of one rather obvious interpretation of the reference: in medieval alchemy, the Great Work (capitalized, as Kushner has it in the script) is the "alchemical marriage," the making of pure gold from base lead. This alchemy symbolizes the transformation of the inner soul of the alchemist from his (or her) basic instinctual self into a higher spiritual being. That Great Work is, indeed, a great struggle—a wrestling with an angel (as in the dream of Jacob in the Old Testament). It is a difficult, prolonged battle that is, among other things, a trial by fire leading to purification, clarification, and rebirth.

Such an interpretation in no way negates the dramatic, psychological, or political resonances of Kushner's work: Prior's transformation in *Perestroika* certainly manifests itself in rather straightforward political rhetoric, just as his call-to-arms is staged in rather secular (and indeed sexual) imagery. Kushner is also a tour-de-force writer, whose dialogue absolutely sings and whose characters come to life with an incandesence rare in contemporary theater. But beyond these effects there are also very big ideas, which can be seen on a number of different levels: dramatic, political, and spiritual.

It is this multi-level approach that has paid off, winning the praise of critics and audiences alike in productions in Los Angeles, New York, and London, although even the most enthusiastic find the work problematic to categorize. "'Angels in America' has no theatrical precedent that I can think of," wrote Vincent Canby in the *New York Times*. "It has something of the dark freedom expressed in novels of magic realism, but it's not a novel. It's an occasionally uproarious, often brutal and sorrowful circus with what might be called novelistic tendencies and a theatrical heart. It takes its spirit and method from its central character, Prior Walter, the acid-tongued sometime drag queen who, in life and in his extensive hallucinations, refuses to knuckle under to AIDS."[3] Frank Rich, writing his final daily drama review for the same paper (before shifting posts), waxes even more enthusiastic, calling *Perestroika* "a true millenial work of art, uplifting, hugely comic and pantheistically religious in a very American style."[4] John Lahr of the *New Yorker* called the fall 1992 production at the Mark Taper Forum in Los Angeles "a victory for Kushner, for theatre, for the transforming power of the imagination to turn devastation into beauty."[5]

And for those willing to look a bit deeper, something else is also going on, beyond politics or onstage pyrotechnics. To suggest such an esoteric interpretation is hardly cockamamie, considering the complex allusiveness of Kushner's writing,[6] and his own knowledge in medieval magic as exhibited in his best-known play prior to *Angels in America:* an adaptation of Corneille's *The Illusion,* a play within a play about a sorcerer's apprentice in the early seventeenth century. At one point in that earlier work, the main character insists: "My visions are concocted through a violent synthesis, a forced conflagration of light and shadow, matter and gossamer, blood and air.... I am a chemist of emotions.... The heart chases memory through the cavern of dreams."[7] (In that play, as in *Angels in America,* Kushner maintains a sardonic, agnostic distance from the mysteries being discussed—and all the magic turns out to be just an illusion in the end—but he clearly has done his research and knows exactly what he's talking about.)

But to understand how he's used the metaphor of spiritual alchemy, we need to first take a look at the basic plot of Kushner's massive, two-part "gay fantasia on national themes," keeping in mind that AIDS itself, in all its horror, ironically may be the very Philosopher's Stone that the characters in the two plays—and the collective America that they represent—must "possess" in order to achieve the necessary transformation, be it political or spiritual.

Both plays center around the telling, as Nicky Silver put it, of "three small stories at once." Two of those stories center on two couples, one gay and one straight, who are on the verge of splitting up; the third involves lawyer and loner Roy Cohn, who is facing the only separation he can comprehend, his own death. The gay couple, Prior and Louis, are fighting primarily because Louis can't deal with Prior's diagnosis with AIDS. Joe and Harper Pitt, a Mormon couple living in New York City, are moving closer and closer to divorce, partly because of Harper's deteriorating mental condition and partly because of Joe's latent homosexuality. Louis and Joe work in the same federal courthouse (Louis as a word processor, Joe as a chief clerk), and Joe is also being wooed professionally by Cohn, who wants him to move to Washington to do his dirty work. Roy is also gay, though viciously homophobic, and he has AIDS, which aligns him thematically (but hardly tempermentally) with Prior. Prior becomes seriously ill and is rushed to the hospital; Louis's devotion falters and he vanishes from the scene. Harper, Joe's wife, goes increasingly (and intriguingly) bonkers and takes more and more pills. Joe calls his mother Hannah in Salt Lake City to tell her he's gay, and she decides to sell her home and head for New York City.

At about that point, near the end of the first part of *Angels*, which is called *Millennium Approaches,* the Angel first appears to Prior. Kushner describes her in the cast of characters as: "four divine emanations, Fluor, Phosphor, Lumen and Candle, manifest in One: the Continental Principality of America. She has magnificent steel-gray wings." Prior finds the whole situation "very Steven Spielberg" and gets an erection.

In *Perestroika*, Roy's nurse is a black drag queen named Belize, a former lover of Prior who is also Louis's political sparring mate on questions of political correctness. Louis starts an affair with Joe shortly after leaving Prior; good bedfellows, the two are strange political soulmates: Louis is stridently leftist; Joe, adamantly conservative. Joe is also a Mormon, something totally beyond the ken of Jewish-agnostic Louis. Joe's mother Hannah arrives in New York City, where she gets a job at the Mormon's Visitor Center and tries to bring Harper back to reality (just after Harper is arrested for trying to gnaw down a tree in Brooklyn's Prospect Park, thinking she's a beaver and that she's in Antarctica) and to reunite Heather and Joe.

The Angel comes back and brings Prior the Sacred Prophetic Implements, a pair of weird glasses and a Book with steel pages. He doesn't much like what he sees through the spectacles, but the Book allows him to achieve his first orgasm in months. The Angel attempts to deliver a sermon to him advocating a life of absolute religious, political, and sexual conservatism, insisting that the only thing that will bring God back (he disappeared during the San Francisco earthquake in 1906) is if people STOP MOVING (don't migrate, don't intermarry, and certainly don't engage in some of the activities Prior recently found integral to his life and identity). Prior ignores the message, which seems rather unrelated to the sexual shenanigans of the Angel anyway.

Roy Cohn has gotten sicker and starts being tormented by the ghost of Ethel Rosenberg, whose execution he had masterminded by influencing the judge at her trial. Joe and Louis fumble at a relationship. Louis visits Prior and tries to rekindle the relationship; Prior tells him to get lost. Louis argues with Joe over his Roy Cohn connection, and Joe beats him up. Cohn dies, and Ethel's ghost helps Louis (who has come to the hospital to steal Cohn's hoard of AZT, to give to Prior) say Kaddish for him. Hannah meets Prior just as he collapses one day in Central Park and helps get him to the hospital; they form a unexpected alliance. Joe visits Harper and tries to rekindle their relationship; Harper tells him to get lost. Prior wrestles with the Angel and follows her to heaven, where he gives back the Book and insists on his blessing, which is simply "more life."

Four years pass. Belize and Louis are still arguing politics. Hannah has become acclimated to life in New York City. Both Harper and Joe are absent. Prior is a survivor, having lived with AIDS for five years (six months longer than his relationship with Louis, he points out). Having refused the Angel's anti-migratory message of stasis, he has, through the experience and the struggle with her, achieved the necessary transformation to go on, a spiritualized conscience that allows him to stand up and lead: "This disease will be the end of many of us, but not nearly all, and the dead will be commemorated and will struggle on with the living, and we are not going away. We won't die secret deaths anymore. The world only spins forward. We will be citizens. The time has come." [8]

The changes Prior experiences in the two plays correspond interestingly to the various stages of spiritual alchemy described by such historians of religion as Titus Burckhardt and Mircea Eliade. Alchemy is thought by them to be an ancient science of self-knowledge and transformation, inherent in many religious traditions, both East and West, its real secret goal having been disguised in the myth that the "science" is merely about transforming lesser metals into gold (which may have been possible as well, but which is more or less beside the point). The real goal of it all, put in Prior's words, would simply be "more life." Or as Mircea Eliade wrote: "The writings of Chinese, Indian, Islamic and European alchemists refer to methods, experiments and recipes capable of healing men and thus prolonging human life indefinitely...and consequently able to grant human immortality." [9]

The process of alchemy, like the structure of the play *Angels in America*, consists of two parts. In the spiritual discipline, these are called the Lesser Work and the Greater Work. Each has three stages, related to an astrological planetary symbol. The Lesser Work begins with Saturn-dominated "blackening, putrefaction, mortification" and a period "dying to the world"[10]; then goes through the Jupiter-driven phase of expansion of the soul "rising out of chaos"; and reaches a white or Moon-related stage when "All the potentialities of the soul contained in the initial chaos have now been fully developed and have united with one another in a state of undivided purity." In Part One of the play, Prior goes through a similar physical, mental, and emotional blackening, putrefaction, and mortification with his first brutalizing AIDS symptoms; he reacts with spunk and resilience, refusing to accept the chaos; and then the Angel, dressed in white, arrives to announce his challenge.

According to Burckhardt, "The first three stages correspond to the 'spiritualization of the body,' and the last three to the 'embodying of the spirit.'" This second half of the process, the Greater Work, combines the Venus-ruled "volative power of feminine Quicksilver" (quite probably the virus itself, but more on that in a moment) with the Mars-ruled "incarnation of the Divine Word" to achieve in the completion of the Great Work, the victory of the Spirit represented by the Sun: "What was only principally and potentially present in the early stages is here manifest." Correspondingly, in Part Two of *Angels in America*, Prior again falls prey to the devastations of the virus, then confronts the Angel and returns the Book to Heaven, allowing him to wrest the blessing of "more life" from those in charge and return to Earth with his new message, the "gold" of his struggle.

In order for any of this transformation to take place, physical elements must be reduced to basics, the *materia prima*, of nature. This can take place in alchemy only through a kind of marriage, or commerce of such contrary or opposing powers:

> The two phases of Nature—dissolution and coagulation—which seem opposed from a superficial point of view but which in reality are mutually complementary, can in a certain sense be related to the two poles, essence and substance.... Within Nature it is alchemical Sulphur which corresponds to the active pole, and alchemical Quicksilver which corresponds to the passive pole.

Sulphur and Quicksilver are the key elements necessary so that matter (the physical body) can be healed and transformed. According to the alchemists, "In the soul Sulphur represents the essence or spirit, whereas Quicksilver corresponds to the soul itself in its receptive and passive role." And Quicksilver is "present in blood and semen" and is known for the incredible speed of its movements and its "great 'desire' to combine with related metals." What better symbolic description of the deadly, mysterious virus called AIDS: "The dissolving and disintegrating power of Quicksilver has a terrible aspect. It is the 'poisonous dragon' which devours everything; it is the water which makes one shudder and which brings the presentiment of death."

What then is Sulphur, which must be married to Quicksilver in the crucible of the human body to stop its destruction and to create the marriage, the transformation? For Prior, could it be other than Fluor, Phosphor, Lumen, and Candle Herself, the principality with whom he has sex, by the Book?

When Prior visits Heaven, he undergoes the first change, shedding his black prophet robes (the *nigredo* or blackening phase of alchemy), revealing his white hospital robe underneath (*albedo*, the bleaching/whitening phase) and approaches the final *rubedo* or reddening phase: "Black is the absence of colour and light. White is purity; it is undivided light—light not broken down into colours. Red is the epitome of colour, its zenith and its point of greatest intensity." This corresponds to the Angel's new warning of what Prior's request for "more life" will entail, for more life equals more suffering:

> When all your ravaging returns to you
> With the rising, scorching, unrelenting Sun:
> When morning blisters crimson
> And bears all life away,
> A tidal wave of Protean Fire
> That curls around the planet
> And bares the Earth clean as bone.[11]

"Bless me anyway," Prior insists. People living with AIDS have been through that, he declares—and worse: "When they're more spirit than body, more sores than skin, when they're burned and in agony, when flies lay eggs in the corners of the eyes of their children, they live. Death usually has to *take* life away.... We live past hope.... Bless me anyway. I want more life."[12]

As Prior knows only too well, this last phase is not a blissed out state

of angelic whiteness, purity, and peace, but something much more startling and unforgettable, like blood and fire and even the royal purple
like the lesions that mark this rite of passage, as Burckhardt puts it:
"After the 'spiritualization of the body'—which in a certain sense corresponds to bleaching, and supersedes the initial blackness of corruption,
comes, as the completion, the 'embodying of the spirit' with its royal
purple-red colour."

The chemical marriage is complete, on Earth (and in America in the
Age of AIDS) as it is in Heaven. As Eliade states:

> To conclude, we may say that the alchemist completed the last
> stage of the very ancient program, begun by early man the moment
> he undertook to transform nature. The concept of alchemical trans-
> mutation is the last expression of the immemorial belief in the pos-
> sibility of changing Nature by human labor. The myth of alchemy
> is one of the rare optimistic myths. Indeed, the *opus alchemicum* not
> only changes, perfects, or redeems Nature, but also brings to per-
> fection human existence: it confers health, perennial youth, and
> even immortality. In the perspective of the history of religions, one
> can say that through alchemy man recovers his original perfection,
> the loss of which is recounted in so many tragic myths from all
> over the world.[13]

What exactly is going on here? Has Kushner taken his viewers somewhere out into the ether of ecstatic spiritual bliss or New Age religiosi-
ty? Hardly. Remember when Prior gets to Heaven in his dream, he's not
ready to buy into any of the stuff that's going on there. "Bless me anyway," he insists, indicating Kushner is far too agnostic—and seriously
political—a thinker for that. The audience is never really expected to
believe that the Angel is real, but at the same time she's never quite
merely the product of Prior's imagination—not simply an airy phantom
like the play magic in his Kushner's earlier play, *The Illusion.*

Similarly, the alchemical metaphors just mentioned should be taken
more as gentle underpinnings of an already strong piece of dramatic
inspiration. They reinforce Kushner's basic theme, symbolically, but
they're not really necessary to his message, which is as much political as
spiritual, and far more pragmatic than esoteric.

When *Time Magazine* did a special cover story on "Angels," Kushner
gave an interviewer some answers that clearly didn't jibe with the tone

of the rest of the article. "I'm certain that if we are to solve the problems on earth, we will have to do it ourselves," he said, adding, "New Age theology says we live in a benign universe where all you have to do is ask an angel for help. This makes things like Sarajevo difficult to understand."[14] The *Time* writer concludes, "The angel in his play in no way is meant to absolve humans of tough choices and hard spiritual work"—almost an understatement about the job of living with AIDS.

A similar attitude is reflected in a note Kushner posted on the backstage bulletin board when the original double-bill of *Millennium Approaches* and *Perestroika* opened at the Mark Taper Forum in Los Angeles:

> And how else should an angel land on earth but with the utmost difficulty? If we are to be visisted by angels we will have to call them down with sweat and strain, we will have to drag them out of the skies, and the efforts we expend to draw the heavens to an earthly place may well leave us too exhausted to appreciate the fruits of our labors: an angel, even with torn robes and ruffled feathers, is in our midst.[15]

What the Angel in the plays represents is hope, struggle, resistance: she is the force (and perhaps the only force) which can meet AIDS head-on and combat that other brutally real/unreal mysterious phantom force in a fight to the finish. Once Prior has known her, he can face that same struggle in himself.

AIDS has transformed many of its combatants in just such a way. Kushner is unique in his ability to capture the metaphor so powerfully onstage in the brilliance of his language, characterization, and plot, but there are dozens of other examples throughout this book of the change and crystallization of body, mind, and spirit that AIDS has demanded of its subjects. And the art of AIDS will go on, turning anger and horror into beauty and hope, until it is no longer necessary.

POSTLUDE

Word Is Out

If this study has focused exclusively on the representation of AIDS in the performing and visual arts, leaving out the literary arts, it has done so not with any intention to belittle the very important work being done in the areas of fiction or poetry—or indeed of diaries and journals, criticism and essays, or even the various forms of journalism devoted to the epidemic. There have been major contributions in all these areas (subject, perhaps, for another volume), and the impact of works like Paul Monette's *Borrowed Time*, a heartfelt journal of his caretaking a lover dying with AIDS, or the accounts by Jeffrey Schmaltz or Harold Brodkey of their own battles with the condition, published in the *New York Times* and the *New Yorker*, respectively, are as important in their way as a movie like *Philadelphia*, the cable TV version of *And the Band Played On*, Salt-n-Pepa rapping out "Let's Talk About AIDS," or the dances of *A Demand Performance*. In each case, the message is being spread to a particular audience, some of whom admittedly are somewhat elite (gay, well-educated, white—for starters), but others of whom are fairly uneducated or ill-educated about AIDS. Hatred, discrimination, and fear thrive on ignorance. Once the word is out about the facts and truths of this condition—and its transmission—such misrepresentations and misinterpretations begin to loose their force. Once the false equations are challenged—those which erroneously confuse AIDS the condition (which does not discriminate) with those who have it—some sort of honest dialogue can begin. Once AIDS is seen as a medical and personal problem, not social stigma, the Great Work can begin, both realistically *and* metaphorically, to confront both it and the equally insidious epidemics of intolerance and fear that attach themselves to it.

AIDS must not be invisible, unmentionable, unthinkable. Every single red ribbon or SILENCE = DEATH button or condom ad on TV or *Red Hot + Country* cassette gets this word out. So do Doonesbury cartoons featuring a character with AIDS, and appearances by characters with AIDS (gay, straight, or indifferent) on TV sitcoms and dramas. So do New York subway posters (in Spanish and English) about the trials of Julio and Marisol in the age of AIDS. So do obituaries which list not only the cause of death (not just for celebrities but for ordinary people as well), but also the names and identities of the longtime companions of the deceased and details of the commitment of the person to AIDS-related causes. Each single piece of information adds to the store of data in each reader or viewer's mind about AIDS, making it real, ordinary, graspable—and at the same time showing that each case is unique and individual, so that the total picture is far from simplistic.

Bit by bit, these pieces of information add up to make AIDS not something that "happens" to faceless strangers, but to real people with families, with lovers, with careers and hopes and dreams like everyone else. When these people happen to be role models already, for young blacks, for example, or young Latinos, or young gays, what a power of example those facing it could be by choosing to acknowledge their condition and/or their sexuality in public: self-"outing" as both personal and peer group empowerment. This epidemic needs to be more than secrets revealed in obituaries. It needs to be shared information, shared struggle, shared hope.

Other stories need to be told as well, those of the "worried well"; those of people who test positive for the HIV virus, but never become ill; those who live full and happy lives even after being diagnosed with full-blown AIDS (as Michael Callen did for over 12 years); those who refuse to give up, even under what sometimes seem the bleakest of circumstances. Not everyone automatically dies of AIDS. Not everyone who tests positive will develop AIDS. And not everyone who dies a sad, sudden, premature, or mysterious death dies of AIDS. All these stories also deserve to be told and shown, heard and viewed.

What we need is a kind of permanent repository for these stories, these works of art—a safe place where people with AIDS can know that their words, their visions, will not be forgotten. We need, in a way, our own holocaust museum. Various projects have been started in each of the arts, but much more needs to be done.

Otherwise, as Jeffrey Schmaltz worries in his last article for the *New York Times*, AIDS burnout may start to set in: "I usually say that my epitaph is not a phrase but the body of my work. I am writing it with each article including this one. But actually, there is a phrase that I want shouted at my funeral and written on the memorial cards, a phrase that captures the mix of cynicism and despair that I feel right now and that I will almost certainly take to my grave: '*Whatever happened to AIDS?*'"[1] Schmaltz died shortly after completing the article, which was published three weeks after his death. His final message is chilling: what if people simply start to forget? Will all this work, all this protest, all this art have been in vain? The solution is clear: Without that terrifyingly *personal* identification that Schmaltz exhibits in this *cri de couer*, AIDS has no real or lasting meaning for any of us.

But through that personalization, transformations continue to happen regularly, including one very important one that perhaps Schmaltz couldn't see because it was taking place right in front of him: Confronted with a death in the family, the *Times* itself changed from an uptight bastion of strident homophobia to a paper that now contains some of the best AIDS reportage in the nation—a paper that could openly chronicle Schmaltz's medical condition and sexual identity, then genuinely mourn his death; a paper whose new publisher could give the keynote address at a 1993 convocation of gay and lesbian journalists. That change occured thanks, by and large, to one man's presence and courage. Like the slave in the Negro spiritual, Schmaltz had a lonesome highway to walk (even if it was just across a newsroom): Nobody else could walk it for him; he had to walk it by himself.

Nothing will ever explain AIDS; nothing will ever excuse or justify it, make it understandable, acceptable, or in any way "right." Yet its incontrovertible presence gives it an uncanny strength and power as a contemporary metaphor, not just as a symbol of the incomprehensible but as a challenge to everything that is decent, humane, and fair. Without its stigma—without, perhaps, even its very horror—today's society might not have been moved to discover its own conscience.

Like any state of suffering, AIDS arrived bearing an oblique, secret gift: clarity of vision achieved through facing the pain and rage of its very meaninglessness—a clarity available not only to the person suffering, but to those around him or her, the friends and family, the caretakers and caregivers, and perhaps even to society as a whole. The gift moves out in quiet circles: those closest feel the vibrations most strongly; those farther away experience only a ripple effect, but something in them is touched, glimpsed, half-recognized; later coming closer, the waves become impossible to ignore.

What began as stigma—not always as open hatred, but more as fear, protectiveness, exclusion of everything perceived as alien, as dis-ease—is met head on by this new force, this conscience, and something else must arise out of the struggle between the two, as between all supposed opposites: evil and good, lower and higher, death and life. This third life force, born of stigma and fear meeting conscience and conscious awareness head on, is art, the attempt throughout history to reflect this struggle, this dichotomy, this schizophrenic balancing act between beauty and horror, between meaning and chaos.

When Peter was dying, I went to speak to a woman whose clear-minded teaching and wisdom had helped me through the struggle thus far. She told me that years before, during a time of great personal crisis in her own life, she too had wished to speak to her teacher but had been unable to reach him because of a wartime emergency. Instead, she had been told the following story, which she then repeated to me. The teacher in question had once been approached by yet another student who had traveled a long distance, at tremendous expense, to seek his advice, following a tremendous personal loss. The man could stay only three days. On the first day, the teacher seemed to ignore him, playing with children in the room. On the second day, he spoke only to others who kept coming and going as the man tried to speak of his own grief, his own struggle. On the third day, it was the same. The man left in despair. The teacher's chief assistant, horrified at what she had seen, reproached him for his actions. "Couldn't you see how great his need was to speak with you? How could you refuse him your help?" The teacher shrugged sadly. "But, of course," he said. "That is exactly why I *could not.* I had not the right."

As shocking as it sounds, AIDS too represents this gift of suffering, awareness, and transformation—a right that cannot be interfered with, no matter how great our rage or pain. That's what the struggle—with the Angel, with AIDS, with our individual and collective souls—is all about.

We still have a right to our rage, our grief, our insistence on abolishing this horror from our lives so that someday soon there no longer will be a need for art about living with AIDS, but only about remembering that time of trial. But we must never forget. And until that time, each of us must ultimately face AIDS alone, as our legacy, our gift, our responsibility.

Montana Healing

A POEM CYCLE FOR PETER LaBELLA

There

The week before Thanksgiving, as we made the bed—
That same bed we've shared through eight years of
Loving, fighting, making up, making do—you let
The bomb drop and we both knew there was no
Way to make this go away, to fold or tuck it under the
Mattress and forget about it. "You know, I'm probably
Going to die from this," you said with a shrug. No build-up,
Just the facts, in your own self-effacing way. The words
Froze in the air: we'd left them unspoken for so long,
As if silence could somehow soften them, or at least
Postpone their numbing terror. "What will you do then?"
You wondered, with a half-smile, "You can't even cook."
I moved awkwardly around the half-made bed to try to
Hold you tight, to make everything all right, but instead
Everything collapsed, and all the rage, denial, and hard
Bargaining that Kubler-Ross describes raced through
Me, all mixed up. It's true, I know: in a year, in a month,
In a day, it could happen—suddenly you'll simply not be
There. And still all you seem to worry about is me, how
I'll go on. We've watched the symptoms mount with mute
Despair: swollen glands, night sweats, sudden strange
Fevers and losses of weight, energy, and will. Yet you
Seem to face each setback with a particular proud fury,
As if that anger could negate at least some of the fear
And frustration that shakes inside you every minute of
Each day. Now, if I close my eyes, and the roaring stops,
I see you standing there by the jukebox in Julius's,
Eight years ago this month. Only our eyes spoke then,
And I left with friends to go home to take care of
Some long unfinished business. The next night I came
Back to the bar, knowing somehow that I'd find you
There, by the jukebox, waiting to help me make the bed.
—October 14, 1986

Ties That Bind

You held on, in spite of all the doctors' dire
Predictions, and we had one last Thanksgiving
Meal together, right down to the yellow turnips
You loved so much. Nine years, nine turkeys;
It was always our favorite day. Then three
Nights later you left, quietly, softly, without
A word. But who needs long goodbyes after all
Our hellos? I'm holding up pretty well, I guess,
Unless I hear the score from *Les Misèrables* —
"Empty Chairs at Empty Tables," especially, or
"Bring Him Home." But even that, though it
Drains so much out of me, doesn't diminish me.
How could I be anything but full, after all we
Shared, right down to your last "I can't" as the
Thermometer fell? Dying is a part of life, its
Last and deepest mystery. We watched it, just as
We sat through nine years of dance and "Dynasty":
Together, linked, inseparable even (especially) now.

—December 29, 1987

Mirrors

It doesn't get easier, which is the one thing
(Well, maybe not the only thing) they never
Tell you. You wake up next to emptiness,
And your day begins alone, hollow, without
Any real reason or flow. Your foot touches the
Cold floor that only cat feet, or your own,
Touch now. The bathroom mirror sends out
Only solo reflections. You shave, you wash,
You brush your teeth. His toothbrush is
Still there. You can't quite bring yourself
To throw it away. Nine years take their
Toll, as blessings fade to brittle memories.
Inside, the mirror shatters, as you blink,
Shivering slightly, and face another day.

— March 17, 1988

Montana Sky Time

This is the quiet hour, the limbo stretch
When the only clock is the sky or the
Heart. Birds still flutter and mosquitoes
Dart in for the kill, but the hills
And clouds are rigid, ready for night
But restive with life. I have never been
Quite this alone. There is something
Awesome, terrible, and comforting in
All this emptiness, this twilight glow.
The hole you left is there, as always
Despite old adages about what heals all
Wounds), but greeting that, resilient,
Is a deeper pulse, ticking, content
With itself: available, recognizable,
New. I contain it: it doesn't run away
Gopher-shy at the sound of my awkward
Steps, or jerk the line, impatient as a
Hungry trout. It's mine. I belong to it,
Having longed so to synchronize again.

— August 1, 1989

Atop Homer Youngs

How odd to find a butterfly two miles up in the sky,
On top of the highest mountain on the horizon of my
Past two summers. After a six-hour climb, looking for
A rock to rest, I discover it's beaten me to the summit.
Wings flapping, orange and black, treading high air:
Very like a monarch, except smaller and somehow
More mothlike. It shares the space easily with me, and
With the little rodent peeking around the cairn—a space
It's true, belonging to something higher, more free
Than any of us. I sit eyes closed, absorbing the sun, then
Try to map the hidden lakes, the twisting creeks, the
Other peaks around me on three sides. There's an almost
Eerie silence now, after the thunderstorm I climbed above,
Watching it send lightning bolts and hail on the Big Hole
Valley below, veiling for a while those other mountains.

Then sunlight, a panorama stretching from ripening hayfields
In the east to the spot where the sun is threatening to set
Too soon in the west. The descent remains. Already it starts
To nag, to pull me back down to the trail below. This
Is the real shock of climbing: You can't stay. You
Must go back to whatever it was that excitement, hope,
Determination brought you beyond. It waits, gaping. Today
Even if I go down twice as fast as I came up, I'll
Barely make it down to the lake below by twilight,
And even then, there remains a five-mile trek through
Woods, across creeks and meadows, in almost pitch-black,
On a night with no moon. How foolish to climb alone,
To ignore the storm, to wait so late to start back, without
Even a flashlight against the dark. Butterflies live just
A single summer, after a long winter trapped in a cocoon.
Still, who's to say what they then see, alone, above and free?
                                        —July 24, 1990

A Naming

Today I named a lake for you, a little alpine lake
Cradled high in the Bitterroots. It's what they call
A cirque, surrounded on three sides by rocky cliffs:
A half-bowl set into the mountain, with water of the
Deepest bluish-green. I spotted it there a week ago,
Looking down from a peak above, and knew it was my
Next climb. Maps out here mix things up a bit: most
Don't name this spot at all—or even indicate that it
Exists—and one insists that it's called Little Lake,
Though actually that one (which is perfectly nice and
Isolated: it, too, was visible from up on Homer Youngs
And even had a mountain goat) is several miles away
And much lower down. Perhaps these high, elusive lakes
Get named and named again by wanderers like me: who's
To say what dignifies the nomenclature of a map? But
Nearby are Little Joe's Lake, Heart Lake, Little Lake
And several without names. The posted trail to Little Lake
Took me quite a way astray: I had to backtrack along
A rocky ridge to get to where I knew our lake must
Be, having mapped it in my head, from up there, the week

Before. I found it at last, just as a heavy, sudden rain
Began, then hail: I couldn't linger, but still I stayed
Long enough to sense a power of place: something sacred,
Something really mine. I named it Little Peter's Lake
Without hesitation, not knowing why you'd seemed so close
To me today—not unusual, that feeling, but why particularly
Today? I thought maybe it was the novel, of which you are
Also so much a part, that's being written in my head as I
Walk these Montana mountains. But then as I turned back
And started down the trail towards the green Toyota jeep,
Something nagged at me, something not quite clear, and
There it was: your birthday—today you'd be thirty-seven.
Four years ago, I bought you that shirt you loved to wear:
Yellow, with little green stripes. I saw you shrink in it
To almost nothing, skeletal and afraid, but still you always
Chose it on special days. You weren't "diagnosed" yet then
But I think we both knew—without saying it. Three years
Ago, another hospitalization (all our holidays by then were
Marked by crisis: my birthday and yours, Palm Sunday, Easter
And that final Thanksgiving): this time I brought you those
Shorty pajamas, a pair of shoes (I think, hoping against
Hope you would walk again, in them), and a little purple
Crystal, which you kept by your bed until the end. I often
Found you holding it, tightly, those last months: I hope it
Helped. It seemed so feeble a gift. And now, today, this lake.

                                            —July 28, 1990

Three Oaks

Three oak trees guard you in a lopsided
Triangle of coincidental power. Their
Leaves fall all around,everywhere except
On the grass above you. The ground there
Looks swept clean by the sky. My roses
(Five yellow, one red, with tiny daisies
That at first I mistook for baby's breath)
Tremble softly above your head. The air
Here is brisk and cool, but the flowers
(Especially the daisies, which I'm sure
You chose, knowing you and daisies)
Seem to have a movement of their own,
Stirring with life in spite of stems cut

Short and no water available for the
Vase. Hazrat Inayat Khan says that all
Movement, all life, is music. Even though
It's been three years, today, since I last
Heard your voice, its vibration echoes inside,
Filling me with sound. After I leave today,
Remember: the roses and daisies will still
Sing for you, as will the leaves and grass
And sky, the oak trees standing watch.
Listen softly: my heartbeat will be
There, too. Inside the triad, we continue.

       — November 29, 1990
       Pinelawn Cemetery, L.I.

Day Without Art

Anticipation meets memory as I wait
For the train to Yale, where Daniella has
Made a piece about us for A Day Without
Art, itself a part of today's international
AIDS awareness forum: her sculpture,
My words, your life, and the loss, the
Anger, the hard acceptance that unites the three.
Midway through your struggle, you
Kept a journal, briefly, jotting down
Your thoughts about that loss, that anger,
That acceptance. You called it, on a folded
Page, "Thoughts by P—Feeling." I glanced at it
This morning and saw that the last entry was
Exactly four years ago today. You'd had a tooth
Pulled and were home alone, feeling bored,
You said, and not too well. "I try to deal
With this," you wrote. "God, it's so hard."
Then—and it astonishes me, even now—
You closed with: "I'm sure there's a reason
For all this (I WILL DEAL)." Then nothing but
Empty pages all the way until the end of the
Book, except for one little doodle: a rough
Jagged line that could be the edge of a
Christmas tree, and there, right next to it,
Two hearts, drawn one inside the other,
Around the inscription, "Rob + Me."

       — December 1, 1990

Metro North

The Hudson's full of Canadian geese today
Stopping on their way south, confused
By the topsy-turvy mix-up of seasons:
Winter is only three weeks away and
Fall is still not here: a year without
Autumn, leaving even the leaves
Surprised. We often took this train to
Visit Joseph, our teacher, a round jolly
Man with piercing eyes and a deep sense
Of peace. He spoke to us of symbols and stars,
The Tarot, runes, the Four Temperaments:
I listened with my head, always taking
Notes; you responded from a deeper
Place, and he recognized that, sensing
In you a healing power. Ironic, I
Suppose. In the end, you couldn't heal
Yourself or the mother whose loss
Shattered you so, robbing you, I've
Always felt, of your own will to go on.
One day in Philadelphia, a pigeon came
To our balcony. You always insisted
That it brought you word: Annie was OK,
Go on with your life. There was a sign:
I've forgotten what—something about a
Numbered band on the pigeon's leg that
Matched your Annie's birth date—but you
Knew. The geese swim against the current
As I watch, longing for my own pigeon.
                              —December 1, 1990

Wishbone Reliquary

The sculpture's up: a simple diptych, a kind
Of secular altarpiece, enshrined in the
Far corner of the student gallery at Yale.
My poems are on translucent paper
Over photographs of you: in between
Are wishbones and, boxed in, at the lower
Right-hand corner, there's a plastic box
With a piece of your green-striped yellow

Shirt and the memorial card from your
Funeral (three years ago today). The box,
Daniella says, can be opened, the objects
Touched. It's like the reliquary she once
Made (of feathers, animal bones, sequined
Glitter and other fragments of life and
Living). That reliquary is now back at her
New apartment, just a few feet across the room
From the table you bought for us—you and me,
That is—in Philadelphia; in the next room
Is the oak hutch we finished and varnished
Together, all those wonderful years ago.
So many reminders remain, wherever
I go, denying the disjointedness I feel,
The leaden hollow ache. For Joseph was right
About you: I feel your touch, moving and healing
Me, here, now, all these hours after our goodbye.
                              —December 2, 1990

Here

The sun's been down an hour or so, just long
Enough to turn the mountains into a two-
Dimensional decoupage: no depth of field,
No definition—even the snowfields melt
Into a uniformity of black, a jagged cut-
Out rimming the whole horizon to the west.
I'm back. Here in these Montana mountains:
Their solid silhouette helps me to heal
Again. The sky takes on a deeper, darker
Blue, while a yellowish hue still hovers
Just behind the jutting line of peaks, and
Jupiter, glowing immense and bright, has
The Big Sky all to itself, with no stars
Daring to challenge its supreme rule. New
York almost got to me this time: I've been
Desperate for Montana since the first signs
Of spring. That hole you left—I can't
Go anywhere in the city without passing
Fragments of our life: streetcorners,
Stores, places where restaurants used to be.
Everything reminds me. At home I see our

Furniture, our records and videocassettes,
Your dishes, the little hutch you stained
(Back home again, after visiting Daniella).
I hear your laugh, your squealing "Good answer!"
Along with the audience of TV's "Family Feud,"
Your imitation of Roz Russell telling Natalie
Wood to "Dip, Louise!" in the movie *Gypsy*.
On Sundays, I can smell your meatballs and
Sauce simmering on the stove. I've tried to
Match it a dozen times, but like my Aunt
Addie's biscuits or Granny's cornbread, even
With recipes I can't come close. It's been a steep
Trail from then to now, from there to here,
From "we were" to "I am." I lose the blazes,
Wander off the path, not really lost but
Not really found ("not going left, not going
Right," as Dorothy Collins sang in Stephen
Sondheim's *Follies*). I want to let you go,
Let myself go, but the path keeps twisting,
Spiraling down then up, as I struggle along,
Hoping for a sign, something to guide me.
At least it's easier away from city lights,
Here where the mountains nightly merge to form
One long unbroken chain: black and strong
And connected until the dawn startles
Them back into individual, solitary giants:
Beckoning, snow-clad, waiting to be climbed.

(P.S.: Two day later, a baby robin came. When
I climbed the stairs at dusk, I found it sitting
There, just outside my room. I approached;
It flew away. Early the next morning it was
Back. I hurried to find a box and pillow, but
By the time I returned, it had gone again. I
Knew that at sunset it would be back, perched
Just outside my door; it was. Our eyes locked
For a long brief moment. Acknowledging my gift,
My sign, I walked back into the empty room,
Knowing now that the robin would not return
Again and that you and I were finally free.)

— July 26-30, 1991

ENDNOTES

Chapter 2: Being in Philadelphia

1. The version used is from a recital disc Callas made in a recording studio in London in September 1954 with Tullio Serafin conducting. John Ardoin, the preeminent Callas discographer, dismisses the reading as having "a rather too slow-burning fire," in his *The Callas Legacy* (New York: Charles Scribner's Sons, 1991), preferring her version of the aria the following January at La Scala. The recital collection was released by EMI in Europe and Angel in the United States; it is also included on the CD and cassette versions of the soundtrack to *Philadelphia*, released by Epic Soundtrax.

2. Quotes from the dialogue of *Philadelphia* in this chapter are from the Jonathan Demme film written by Ron Nyswaner and released by TriStar Pictures in December 1993. A novelization of the film (a book created from the screenplay) was published by Bantam Books, New York, in January 1994, written by Christopher Davis based on Nyswaner's screenplay. Quotes in this chapter have been checked against the novelization, which, like the film, is copyright © 1993, TriStar Pictures, Inc.

3. Ron Nyswaner, "The 'Philadelphia' Scribe Fights Back," *New York Times* Arts & Leisure Section, January 23, 1994.

4. See Douglas Crimp's essay, "Right On, Girlfriend," in Michael Warner's *Fear of a Queer Planet* (Minneapolis: University of Minnesota Press, 1993), especially pp. 309-11.

5. Demme in an interview in *New York Times*, Arts & Leisure Section, Feb. 28, 1993, p. 26.

6. See the lyrics of Bruce Springsteen's "Streets of Philadelphia" (© 1993 Bruce Springsteen ASCAP) and Neil Young's "Philadelphia" (© 1993 Silver Fiddle Music ASCAP) on the *Philadelphia* soundtrack, Epic Soundtrax.

7. See the studio production notes in the *Philadelphia* folder in the Theatre Collection clippings file of the Lincoln Center Library of the Performing Arts, New York.

Chapter 3: Hollywood Silence vs. Independent Voices

1. Mary Murphy, "Denial/Secrecy/Dread: The AIDS Scare—What It's Done to Hollywood and the TV You See," *TV Guide*, Oct. 22, 1988, p. 5.

2. The Davis letter is quoted in a news story by Aljean Harmetz, *New York Times*, Sept. 12, 1991, p. C15.

3. Michael Musto, "La Dolce Musto," *Village Voice*, Jan. 4, 1994, p. 36.

4. See John Horn's Associated Press interview with Schumacher, *New York Daily News*, July 4, 1991, p. 27.

5. One reader of a draft of this manuscript, New York critic William Harris, has suggested that even openly gay directors have sometimes dealt obliquely or circuitously with AIDS in some of their works. He suggests Tom Kalin's *Swoon*, a revi-

sionist gay look at the case of Leopold and Loeb, and Gus Van Sant's *My Private Idaho*, along with Todd Haynes's *Poison* (which seems particularly apt, and not all that oblique). I would also add Van Sant's *Drugstore Cowboy* and especially his early black-and-white feature, *Malo Noche*.

6. See Kevin J. Harty's "'All the Elements of a Good Movie': Cinematic Responses to the AIDS Pandemic," in Emmanuel S. Nelson's *AIDS: The Literary Response* (New York: Twayne, 1992), pp. 115-16.

7. Thomas Waugh, "Erotic Self-Images in Gay Male AIDS Melodrama," in *Fluid Exchanges: Artists and Critics in the AIDS Crisis*, edited by James Miller (Toronto: University of Toronto Press, 1992), p. 123.

8. Harty, p. 118.

9. John M. Clum, "'And Once I Had It All': AIDS Narratives and Memories of an American Dream," in *Writing AIDS: Gay Literature, Language, and Analysis*, edited by Timothy F. Murphy and Suzanne Poirier (New York: Columbia University Press: 1993), p. 207.

10. Ibid., p. 223.

11. Craig Lucas, the screenwriter of *Longtime Companion*, is also a significant playwright on the New York theater scene. His best-known play, *Prelude to a Kiss*, made it to Broadway and was also adapted as a movie starring Adam Baldwin and Meg Ryan. It also raised eyebrows among some AIDS activists, presenting the story of a young couple whose marriage goes awry when the bride is kissed by an old man at their wedding and begins to age and slowly waste away, like the characters in Stephen King's novel, *Thinner*. Lucas, like King, has denied that the work is intended to refer to AIDS. In *Prelude*, the final explanation—metempsychosis, or soul exchange between two characters—seems a bit too easy an out, considering the complexity of the issues Lucas is really raising.

12. Gregg Araki, from unpublished production notes to *The Living End*, distributed by October Films, New York, New York.

13. Ibid.

Chapter 4: Three Iconoclasts: Derek Jarman, Cyril Collard, & John Greyson

1. From *Blue*, written by Derek Jarman with music composed by Simon Fisher Turner. Published and copyright © by Mute Records Limited, London. *Blue* is a Basilisk Communications/Uplink production for Channel 4 in association with the Arts Council of Great Britain, Opal and BBC Radio 3. Written and directed by Derek Jarman, © Basilisk Communications 1993. All quotes herein are from the Mute Records CD libretto for the film.

2. See David Wojnarowicz, *Close to the Knives: A Memoir of Disintegration* (New York: Random House Vintage Books, 1991), a powerful account of the death of Wojnarowicz's friend, photographer Peter Hujar, and Wojnarowicz's own long illness.

3. Hervé Guibert's *To the Friend Who Did Not Save My Life* (London and New York: High Risk Book/Serpent's Tail, 1994) is a thinly disguised account of the death of Guibert's friend, philosopher Michel Foucault, from AIDS and then

Guibert's own diagnosis and battle with the condition. Guibert's novel was published in France in 1990; a translation into English was first brought out by Macmillan. Another novel detailing his own condition was published in France as *Le protocol compassionel* in 1991 (Guibert himself died that December); it has not been translated into English. See also Emily Apter's "Fantom Images: Hervé Guibert and the writing of 'sida' in France," in *Writing AIDS*, op. cit.

4. See the *American Heritage Dictionary* (Boston: Houghton Mifflin Company, 1992), Third Edition, p. 666, as well as program notes to the American release of *Savage Nights* from Gramercy Pictures, p. 11.

5. From the production notes to *Savage Nights*, released by Gramercy Pictures, p. 4-5.

6. Randy Shilts, *And the Band Played On: People Politics, and the Epidemic* (New York: St. Martin's Press, 1987), especially pp. 136-38, 196-97, 251-52.

7. Telephone interview with John Greyson, February 1994.

8 John Greyson, "Parma Violets for Wayland Flowers," in *Fluid Exchanges*, p. 136.

9. Douglas Crimp, "How to Have Promiscuity in an Epidemic," in *AIDS: Cultural Analysis, Cultural Activism*, edited by Douglas Crimp (Cambridge, Mass: MIT Press/October Book, 1988), p. 270.

9. Greyson, "Parma Violets," p. 137-38.

10. Ibid., p. 140 (subsequent block quotes also from "Parma Violets").

11. Livingston's documentary of the "voguing" at drag balls was a surprise hit on its release and has brought this underground show of rebellion to wide public attention. I am especially indebted to the insights in Julie Byrne's "Identity Goes Up in Flames: Queer Ethics, the Politics of (Non)Representation, and *Paris Is Burning*," unpublished paper presented at the American Academy of Religion, November 22, 1993. Byrne stresses the radical "outsider" politics of the transvestites in the film—a stance adopted, in some sense, by AIDS activist groups like ACT UP.

12. Charles Ludlam and John Vaccaro are credited with being the founding fathers of the "ridiculous theater" movement in New York. After working together on one production, appropriately called *When Queens Collide*, in the mid Sixties, they formed separate troupes called the Ridiculous Theatrical Company (Ludlam's troupe) and the Play-House of the Ridiculous (Vaccaro's group, which performed chiefly at Ellen Stewart's LaMama). Both troupes involved extensive use of camp and transvestism in their iconoclasm of theatrical, sexual, and social stereotypes. Lots of other performers, some of whom worked with Ludlam or Vaccaro and some of whom did not, used theatrical transvestism: Candy Darling, Jackie Curtis, Holly Woodlawn, Agosto Machado, Ethyl Eichelberger, the Hot Peaches troupe, the Angels of Light, Ekathrina Sobechanskaya and Her Trocadero Gloxinia Ballet, and many more. Curtis and Eichelberger took their own lives after being diagnosed with AIDS; Ludlam died of the epidemic in 1987.

13. Agitprop is a form of art that tries to incorporate a political message within the context of the work of art (painting, film, novel, etc.) itself, so that the audience or viewer is quietly won over to the artist's point of view. The term is usually used by critics on the right to dismiss such art by leftists. Even the usually even-handed

American Heritage Dictionary (p. 34) gives a first definition as "Communist-oriented political propaganda disseminated especially through drama, art, or music." The third definition is only slightly less judgmental: "Something, such as a film, that is designed to impress a certain political or social perspective on its audience, with little or no consideration given to accuracy." None other than conservative guru George F. Will is cited as the contextual quote, declaring: "It also is a conspiracy movie, agitprop against today's targets, big government and big business." *AHD* doesn't say which movie is so maligned, but I imagine ACT UP or John Greyson would be delighted to be so designated, having proudly stolen a put-down from the opposition and turned it into a stridently open and (HIV) positive statement.

Chapter 5: Bringing the Battle Home: *And the Band Played On* & *A Time of AIDS*

1. Betsy Sharkey, "'And the Band Played On': Searching for Truth," *New York Times*, Arts & Leisure Section, Sept. 5, 1993, p. 24.
2. Ibid.
3. Shilts quickly moved to disassociate himself with the "Patient Zero" question to Sharkey, for example, stating that he had turned down a Japanese producer who wanted to focus on the Gaetan Dugas issue (although he himself was a chief perpetrator of the myth). See Sharkey, p. 1.
4. John J. O'Connor, "Beyond the Re-editing, Rage Over AIDS," *New York Times*, Sept. 10, 1993.
5. Ibid.

Chapter 6: From *An Early Frost* to Today: Dramatizing AIDS on TV

1. See Paula Treichler, "AIDS Narratives on Television: Whose Story?" in *Writing AIDS*, pp. 161-99. She cites often-quoted complaint by Vito Russo (author of *The Celluloid Closet*, the classic study of the representation of homosexuality in the movies) that such movies are really just "gay movies for straight people." (p. 165)
2. See Treichler's essay, "AIDS, Homophobia and Biomedical Discourse: An Epidemic of Signification," in *AIDS: Cultural Analysis, Cultural Activism*, pp. 31-70.
3. Treichler, "AIDS Narratives," p. 164.
4. Waugh in *Fluid Exchanges*, p. 123.
5. Treichler, "AIDS Narratives," p. 186.
6. Harty, pp. 123, 213 (note 19).
7. See Simon Watney, *Policing Desire: Pornography, AIDS, and the Media* (Minneapolis: University of Minnesota Press, 1987), pp. 137-138.
8. Harty, p. 119.
9. Ibid., p. 120.

Chapter 7: *Common Threads* & Other AIDS Documents

1. From Marlon Riggs' documentary, *Tongues Untied*, first presented on Public Television's "Point of View" series July 16, 1991. From a poem by Essex Hemphill.
2. From a poem by Essex Hemphill, recited in *Tongues Untied*.

Chapter 8: Rock & Roll Television

1. David A. Keeps, *New York Times*, Arts & Leisure Section, , July 19, 1992.

2. Jon Pareles, "Talking 'Bout the Retrovirus," *New York Times*, Week in Review Section, March 27, 1994.

3. Michael Callen and Marsha Malamet, "Love Don't Need a Reason," Warner Bros. Publishing Co. (ASCAP), Tops and Bottoms Music, Malamutton Music (BMI). From the album *Purple Heart* by Michael Callen, © 1988 by Significant Other Records.

4. John Carlin, personal interview, Januray 1994.

5. From the liner notes to *Red Hot + Dance: A Benefit for AIDS Research and Relief,* © 1992 Sony Music Entertainment (UK) Limited/Compilation. (P) 1992 Leigh Blake and John Carlin.

6. "All Your Jeans Were Too Tight," by American Music Club, written by Mark Eitzel, © PolyGram Music/I Failed in Life Music (BMI). Included on *No Alternative*, compilation (p) and © by The Red Hot Organization.

7. "Take a Walk," by Urge Overkill. Written by Urge Overkill. © King/Kato Ltd. (BMI). Included on *No Alternative*, compilation (p) and © by The Red Hot Organization.

8. Brian Hanna, personal interview, January 1994.

Chapter 9: Anthems & Mourning Songs

1. Barry Walters, "Everybody Hurts: Grief and Transcendence in Today's Pop," *Village Voice*, Rock & Roll Quarterly, Fall, 1993, p. 13, 19.

2. "The Day After That," from the Broadway musical *Kiss of the Spider Woman*, by Fred Ebb and John Kander. The Liza Minnelli CD single was released by Columbia.

3. Jim Fouratt, personal interview, February 1994.

4. See especially Michael Callen, *Surviving AIDS* (New York: HarperCollins, 1990).

Chapter 10: Dance: At the Vanishing Point

1. Jeremy Gerard, *New York Times*, June 9, 1987, p. C15: "Five prominent choreographers with the Dancing for Life benefit—Jerome Robbins, Mikhail Baryshnikov, Twyla Tharp, Peter Martins, and Lar Lubovitch—issued a statement in response to questions from The Times, taking strong exception to any suggestion that AIDS has had a special effect on the arts."

2. Joanna Simon, "AIDS and the Arts," a special segment on "The MacNeil-Lehrer Report," Public Broadcasting System, July 1987.

3. Gerald Arpino, personal interview, Feb. 24, 1994.

4. Wendell Ricketts, "AIDS Onstage," *Dance Ink* IV:3 (Fall 1993), p. 16.

5. Maya Wallach, September 1989 interview with Demian Acquavella, in the AIDS Oral History project at the Dance Collection, New York Library of the Performing Arts, Lincoln Center in New York City.

6. Deborah Jowitt, *Village Voice*, Sept. 7, 1993.

7. Jennifer Dunning, "Gary Chryst: A Dancer With a Distinct Difference," *New York Times*, Arts & Leisure Section, Aug. 29, 1993, p. 8.

8. Arpino, interview.

9. This videotape, available in the Dance Collection, New York Library of the Performing Arts, features a performance of "Lacrymosa" as well as an interview with Stierle about the making of the piece. Stierle's statements here about "Lacrymosa," unless otherwise indicated, are taken from the videotape.

10. Janice Berman, interview with Edward Stierle, *New York Newsday*, TK

11. Stierle, videotape of "Lacrymosa."

12. Berman interview with Stierle.

13. Arpino, interview.

14. Berman interview.

15. Arpino interview.

16. Arnie Zane interview in Dance Collection Oral History Project, Dance Collection, New York Public Library. Interview conducted by Lesley Farlow, Dec. 23, 1987.

17. Simon, "AIDS and the Arts."

18. Acquavella interview.

19. Burton Taylor interview, AIDS Oral History Project. Interview by Lesley Farlow, Oct. 16, 1990.

20. Ted Hershey interview, AIDS Oral History Project. Interview by Lesley Farlow, Feb. 25, 1991.

21. Clark Tippet interview, AIDS Oral History Project. Interview by Lesley Farlow, April 15, 1991.

Chapter 11: Music: Of Rage and Remembrance

1. Liner notes by John Corigliano, *Symphony No. 1*, © Erato Disques, S.A. 1991.

2. Ibid. All succeeding quotes about the symphony are from Corigliano's liner notes to the symphony.

3. Diamanda Galas, *Plague Mass: Give Me Sodomy or Give Me Death*, Mute Records, published by Mute Song.

4. Galas as quoted in the liner notes to *Plague Mass*.

5. William Parker, quoted in Will Crutchfield interview, "A Baritone Gives Voice To a Patchwork of Emotions," *New York Times*, Arts & Leisure Section, May 31, 1992.

6. Philip Caggiano, personal interview, January 1994.

7. Crutchfield, "A Baritone Gives Voice."

8. From *The AIDS Quilt Songbook*, music © copyright 1993 by Donald Wheelock, to the poem "Fury" by Susan Snively. Used in the collection by permission of the author. The songbook is published by Boosey & Hawkes, New York, and is available on CD and cassette from Harmonia Mundi Records, Los Angeles.

9. Richard Pearson Thomas, "AIDS Anxiety," © 1993 by Richard Pearson Thomas.

10. Melvin Dixon, "Heartbeats," used in the collection by the permission of the

Estate of Melvin Dixon.

11. Parker quoted in Brian Kellow, "Art in the Age of AIDS," *Opera News*, June, 1992, p. 42.

12. Perry Brass, "Walt Whitman in 1989." Used in the collection by permission of the author. Brass has dated his poem Sept. 18, 1989, Orangeburg, New York; he dedicates it "for a generation taken by our war."

Chapter 12: The NAMES Project AIDS Memorial Quilt.

1. Melvin Dixon, "Aunt Ida Pieces a Quilt," in *Confronting AIDS Through Literature*, edited by Judith Laurence Pastore (Urbana: University of Illinois Press, 1993), p. 149.

2. Cindy Ruskin, *The Quilt: Stories from the NAMES Project* (New York: Pocket Books, 1988), p. 9.

3. Ibid., p. 10.

4. Elinor Fuchs, "The Performance of Mourning," *American Theatre*, January, 1993, p. 15.

5. Peter S. Hawkins, "Naming Names: The Art of Memory and the NAMES Project AIDS Memorial Quilt," *Critical Inquiry* (Vol. 19, No. 4), Summer 1993, p. 752.

6. Ibid., p. 754.

7. Ibid.

8. Ibid., p. 760.

9. Ibid., p. 770-71.

10. Ibid., p. 774.

11. Robert Dawidoff, "The NAMES Project," in *Personal Dispatches: Writers Confront AIDS*, edited by John Preston (New York: St. Martin's Press, 1988), p. 155.

12. Ibid., p. 159.

13. Ibid., p. 157-58.

14. Richard D. Mohr, *Gay Ideas: Outing and Other Controversies* (Boston: Beacon Press, 1992), p. 120.

15. Susan Grant Rosen, "The NAMES Project Quilt: Sacred Symbol for the Age of AIDS?," unpublished paper delivered at the American Academy of Religion, November 21, 1993, p. 8 of manuscript.

16. Judy Elsley, "The Rhetoric of the NAMES Project AIDS Quilt: Reading the Text(ile)," in *AIDS: The Literary Response*, p. 188.

17. Fuchs, p. 17.

18. Ibid., p. 17-18.

19. Rosen, p. 9.

20. Ibid., p. 10.

21. Ibid.

22. Ruskin, *The Quilt*, p. 63.

23. Timothy F. Murphy, "Testimony," in *Writing AIDS*, p. 314.

24. Dixon poem in *Confronting AIDS Through Literature*, p. 150.

25. Ibid., p. 151.

Chapter 13: Confrontations & Critical Agendas

1. Crimp, *AIDS: Cultural Analysis*, p. 7.
2. David Wojnarowicz, *Witnesses: Against Our Vanishing* catalogue, Artists Space, p. 7; a somewhat altered version appears in Wojnarowicz's *Close to the Knives*, p. 114.
3. Wojnarowicz, *Witnesses* catalogue, p. 10; *Knives*, p. 120.
4. *Witnesses: Against Our Vanishing* catalogue, p. 4. The following quotes from the exhibition are all from the catalogue.
5. Nan Goldin, from the introduction to the exhibit catalogue, p. 4.
6. Ibid., p. 5.
7. Ibid.
8. Ibid.
9. Douglas Crimp and Adam Rolston, *AIDS DemoGraphics* (Seattle: Bay, 1990), p. 13.
10. Ibid., p. 16.
11. Ibid., p. 14.
12. Crimp, *AIDS: Cultural Analysis*, p. 7-11.
13. Lois Nesbitt, "Out of the Studio and Onto the Streets: Guerrilla Art and AIDS," *Public Art Issues* (New York: Public Art Fund, Inc., 1992), p. 24.
14. From the catalogue of *From Media to Metaphor: Art About AIDS*, a traveling exhibit organized by Independent Curators Incorporated, New York, catalogue, p. 22.
15. Thomas Sokolowski, personal interview, January 1994.
16. Crimp, *AIDS: Cultural Activism*, pp. 237-70.
17. Watney, *Policing Desire*, pp. 115, 132.
18. Quoted in *Fluid Exchanges*, pp. 39-40.

Chapter 14: What the Camera Saw: Mapplethorpe & Other Photographic Responses

1. William Harris has suggested contrasting Mapplethorpe's glossy, studied self-portraits with the powerful snapshots that Mark Morrisroe made of himself both before and after his diagnosis (including the harrowing portrait he made shortly before his death, which was included in the *Witnesses:Against Our Vanishing* exhibit, mentioned in Chapter 13). Morrisroe's snapshots have not been published, but his work is represented by Pat Hearn of the Pat Hearn Gallery in New York.
2. Preston, p. xii.
3. Marvin Heiferman, introduction to *The Indomitable Spirit* (New York: International Center of Photography Midtown, 1990).
4. Ibid.
5. Ibid., preface by Andy Grundberg.
6. Nicholas and Bebe Nixon, *People with AIDS* (New York: David R. Godine, 1991), p. vii.
7. Again William Harris suggests contrasting the photos by the Nixons or Solomon with those of Brian Weil, who works from within the AIDS community (his photography grew out of his volunteer service at Gay Men's Health Crisis)

rather than as an outsider. As a result, his photos span a broad demographic of ethnic, racial, and sexual categories; he has also photographed PWAs abroad, in Haiti, Africa, and Southeast Asia. And unlike the stark, arty look of the Nixons or Solomon, he opts for grainy, almost blurred images of his subjects, which give his representations an aura of grace and respect.

8. Rosalind Solomon, "Artist's Statement," from the exhibit catalogue, Grey Gallery, New York

9. Introduction by Thomas Sokolowski to the Solomon exhibit catalogue.

10. Ibid.

11. Ibid.

Chapter 15: Frank Moore: Canvases from an Epidemic

1. David Hirsh, "Frank Moore: A Subverted Vision of The Peaceable Kingdom," *New York Native*, January 11, 1993, p. 16.

2. Personal interview with Frank Moore, Oct. 15, 1993.

3. Hirsh, p. 18.

4. Ibid.

5. Moore, interview.

6. William Harris, "Art and AIDS: Urgent Images," *ARTnews* (May 1993), 123.

Chapter 16.: Days Without Art

1. Media release from Visual AIDS, 131 W. 24th St., New York, dated November 22, 1993.

2. John Follain, Reuters newswire, Dec. 1, 1993.

3. Ibid.

4. Michael Christie, Reuters newswire, Dec. 1, 1993.

5. Reuters report from Rabat, Morocco, Dec. 1, 1993.

6. Amba Dadson, Associated Press newswire, Dec. 2, 1993.

7. United Press International newswire, Dec. 1, 1993.

8. Ibid.

Chapter 17: Early Stages: Larry Kramer, William M. Hoffman, & Robert Chesley

1. See Randy Shilts's account in *And the Band Played On*, pp. 556-57.

2. Ibid., pp. 108-9.

3. Ibid., p. 109.

4. Michael Musto, *Village Voice*, Jan. 4, 1994.

5. Larry Kramer, *The Normal Heart* (New York: New American Library, 1985), p. 114.

6. James M. Jones, "The Sick Homosexual: AIDS and Gays on the American Stage and Screen," in *Confronting AIDS Through Literature*, p. 118.

7. Larry Kramer, *The Destiny of Me* (New York: Penguin Plume, 1993), p. 108-9.

8. Ibid., p. 109.

9. Ibid., p. 122.

10. Ibid., p. 4.

11. William M. Hoffman, *As Is*, in *The Way We Live Now: American Plays & the AIDS Crisis*, edited by M. Elisabeth Osborn (New York: Theatre Communications Group, 1990), p. 7.

12. Ibid., p. 61.

13. William M. Hoffman, personal interview, December 20, 1993.

14. Joel Shatsky, "AIDS Enters the American Theatre: *As Is* and *The Normal Heart*, in *AIDS: The Literary Response*, p. 134.

15. Hoffman interview.

16. Robert Chesley, *Hard Plays/Stiff Parts: The Homoerotic Plays of Robert Chesley* (San Francisco: Alamo Square, 1990). All Chesley quotes are from the introductions to the three plays (*Night Sweat, Jerker,* and *Dog Plays*) or from the plays themselves, as indicated.

Chapter 18: Further Confrontations Across the Proscenium Arch

1. Michael Feingold, introduction to *The Way We Live Now*, p. xvii.

2. Ibid., pp. xiii-xiv.

3. Michael Kuchwara, Associated Press newswire, March 12, 1992.

4. Quoted in C. Carr, "Show Me the Way to Go Home," *Village Voice*, Aug. 17, 1993, p. 37.

5. Ibid.

6. Robert Massa, *Village Voice*, January 17, 1989, p. 93.

7. The complaint was made by an AIDS group in Paris, according to the Reuters newswire, Oct. 6, 1993. Their bid to stop the appearance of the ads was unsuccessful.

8. Scott McPherson, *Marvin's Room*, introduction (New York: Plume, 1992) p. xxii.

9. Kramer in McPherson, p. viii.

10. David Richards, "A Working Playwright Edges Into Fame," *New York Times*, Arts & Leisure Section, Aug. 29, 1993, p. 5.

11. Rich in William Finn and James Lapine, *Falsettos* (New York: Plume, 1993), p. 246.

12. *Falsettos*, p. 162.

13. Ibid., p. 172.

14. Ibid., p.174.

15. Jean-Claude van Itallie, *Ancient Boys*, in *Gay Plays: An International Anthology*, edited by Catherine Temerson and Françoise Kourilsky (New York: Ubu Repertory Theater Publications, 1991), p. 366.

16. Ibid., p. 370.

17. Copi, *Grand Finale*, translated by Michael Feingold, in *Gay Plays*, p. 198-99.

18. Ibid., p. 205.

19. Harvey Fierstein, "Manny and Jake," in *Safe Sex* (New York: Atheneum, 1987), p. 12.

20. Harvey Fierstein, "Safe Sex," in *Safe Sex*, p. 56.

21. Harvey Fierstein, "On Tidy Endings," in *Safe Sex*, p. 96.

22. Harry Kondoleon, *Christmas on Mars*, in *Self Torture and Strenuous Exercise: The Selected Plays of Harry Kondoleon* (New York: Theatre Communications Group, 1991), p. 109.

23. Harry Kondoleon, *Anteroom*, in *Self Torture and Strenuous Exercise*, p. 232.

24. Harry Kondoleon, *Zero Positive*, in *The Way We Live Now*, p. 209.

25. Ibid., p. 264.

26. Ibid., p. 279.

27. Paula Vogel, *The Baltimore Waltz* in *American Theatre* (September 1991), insert p. 2.

28. Susan Sontag, "The Way We Live Now," dramatized for the stage by Edward Parone, in *The Way We Live Now*, p. 103.

29. Ibid., p. 109.

30. Ibid., p. 127.

31. A videotape version of the performance is in the Theatre on Film and Tape (TOFT) Archive at the New York Library of the Performing Arts at Lincoln Center. A film version, directed by Jill Godmillow and produced by Jonathan Demme, is currently being edited.

32. Greg Mehrten, personal interview, Jan. 11, 1994.

Chapter 19: Allowing Laughter: *Jeffrey* & *Pterodactyls*

1. Edmund White, "Esthetics and Loss," in *Personal Dispatches*, p. 151. The essay originally appeared in the January 1987 issue of *Artforum*.

2. Ibid., 146-47.

3. Ibid., p. 151.

4. Paul Rudnick, personal interview, Jan. 11, 1994.

5. Frank Rich, "Laughing at AIDS Is First Line of Defense," *New York Times*, Feb. 3, 1993, p. C18.

6. Nicky Silver, *Pterodactyls*, in *American Theatre*, February, 1994, p. 30.

7. Ibid., p. 28.

8. Nicky Silver, personal interview, Oct. 28, 1993.

9. David Richards, "Humans Are the Dinosaurs in 'Pterodactyls," *New York Times*, Arts & Leisure Section, Oct. 24, 1993, p. 5.

10. Ben Brantley, "Mining the Humor From the Decline of a Class," *New York Times*, Oct. 21, 1993, p. C15.

11. Silver, interview.

12. Nicky Silver, Playwright's Notes to *Pterodactyls* in *American Theatre*, p. 29.

Chapter 20: Alchemy & *Angels in America*

1. Titus Burckhardt, *Alchemy: Science of the Cosmos, Science of the Soul* (London: Stuart & Watkins, 1967), translated from the German by William Stoddart, p. 23.

2. Tony Kushner, *Angels in America—Part One: Millennium Approaches* (New York: Theatre Communications Group, 1993), p. 119.

3. Vincent Canby, "Two 'Angels,' Two Journeys, In London and New York,"

New York Times, Arts & Leisure Section, Jan. 30, 1994, p. 5.

4. Frank Rich, "Following an Angel for a Healing Vision of Heaven on Earth," *New York Times*, Nov. 24, 1993, C11.

5. John Lahr, "Beyond Nelly," *The New Yorker* LXVIII: 40 (Nov. 23, 1992), p. 130.

6. See William Harris, "The Secrets of 'Angels,'" *New York Times*, Arts & Leisure Section, March 27, 1994, p. 5, for an examination of such allusions.

7. Quoted in a review of *The Illusion* by Rosette C. Lamont in *Theater Week*, Vol. 7, No. 29 (Feb. 21, 1994), p. 53.

8. Tony Kushner, *Angels in America—Part Two: Perestroika* (New York: Theatre Communications Group, 1994), p. 148.

9. Mircea Eliade, "The Myth of Alchemy," *Parabola* III: 3 (August 1978), p. 9.

10. Burckhardt, pp. 185-86. The following quotes relating to the traditional alchemical process are all from Burckhardt, pp. 123-91.

11. *Perestroika*, p. 135.

12. Ibid., p. 136.

13. Eliade, p. 19-20.

14. Tony Kushner quoted in "Angels Among Us," *Time* (December 27, 1993) p. 65.

15. Quoted by Lahr, p. 130.

Postlude: Word Is Out

1. Jeffrey Schmaltz, "Whatever Happened to AIDS?," *New York Times Magazine*, Nov. 28, 1993, p. 86.

INDEX